To my wife, Leigh.

It just gets better and better.

Grace and Peace

CONTENTS

ACKNOWLEDGMENTS

One of the pitfalls of interim ministry is that it doesn't allow you a lot of time to get to know the people in the churches you serve. Since each assignment only lasts about a year, I'm generally packing up my study at just about the same time that I'm finally confident that I'm calling people by the right name. My farewell sermon typically includes the line, "If I haven't been to see you this year, count your blessings, because that probably means that you haven't been sick, in jail, separated from your spouse or deceased."

That being said, a year is plenty long for each congregation to become special in its own way, and I want to begin by expressing my heartfelt gratitude to:

First Reformed Church of Oostburg, Wisconsin (did we ever have a meeting without cheese?)

Hope Reformed Church of South Haven, Michigan (did we ever have a meeting without blueberries?)

Covenant Life Church of Grand Haven, Michigan (whose idea was it to buy all the chairs with wheels?)

Resurrection Reformed Church of Flint, Michigan (sorry about having the only non-GM car in the parking lot.)

Good Samaritan Reformed Church of Gahanna, Ohio, now part of CenterPoint Church (so, how are your Buckeyes going to do this year?)

Third Reformed Church of Grand Rapids, Michigan (one last time: eighty percent full is full. Really.)

Gun Lake Community Church of Wayland, Michigan (did that guy with the gun ever come back?)

First Reformed Church of Grandville, Michigan (see Third Reformed Church, above.)

Calvary Reformed Church of Holland, Michigan (you could give seminars in knowing how to be about something—except that you're too busy being about something!)

Forest Hills Presbyterian Church of Grand Rapids (Best. Coffee. Ever.)

Central Reformed Church of Oskaloosa, Iowa (now that's what I call a farewell gift: track time in both a Porsche 911 Turbo *and* a Ferrari 360 Modena!)

First Presbyterian Church of Hastings, Michigan (can you tell me one more time how those doors know when to unlock themselves?)

Church of the Savior, South Bend, Indiana ("... and the award for best use of screens in worship goes to: Church of the Savior!")

Central Reformed Church of Grand Rapids, Michigan (it was a joy to look down at the tops of your heads from that really high pulpit.)

Bethany Reformed Church, Sheboygan, Wisconsin (back in Wisconsin after 14 years, and they still didn't fix Interstate 43).

The Peoples Church, East Lansing, Michigan ("unique: adjective, 1. Being the only one if its kind; unlike anything else." That sounds about right.)

Since Covenant Life Church is at the heart of this book, a few people who were there with me at the time deserve special mention: I was supposed to be mentoring Bob DeVries, but I think it ended up going the other way just as much. I wish I could have had Cec Bradshaw's administrative skills—not to mention his positive attitude—at every church I served. I learned a lot about worship from Steve Caton; I can't begin to count how many times I've shared his reminder that 52 Sundays a year isn't that many, and that we shouldn't waste a moment of any of them. Trudie Kok always managed to pray for me exactly when I needed it most.

Although I mostly try to keep my children, their spouses and their families out of my writing in any direct way, they are still present on every page, if only in their insistence that I not use words and phrases that I learned in the 1960s—or last week. Even though I don't say it often enough, I hope you all know how much I love you.

Finally, I want to thank my wife, Leigh, for all her patience, kindness, forgiveness and love. After 37 years, it just keeps getting better.

INTRODUCTION

I wish I had such a rich vocabulary that I could just jot down a few words or phrases and have you know exactly how I felt as I experienced the ideas that led to this book. It happened in a very short amount of time—minutes, not hours or days. Not only did it come to me quickly, it also came nearly complete. One moment, I was driving along, probably speeding (okay, definitely speeding), singing with the CD player; the next, I knew that I was going to be writing on the subject of obedience.

Before I say more, it might be helpful for you to know that I'm not generally given to mystical experiences or ecstatic trances. I don't usually lean toward the experiential side of things, theologically; I've never been much of a wonderer or dreamer. I tend to be more of a rational, reasoning, show-me-the-facts kind of person. Many years ago, I did experience one exceptionally vivid dream that I believe was God's way of helping me deal with a tragedy that I had witnessed (you'll read about that later); but other than that, I'd never had anything that I would call a sudden revelatory experience.

Until that moment in the car.

Here's how it happened: On a gorgeous early summer morning, while serving as the interim pastor of a church near the eastern shore of Lake Michigan, I was beginning the day with devotions. At the time, I was working my way through the early chapters of Joshua, and I had just finished reading about the renewal of the covenant sign which God required of all the men of Israel before the people could enter the Promised Land

(Joshua 5:1-12). If you're thinking "ouch" (or more accurately, "OUCH!") you're remembering the story correctly.

In my study Bible, there is a break at verse 12, which is followed by several paragraphs of introductory material leading into the next section of the text. This is where the story of Jericho begins, and I thought about leaving this extra reading and the few remaining verses of chapter five for the next day. But instead, I kept going. I'm nothing if not methodical (yes, I sort my jelly beans by color, lining them up on my desk, after which I eat them in sequence so that I don't eat the same color twice in a row). So, adhering to my dutiful, chapter-a-day routine, I read to the end, and ended up puzzling over those last few verses for the rest of the day.

Here's what they say:

Once when Joshua was by Jericho, he looked up and saw a man standing before him with a drawn sword in his hand. Joshua went to him and said to him, "Are you one of us, or one of our adversaries?" He replied, "Neither; but as commander of the army of the Lord I have now come." And Joshua fell on his face to the earth and worshiped, and he said to him, "What do you command your servant, my lord?" The commander of the army of the Lord said to Joshua, "Remove the sandals from your feet, for the place where you stand is holy." And Joshua did so (Joshua 5:13-15 NRSV).

Having been in church since before I can remember, followed by Christian school through grade six, four years at a Christian college, three years of seminary, and 21 years of parish ministry, I knew that I had either heard or read the account of Israel's victory over Jericho many times before. Yet, for some reason, it almost seemed as if I was reading this opening scene, Joshua's encounter with the commander of the Lord's army, for the first time. I remembered some of the details, but I couldn't recall ever giving much thought to what was actually taking place during the sudden appearance of this unearthly warrior.

As readers, I think we are supposed to be surprised when this commander doesn't immediately state that he is on

Joshua's side. Wouldn't that be the logical reason for God to send the head of heaven's army? To help Israel in their first battle for the Promised Land? But that's not what the commander said.

Joshua's response—and I'm thinking here that he was probably recalling some of the things Moses had told him about his encounters with God—was to immediately fall to the ground, asking if the commander had a message from the Lord. Joshua was told to take off his sandals, which would have been a confirmation that he was in the Divine presence (see the story of Moses and the Burning Bush in Exodus 3). He then received God's peculiar instructions about how Jericho was going to be defeated. Yes, I know, this is actually in the beginning of chapter 6; amazingly, I bent my own arbitrary devotion rules and read ahead.

Joshua and his army were told to march around the city once a day for six days, and seven times on the seventh day. After that, the walls would simply collapse. There were a few more details in the instructions about the sounding of trumpets and carrying the Ark of the Covenant, and there was supposed to be some shouting at the end, but the gist of the message was to simply march around the city as instructed until the walls fell down.

As I said, I wondered about the strange closing verses in chapter 5 for the rest of the day, and I must have still been thinking about them when I got in my car to drive home. Normally, I listened to National Public Radio during my 40-minute commute, but on this day, I put a CD into the changer, k.d. Lang's "Hymns of the 49th Parallel." No, it isn't a worship CD, (unless you think Canada is heaven); it isn't even a Christian CD. Rather, it's a CD of songs written by Canadian composers, one of whom is Joni Mitchell. k.d. covered her 1977 release, "Jericho" on track nine.

When that song started playing, and k.d. sang Joni's lyric, "Just like Jericho, I said, let the walls come tumbling down," I suddenly knew what those last few verses in Joshua 5 were about. Not only that, but in the space of just a few minutes, I had a crazy idea for how a congregation could share in the Jericho experience. I also had the beginnings of an outline for a book (you're reading it). It was the weirdest thing; as I later described it to my wife, Leigh, it was as if God had just opened up the top of my head and poured in a pitcher of thoughts, all at once.

Now, you have to understand that there was nothing revolutionary or even very original about what I experienced as I was driving; it was just incredibly new—maybe a better word would be *real*—to me. The key to my understanding of Joshua's brief encounter with the commander of the Lord's army was obedience.

When Joshua asked him whose side he was on, and he answered "Neither," I suddenly understood that the angelic commander wasn't the least bit interested in aligning himself with either Israel or Jericho. What he—and God—wanted to know was whether or not Joshua would choose to align himself with God. In other words, God's commander wasn't there to do things Joshua's way, but rather to see if Joshua would dare to approach Jericho God's way. Would he trust God? Would he persuade his own commanders to obey God's bizarre instructions for how to defeat the walled city? Or would Joshua choose to do his own thing and go his own way, forfeiting the Lord's help as he attacked the city in a more conventional manner?

Joshua was being challenged to commit himself to a course of radical (some might say ridiculous) obedience. It was clearly God's desire to give Jericho, and by extension, the entire Promised Land, to the Israelites, but God wanted them to do it in a different way.

Do it a different way.

Try it a different way.

Try it God's way.

Try it God's way, for a change.

The Jericho effect: What if we tried doing things God's way, for a change?

That was it. What if *we* tried to be obedient to God in the way that Joshua had been challenged to be obedient? What might the commander of the Lord's army be able to accomplish on our behalf? What walls might we be able to bring down through the simple act of choosing to do things God's way?

At this point, my thoughts began to race from one thing to another: Different kinds of obedience; God's way seeming so unusual compared to our way; the power of the Lord's army; sin building walls; obedience bringing them down. In the middle of all these thoughts, one particular image stood out very clearly: a congregation of God's people marching together in obedience.

It was as if I could already hear the seven trumpets as I imagined the Word of God leading God's people. I didn't know who or what or when or where, or even if it would ever actually happen, but I had this amazingly clear conviction that the story of Jericho could become the motivation for a group of people to choose obedience in order to bring down walls built by sin.

That's what this book is about; how I've been challenged to align myself with God's will, and how a congregation took a risk and lived out the story of Jericho. Along the way, I'm pretty sure that I'll wander off in seemingly random directions; I know without a doubt that I will use a lot of parentheses (I tend to think parenthetically); and you may occasionally wonder if I'm ever going to get to a point (I make no promises about that). I will address half a dozen different areas of obedience, thinking about how God's way is different than our way. We'll think about how our disobedience builds walls, and then we'll see how trying to do things God's way can bring them down.

The many stories that I will share along the way are all true, but I have changed some of the details to protect the identities of the people involved. I've tried really hard not to let this book build any new walls.

"Just like Jericho," k.d. was singing, "Let the walls come tumbling down." Divine messages sometimes come through unusual messengers, but God's word for me was perfectly clear. "Why not try it my way, for a change?"

PART ONE: MARCHING WITH JOSHUA

CHAPTER ONE: I READ, GOD SPEAKS

Obedience to the Word of God

"**S**omething kind of strange happened as I was driving home today."

My wife, Leigh, and I were taking our usual evening walk, passing through Centennial Park in the heart of Holland, Michigan, our hometown. We often shared the details of our days as we walked, and I'm sure Leigh expected me to tell her another one of my many commuting horror stories: That I had dodged another herd of kamikaze deer crossing the highway, that a truck in front of me had lost part of its load again (I ran over a gallon of paint on one occasion, a ladder on another), or that someone ignoring a "lane closed ahead" sign had caused another near-collision at a road construction site.

"So, what did you almost hit this time?" Leigh asked. I told her that for once it wasn't traffic-related, but rather that it was an idea that had hit me while I was in the car. I described how I had started the day as usual with my devotions, reading the opening verses of the Jericho story, how I had puzzled over the meaning of the incident between Joshua and the captain of the Lord's army for the rest of the day, and then how it had all suddenly become clear to me as I was listening to my k.d. Lang

CD on the way home (which, by the way, had been Leigh's recommendation; she knows what I like).

I probably talked for twenty minutes straight, explaining my emerging understanding of how this familiar story was all about obedience, beginning with how God wanted to simply give the Promised Land to Joshua and the people, if they were willing to do it a different way. I talked about God's unusual instructions for how the city was to be defeated, Joshua's willingness to obey those instructions, and the collapse of Jericho's wall. I continued with what I remembered about the rescue of Rahab and her family, the secret disobedience of Achan, and the consequence of Achan's sin when Israel attacked the next city, Ai. I went on and on, partly recalling my thoughts from the morning and from the car, and partly thinking out loud, talking about how obedience was so critical to every part of the Jericho story.

Then I told Leigh about how I had experienced the idea of a congregation living out this story, marching together as a sign of their desire to be obedient to God. "Imagine if a church decided to honor God with a sincere effort at obedience for even one week," I said. "I don't mean legalistic, mindless obedience, as if they're going to suddenly try to live by every obscure verse in the Old Testament—you know, not sewing two kinds of cloth together, or not boiling a kid goat in its mother's milk. But what if they simply said, 'For this one week, God, we will try to do things your way'?

"For example, if a questionable TV program came on," I said, "they would be encouraged to turn it off. If they were reading something and saw that God's name was being used in vain, they would put it down. If they were online and clicked on something inappropriate, they would click it off and go somewhere else. For a week, husbands and wives would try not to fight with each other, parents and children would try to get along, no one would use profane language or make racial slurs.

"And those are just a few of the obvious ways we could work at obedience," I continued, rushing on. "I think there could be a special meeting every night during that week for people to encourage each other, and to talk about the walls that we create by our disobedience; and then we could end the meetings by marching once around the church as a symbol of our desire to do things God's way for that week."

I paused for just a moment, still processing all the ideas. "We could call it the Jericho Week, and then end it with a Jericho Sunday, marching around the church seven times, just like Joshua and the Israelites, praying that God would bring down all the walls. Not the literal walls of the church building, but the walls that gradually build up between husbands and wives, parents and children, brothers and sisters, people of different races, men and women, fellow church members. All of us and God."

When I finally stopped talking, Leigh was quiet for a few moments, taking it all in. "That would take a lot of preparation, and it would take a pretty special church," she said. "I'm not sure you could get just anyone to go along with that."

Little did we know that in just a few weeks, God would lead us to that very special congregation, a group of people not only willing, but eager to give the Jericho Week a try.

* * *

Let me back up a moment here and tell you what it is that I do. I am a SIM, a Specialized Interim Minister. SIMs serve churches that are between pastors. We come in for about a year, fulfilling most of the regular pastoral functions —preaching, weddings, funerals, pastoral calling, and so on— but we also help the congregation through an intentional self-study process before they call a new minister. We focus on separation and grief issues related to the departure of the previous pastor, and help the members think about their history, identity, leadership, and new directions in ministry, among other things. We pay special attention to any area where there has been conflict, working to bring about healing before the church begins the process of calling a new pastor.

I never intended to become an interim minister. During the first 19 years of my ministry, I would have told you that that was a job for recently retired clergy whose spouses couldn't stand to have them around the house full time. My goal upon entering the seminary was to become a regular, settled pastor, maybe even one of those warmly beloved ministers who stay in one place long enough to baptize the children of the members they baptized a generation earlier.

It didn't quite work out that way. Leigh and I both graduated from Western Theological Seminary, which is located in Holland, Michigan, in May of 1984. In September of that year, we loaded up our brown Toyota Corolla and took our shiny new Master of Divinity degrees—and our daughter Abigail, too, who was born right after graduation—and moved to Clymer, New York. I had accepted a call to be the pastor of the Clymer Hill Reformed Church, a congregation made up of about 65 families, nearly all of them involved in dairy farming.

I served that church for a little more than three years, learning almost as much about driving a John Deere tractor as I did about being a pastor. Leigh stayed home as we did our part for church growth by adding two more children, our sons Peter and Paul, to the congregation.

In general, I thought I was doing a pretty good job on my "warmly beloved" goal. That is, right up until the evening when one of the elders came to my door with a long list of complaints about my numerous failures and shortcomings. I'm not saying that there was anything on that list that wasn't true, but I felt miffed about it just the same.

As I was pondering the implications of this elder's visit, I was contacted by the Union Reformed Church of Franklin Lakes, New Jersey, a suburban congregation in an affluent bedroom community just a short drive west of where the George Washington Bridge crosses the Hudson River into New York City. I thought this might be my chance for a long-term pastorate, having made all my rookie mistakes at Clymer Hill. Leigh and I both loved the idea of being close to a big city, especially since there would be many more ministry opportunities for her. So we accepted the call and moved from the country to suburbia. While there, Leigh was ordained to hospice chaplaincy, ministering to the needs of the dying, their families and friends, through Northwest Bergen Hospice.

As much as we enjoyed both the area and the people, and as much as Leigh loved her new ministry, we quickly came to realize that this was not the place where we wanted to raise our family. To put it bluntly, in this neighborhood of million-dollar homes, we were always going to be near the bottom, economically. As soon as our children started school, we knew that this was going to be increasingly difficult for them. There was no way that we could rent an entire theater for a first-grade birthday party (as one family did), spend winter vacations either skiing at Vail or cruising in the Caribbean (as many families did), or buy every new fashion as soon as it hit the market (as nearly every family did). I kind of liked the idea of driving a Porsche to the grade school for parent-teacher conferences the way several of the other dads did, but didn't see any way to get that into the deacons' mission budget.

So after a little more than three years of "Green Acres is the place to be," followed by five years of "Give me Park Avenue," we decided to go back to where we started. The Maplewood Reformed Church of Holland had invited me to become their Minister of Worship and Administration, which would be my first experience as the head of a pastoral staff.

That was early in 1993, and at the time I could easily imagine spending the rest of my pastoral career at family-friendly Maplewood. I enjoyed just about everything about my ministry there, especially the gradual transition that took place from being an inwardly-focused church to one which was involved in numerous outreach ministries. Even after seven or eight years, if someone had told me the convoluted sequence of events that would lead to my new calling as an interim minister, I would have told them that they must be thinking about someone else, because I was looking forward to becoming warmly beloved, and I figured it was only a matter of time before I attained that lofty status.

* * *

That afore-mentioned, odd sequence of events began with some writing that I did for the local newspaper. The Holland Sentinel used to have a space on the Friday religion page for local pastors to submit guest columns, and I know this will make me sound egotistical, judgmental and anything but warm or beloved, but I thought a few of them were bad. Bad theology, bad ecclesiology, bad pastoral advice—take your pick. When I sat down with the paper on Friday, Leigh knew that she might hear me start muttering when I got to the religion section.

So one day she said, "Why don't you submit something?" Which I did, 600 words on the pairing of coffee mugs in the dishwasher. It was actually a piece about marriage, based on my observation that at the end of the day, pairs of mugs meant I had probably spent quality time with Leigh, while solo mugs suggested that I hadn't. I called it the Coffee Mug Contentment Measure.

After a few more submissions, a meeting with the Sentinel editor resulted in an offer to write a regular religion column, for pay! (on second thought, never mind the exclamation mark; it was pretty meager pay). A few years later, the arrival of a new editor led to an offer to write a second weekly column for the editorial page. In that one, I was almost completely free to choose my own subjects. Just about the only thing I wasn't allowed to do was endorse a Democrat for public office (in West Michigan, that would be considered a mortal sin).

In spite of this restriction, I still chose to write about state and local government, always a favorite op-ed focus. There are very few things easier to do than find fault with elected officials, and I occasionally experienced mild pangs of guilt as I lobbed yet another written grenade into the political arena. I know that some columnists would be filled with glee if they could goad one of their representatives into calling them late at night, spluttering about the latest thing that was said about them in the paper, but whenever that happened, it only made me feel guilty, knowing that I was doing so little to actually change anything. Ink, like talk, is pretty cheap.

So I'd been ministering at Maplewood for about nine years, and writing in the paper for five when I had another one of those uncomfortable elder visits. This time, there wasn't any list of complaints, just an awkwardly ominous question. "So, Pastor, have you been, you know, getting any inquiries from other churches?"

So much for hanging around long enough to become warmly beloved. I could see that I was probably going to have to move on again, but Leigh and I didn't want to leave Holland. By this time, she was working as a chaplain at Resthaven Care Center, a long term, skilled care nursing facility, a ministry that she loved. Not only that, but all three of our children were at Holland High School.

Conveniently, the State House of Representatives seat for my district was soon going to be open due to term limits, and I judged that with my name recognition from the paper, I had a decent chance to fill it. With Leigh's permission, as well as that of my church (more about that in a moment), I formed a campaign committee, registered with the County Clerk, began raising funds, ordered handouts and yard signs, bought two new pairs of shoes and announced my candidacy.

Before starting the campaign, I had approached the leadership of my congregation for their blessing, describing what I planned to do, and I told them that win or lose, I would be done at Maplewood at the end of the year. If I won, I would obviously be headed to the state capitol in Lansing; and if I lost, it seemed unfair for me to expect that the church would put its ministry plans on hold, waiting around for the outcome of my campaign. I told them that they needed to be able to start planning for their future even while I was still going door-to-door.

I also promised them that during the campaign, my ministry would _always_ come first.

* * *

Looking back, that was an important statement. I gave them my word. Four years later, I think it was one of the first things I thought about when I experienced the whole Jericho idea about obedience.

Here's why: In the middle of the campaign season, I got a call to come to Lansing for what I was told would be an important meeting, a chance to rub shoulders with people who could make a difference in my general election campaign should I win the primary in August. At just about the same time, Joyce, an elderly nursing home resident from my congregation, passed away. Joyce had only a few relatives, none of whom attended my church.

Her sister called me to ask if I could conduct the funeral service, which, of course, was scheduled for the same day I was supposed to be in Lansing. Even though I had called on Joyce often, and counted her as a friend, I did a quick mental calculation, and decided that if I said that I wasn't available to do the funeral that day, it wouldn't cost me anything with my congregation (many of the members had no idea who this woman was). Not only that, but when I told the sister that I had a conflict, and asked if it would be possible to hold the service on another day, she told me that her nephew, also a minister, would probably be able to take care of everything.

When I hung up the phone, I felt relieved—problem solved! —and at the end of the week I was sitting in my "important" meeting in Lansing. It turned out to be a complete waste of time, a bunch of low-level lobbyists nattering at us about how the state government oppressed their clients. In the early afternoon, when I impatiently glanced at my watch, I realized that Joyce's funeral service was just getting under way.

In that exact moment, I knew that I had just lost the election.

I knew it without a doubt. I hadn't kept my word about putting my ministry first, so why would I expect that God would grant me the blessing and responsibility of being a State Representative? Wasn't this the very "lack of integrity" kind of behavior which I had so often criticized in my weekly commentaries?

That's how, six months later, I came to be a Specialized Interim Minister. I lost the election, finished up my ministry at Maplewood (ten years almost to the day, and still not warmly beloved), spent a few months thinking about humility while writing some Bible study guides (on Daniel and I, II, and III John), was invited to take the training for interim ministry, and took my first assignment in Oostburg, Wisconsin.

* * *

Keeping our word is just one of the things that answers the question, "What does it mean to be obedient?" The more I thought about the whole Jericho idea with its emphasis on obedience, the more I knew that whatever form it took, it would have to begin with an emphasis on knowing God's Word.

I already told you about my jelly bean habit—sorting them by color and eating them in sequence—so it might not surprise you to know that I'm also the kind of person who reads the manuals that come with things. Cover-to-cover. I not only know how often to change the oil in my car, I know how to reprogram the electronic key fob. I can set the clock on my microwave oven in less than ten seconds. I assembled the bookshelves for my daughter's first apartment, the ones in the box that ominously said "some tools required," in record time. I can do all these things *because I read the directions*.

We know that following directions makes our lives easier, yet we often think that we can just get by on whatever general knowledge we've picked up along the way. Either that or we think that following directions is for noobs and weenies, and that nothing bad will happen to us if we just do things in whatever way we please.

For example, I once watched my middle brother, Tymon, who at the time was working for a garage that specialized in import cars, reassemble the valve train on a 5-series BMW. Noticing that the car didn't seem to be very old, I asked him how many miles it had on it.

"Hmm, less than 70,000, I think." Not much for a car of this class.

"So why on earth does an expensive car like this already need an engine rebuild?" I asked.

Ty looked up at me. "Because the owner never, ever changed the oil."

I'm guessing that this wasn't due to ignorance. How could anyone not know that a car's oil needs to be changed regularly? Even if you don't read the manual and ignore the maintenance symbol on the dashboard, the reminder postcards from the dealership and the very existence of a zillion quick lube joints pretty much tells you that it needs to be done. This owner just didn't do it, and ended up paying a very high price for his neglect (at least my brother had a big smile on his face as he worked; he may have even been whistling).

So it's one thing to read the manual or the directions or the "how to" guide; it's another to actually obey what we find written there. Both are required, knowing and doing, if we are going to be obedient to God's Word.

* * *

As I said, I'm the guy who reads the manuals, so you may have already guessed that I've read the Bible cover-to-cover. I've actually done it more than once. I take my time, reading at least a chapter a day with my devotions, and one of the main reasons I do it is so that I can learn from the Author what it is I need to know and do as I live my life each day.

I learned the basics of God's Word a long time ago; most of us did. So even though it never hurts to be reminded that stealing is wrong or that gossiping ranks right up there with sins like murder and God-hating (Romans 1:29-30), I actually read now for the more specific, personal guidance that God chooses to reveal to me each day.

Here's a typical example of what I mean. I was recently reading Esther, the one book of the Bible that never mentions God by name (it's as if God is just barely out of sight, working behind the scenes). At the same time, I was dealing with the issue of my ego again, which is easily the size of Montana (I would have said Texas, but I've been to Texas, and those folks are even more convinced of their superiority than I am).

At any rate, my ego was on the table because several weeks earlier, I had been given the chance to apply for two different jobs. The first was a position of some note, the directorship of an important denominational division. It was the kind of career achievement that makes your mother brag to the neighbors. To put it another way, it wasn't an interim position.

When you do interim ministry, many people, including your mother, keep asking "Do you really *like* doing that?" as if to say, "Wouldn't you rather have a *real* job?" This new position would have been a chance for people to say something different to me, something along the lines of "Wow! Congratulations! Good for you!"

The second job possibility was another interim placement, this time at a smallish neighborhood church which was going through an identity crisis. From a prestige perspective, this wasn't anything my mom was going to brag about, and I presumed that just about any trained interim could help this church. The denominational position, on the other hand, clearly required someone with my particular skill set.

While I was still in the middle of the interview process

for the ego-boosting job, I was officially offered the interim placement. Not only did the congregation offer me the position, they offered me a ridiculously generous compensation package which I knew was a huge stretch for them. When I told them about the other possibility and that it would be a couple of weeks before I could give them an answer, they said that they were willing to wait for my answer until that process was completed.

Were these nice people, or what?

After the first round of interviews, reference checks, writing samples, and even a screening session with a staff psychologist, the Mom-worthy denominational people decided that they wanted to run through yet another round of interviews with the candidate finalists, the date for which was almost a month away. I knew that I had to call the church folks who were so graciously waiting for me, but I also knew that I ran the risk of ending up with neither job.

What to do? Accept the humble congregational job, or gamble on the next round of interviews in the hopes of getting the praise-worthy position of note?

You already know what I did, right? I took a chance on the ego-inflating job and didn't get it (I've come to realize that this is something of a pattern with me). On the very day that I was told that it was being offered to another candidate, I called back the church and was told that they too had offered their position to another candidate. Heavy sigh.

So what does all this have to do with my reading the Bible every day? In particular, what did reading the story of Esther during the job interview process have to do with my looming unemployment?

You may recall that two of the characters in Queen Esther's story are Haman and Mordecai, and that Haman had an ego the size of, well, mine (maybe even a bit larger). Haman also considered himself a person of some importance, being the king's right-hand man and all. As he sashayed around the royal city of Susa being all important with himself, it irritated him to no end that Mordecai, a Jew, wouldn't bow down to him. So Haman plotted to destroy Mordecai, as well as the rest of the Jews.

I don't want to give away too much, just in case you haven't read Esther yet, but suffice it to say that egotistical Haman got his comeuppance, while humble Mordecai ended up in royal garments. Just in case I hadn't already gotten the point about my inflated sense of my own importance, on the very day after I lost both jobs, the prayer book that I use as part of my devotions quoted these verses from Paul's letter to the Philippians: *"Do nothing out of selfish ambition or vain conceit. Rather, in humility value others above yourselves, not looking to your own interests but each of you to the interests of the others"* (Philippians 2:3-4). *Frances*

I don't think it was wrong for me to try for the prestigious job, but reading God's Word made it painfully clear to me that I had been seeking it for the wrong reasons (which reminds me: I'm probably writing this book for the wrong reasons, too, but buy some extra copies to give as gifts anyway, okay?)

The point is that we have to read God's Word daily to know how to be obedient. One of the miracles of the Bible is that it truly is a living Word, which means that it has the uncanny ability to speak to each of our unique situations, if we are willing to pay attention to what it says.

In the case of my job search, I should have remembered that those who exalt themselves are often humbled, while the humble are often exalted (see Matthew 23:12). It was right there on the page for me to see—in fact, it was on several pages, both in Esther and in Philippians, and not just on one day of my devotions, but over the course of many days of reading. God was speaking; I just wasn't listening or being obedient.

* * *

That was a rather lengthy example of how I've experienced

God speaking to me through the Bible, challenging me to obedience. There have been countless other times, some of which were so immediate that they were almost scary; others of which have been unfolding over the course of my entire adult life.

As an example of the former, I was once reading the back pages of a weekly news magazine early in the morning (I read while I brush my teeth; you too?) and saw a brief item about a famous movie star which mentioned that she had gotten her start in adult films (by which I mean, you know, *adult* films). I figured that this woman probably had an interesting backstory about overcoming adversity, and I planned to see if I could find out more about it online. Yes, I suspected that I might find inappropriate content there, but hey, I was just interested in how people find success after a rough beginning. Isn't it amazing how we can find ways to justify our disobedience?

Just about an hour later, when I was dutifully reading my devotions before firing up my computer, my daily prayer guide included Psalm 101, in which I was confronted with this verse: *"I will not set before my eyes anything that is base"* (Psalm 101:3). As challenges to be obedient go, it was pretty immediate and pretty direct, and for once I decided not to follow through with my plan to be disobedient.

This example of an immediate word from God also relates to one of the lifelong obedience challenges I've experienced: What it means to be faithful as a husband. This isn't the kind of obedience that we live out by avoiding just one specific kind of behavior, like not stealing, or not lying; neither is it the kind of obedience that only applies in a very narrow situation, like not visiting adult web sites. Rather, it is the kind of obedience which needs to be lived out all day, every day, in every circumstance, "… for as long as we both shall live." Even though Leigh and I have now been husband and wife for more than 37 years, God's Word is still teaching me what it means to be obedient as her husband.

It shouldn't surprise us that so much of what we find in God's Word ends up being about obedience; this is where the Bible begins, after all. In the perfect Garden of Eden, Adam and Eve only had to obey one thing: God told them not to eat from the tree of the knowledge of good and evil (Genesis 2:16-17).

I used to think that this was an unfair setup. How could they not fail? I have no doubt that I would have eaten from that tree, probably before the serpent even got around to tempting me. He'd come slithering up (yes, I know, he hadn't been turned into a legless creature yet), and I'd already be munching away. "Want some?" I'd offer. "I think there's plenty for everyone."

But then, I'm thinking with a mind which has already been corrupted by sin. There's no way that I can imagine what it would be like to never have known sin, so neither can I imagine what it felt like to be Adam or Eve, confronted with this one challenge to be obedient. All I know is that if Eden was perfect, then this tree with its challenge to be obedient had to be perfect, too.

This was another one of those things that I had to think about for a long time. It was when I was writing the Bible study guide to John's three letters that it finally clicked. In his gospel, John recalled something Jesus said at the last Supper: "If you love me, you will keep my commandments" (John 14:15). Later, in his first letter, John expanded on this teaching, making a number of references to how our love is demonstrated by our obedience. For example, in I John 2:3-6, the Evangelist wrote:

"Now by this we may be sure that we know him, if we obey his commandments. Whoever says, 'I have come to know him,' but does not obey his commandments, is a liar, and in such a person the truth does not exist; but whoever obeys his word, truly in this person the love of God has reached perfection. By this we may be sure that we are in him: whoever says, 'I abide in him,' ought to walk just as he walked."

"Whoever obeys his word, truly in this person the love of

God has reached perfection." Suddenly, that tree in the Garden of Eden was starting to make sense. It was a gift, an opportunity for Adam and Eve to experience what it means to give and receive love.

I think the gift aspect of obedience isn't always obvious to us because we live our lives with so many apparently non-spiritual requirements related to obedience; they seem more like tedious demands than gifts. Every once in a while though, we get a chance to be obedient in a way that reminds us of what Adam and Eve may have experienced.

I had this chance when I worked as a Cast Technician in the emergency room of a Grand Rapids hospital (both before I started seminary and during my first year), where I had a supervisor who was so generous and understanding that I was eager to do anything she asked me to do. When I started working for her, and she learned that I was headed for seminary the following year, she bumped up my pay as quickly as she could. When seminary began and I could only work part time, she worked around my class schedule to give me the hours I was available.

I was so thankful for everything that she had done for me that I was glad when she assigned me any additional responsibilities. It was a chance to be obedient in a way that expressed my appreciation. I could give something back.

Maybe that's what Adam and Eve felt about the tree of the knowledge of good and evil, at least until they ate from it. Their obedience was something they could offer to express their love for God, which is still true of our obedience today.

* * *

Throughout the planning for the Jericho project, I was reminded of how important it is for us to know God's Word in order to live God's way. If Joshua had paid no attention to the directions he received about how he was supposed to attack Jericho, he never would have guessed how God wanted it to be done (seriously; would it have occurred to you to do it by walking in circles around the city for a week?)

The same is true for almost any other person we can name from the Bible: If Noah hadn't listened to God, would it have occurred to him to build a boat miles from any water? If Abraham hadn't listened, would he have considered a move from his ancestral home in Ur of the Chaldeans to the distant land of Canaan? If Samuel hadn't listened, would he have chosen David, the youngest of Jesse's sons, to be the king of Israel?

Before they listened to Jesus, would any of the disciples have chosen to follow him? Would Peter and Andrew, or James and John ever have figured out on their own that they were supposed to give up fishing? Would Matthew have left his tax business? Would Paul ever have given up persecution and become an evangelist if he hadn't listened to Jesus on the road to Damascus?

Would Jesus himself, emptied of his glory, have known that the unlikely way of the cross was the way to eternal life for all humanity if he hadn't listened to his Father's voice?

It's when we don't listen, trying to figure things out on our own, that we get into trouble. God's way is so often the opposite of everything else we hear that it's almost impossible for us to guess what God wants us to do, at least until we get some practice at it; and even then, God's Word can still surprise us.

Without knowing God's Word, it's hard to imagine how we could ever be consistently obedient. As God said to Isaiah, *"For my thoughts are not your thoughts, nor are your ways my ways, says the Lord"* (Isaiah 55:8 NRSV). Without obedience, there is no Jericho effect; no walls come tumbling down.

Fortunately, we don't have to learn God's will all at once. No matter where we turn in the Bible, we will find something to guide us. That's where the Jericho effect begins.

QUESTIONS FOR REFLECTION AND DICUSSION

1. Have you ever received a revelation from God, or have you experienced a sudden insight into God's Word? What were the circumstances surrounding that experience? What did it make you want to do?

2. Does "biblical obedience" mean the same thing as "doing everything the Bible says?" Why or why not? How would you define biblical obedience?

3. Have you ever belonged to a church that had a "warmly beloved" minister? What qualities did he or she have that would lead you to use the description? Would you say that he or she was obedient?

4. Describe a time when an unusual series of events led to a significant change in your life. Could you have planned it yourself? Looking back, can you see God's hand in it?

5. On a scale of one to ten, with one being low and ten being high, where would you rate yourself in terms of biblical knowledge? Where would you like to be? What difference do you think that would make in your life?

6. Do you read the directions that come with things? Why or why not?

7. Who would you prefer to spend time with: Someone described as humble, or someone described as egotistical? Which characteristic is more likely to lead to obedience? Why?

8. True or false: Everybody is doing it. What are some other things we say when we are trying to justify our disobedience?

9. What is the relationship between obedience and love? Can you give some examples of how the two are connected?

10. Before moving on to the next chapter, spend a few minutes thinking about the ways that our obedience—or lack of it—affects our family life.

CHAPTER TWO:
I CHERISH, GOD
HONORS

Obedience with My Family

On the day that I read the Jericho story in my devotions, I was finishing up a year as the interim pastor of Hope Reformed Church in South Haven, Michigan. South Haven is a small resort town on the lower left side of the mitten, about 30 miles south of Holland, populated by many part-year and weekend residents from Chicago and Kalamazoo. As a result, when most churches experience their summer slump, Hope Reformed adds a second morning service to accommodate all the extra worshipers.

Their biggest day of the year, attendance-wise, is always the Sunday closest to the Fourth of July, and even though the search committee was ready to name a new pastor—which meant that it was time for me to be on my way—the church's leadership had asked if I would at least stay through the holiday. After that, I would be free to move on to my next assignment.

Unfortunately, I had no idea where that was going to be.

Let me take a moment to get this out of my system: Most of

the denominations that I have served as an interim minister allow their member congregations to pick their own ministers. Not surprisingly, other than the swimsuit competition, this process has a lot in common with a twentieth century beauty pageant. First, there are the preliminary elimination rounds ("Please send a résumé and your responses to these thirty questions"), then there is the talent competition, (we'd like to come to your church and hear you preach), and finally, there is The Interview (substitute "Jesus Christ" for "world peace" and the answers are pretty much the same).

I once asked a woman in my seminary's records office if a congregational search team had ever requested a copy of a candidate's grade transcript. "No," she said, "I don't believe that's ever happened."

Unfortunately, interim ministers are chosen in pretty much the same way. The process is a bit more streamlined, and I've been hired on a couple of occasions without anyone from the congregation even hearing me preach, but churches are free to pick whomever they like as an interim. Most denominations don't have anyone serving as a matchmaker.

What this means is that when a new pastor is on the horizon, interims are pretty much on their own in terms of finding the next church where they can serve. If you're someone like me who has, you know, a mortgage to pay, this can be an anxious time.

As the Fourth of July weekend approached, I had been in conversation with several congregations, none of which seemed to be a good fit. One of them said "No, thank you," when they discovered that my wife was also an ordained minister. Another recoiled in horror when I suggested that the neighborhood around their church was changing, and that this might call for a different kind of ministry. Yet another one told me that all they really wanted was a pastor to keep the doors open and the lights on until their last member passed away. They didn't put it quite that bluntly, but their complete lack of interest in hearing about any of the usual transition work made their wishes clear.

In the middle of running all over southern Michigan and northern Indiana to attend these interviews, I heard about a congregation in Grand Haven, Michigan (about twenty miles north of Holland) which might need an interim. The name of the church was Covenant Life, and it was their founding pastor who was leaving, which meant that it was still quite a young church.

A quick visit to their web site revealed a vibrant, leading-edge congregation that I was certain would never, ever, not in a million years consider someone like me, not even as an interim.

You see, I have no cool factor. At the time, I was a little over fifty and graying. I have some scars on my face, but not the interesting kind that might have been caused by a fencing accident in Heidelberg, or a harpoon incident while serving as a Navy Seal. At five feet ten-and-a-half, I'm neither tall nor short; and even though I work out at the gym four mornings a week, I still mostly look like Popeye before he eats his spinach.

I'm terribly near-sighted, so I either wear thick glasses with bifocals or keep grabbing for my reading glasses if I'm wearing my contacts. My voice is the kind that falls in the bland register where even people with excellent hearing ask me to repeat myself. I dress conservatively: no earrings or tattoos; no woven or beaded necklaces, bracelets or anklets; no vintage rock band t-shirts; no cargo shorts or sandals. Actually, I own a pair of the latter, but it would never occur to me to wear them to church, even though Jesus probably did.

I know that appearance isn't everything, and that there are people who fit my general physical description and yet manage to ooze cool out of every pore. They dominate a room the minute they walk in because they have that hard-to-define "it" factor, something about them that just makes them intriguing.

I'm not one of those people. I'm probably one of the most

forgettable people in any given gathering. If I sat next to you for a semester in college, you would need to read my name tag at the reunion, and even then you would smile politely and say, "Oh, right, Case!" when in fact you didn't remember me at all.

What I saw at Covenant Life's web site was the kind of ministry I had always dreamed about leading, a group of believers who clearly had no interest in being or doing church as usual. Their facility, in the heart of Grand Haven's downtown waterfront, was a reclaimed post-and-beam factory building, the former home of Story and Clark pianos. Pictures of the worship space were filled with guitars, keyboards and drums, surrounded by ancient wooden beams, candles, back-lit scrims, and theatrical lighting. Other ministry pages on the site seemed to be just as creative and forward-thinking; and everywhere I looked I saw pictures of people who seemed to be dripping with cool.

I may have sighed out loud, because I knew that I would never be a fit for this kind of church. I didn't even bother to bookmark the page or jot down any contact information. I just exited the site and went back to wondering what God had in store for me next.

* * *

Thinking about that first encounter with Covenant Life reminds me of another covenant I never thought would happen: Getting married.

My adolescent life plan was to go to college, meet a girl, get married shortly after graduation, begin a lucrative career as a computer programmer, and live the American Dream. A major part of this dream involved a succession of increasingly fine sports cars (my middle brother used to own an MG and a Corvette; I used to drive a Buick Skylark). Long term, I didn't want to settle for anything less than a Ferrari.

This was my approach to dating, too. I figured I would start with some Hondas and Toyotas, move up to a Saab or a Jaguar, and eventually marry my Ferrari. Since there is no possible way that I can continue this analogy without getting into serious trouble at home, I'll stop the car comparisons right here.

I dated quite a bit in high school, mostly because I'm a good listener (and in spite of what I said before about my looks, I'm not hideous, just bland). I could get lots of first dates, and even had several long-term relationships (i.e., beyond the second date), nearly all of which eventually ended in exactly the same way: The girl would sit me down and tell me that she just couldn't take my negative attitude anymore.

Note: In defense of my admittedly pessimistic approach to life, I would just like to say that I was always proven right when I told the girls that they probably wouldn't like me very much when they really got to know me.

Not surprisingly, I graduated from college as a single guy, and moved on to law school, certain that the allure of being married to a wealthy attorney would help me find the wife of my dreams. As it turns out, "law student" isn't the same thing as "wealthy attorney" in women's minds, plus I was still guilty of far too much negativity, which meant that I also left law school as a single guy.

You may have noticed that I said "left" as opposed to "graduated from." I was well into my third year at Wayne State University School of Law when I sensed God's call into ministry. (No, I haven't forgotten that I was talking about getting married or that this chapter is about obedience with my family. I'm getting there.)

What was amazing about this call was that it wasn't as if I was a serious student of the Bible at the time, or that I had even been considering a call into ministry. It really came out of the blue.

Literally.

I was driving from my apartment in Detroit to my parent's home in Grand Rapids early on a beautiful Saturday morning, under a perfectly clear blue sky. Directly ahead of me, as I was headed west on I-96 near Lansing, I saw two dark blue columns in the sky that pointed straight up into heaven. The more I stared, the darker they became, and the more I was convinced that there was something really peculiar going on with the sky.

As I said earlier, I'm not the mystical type, but this got my attention, and I started thinking about God, and whether or not I was seeing something with divine origins. I hadn't been attending church, I hadn't been reading the Bible, and my prayer life was limited to emergency pleas ranging from "Please don't let the professor call on me," to "Please let this girl answer my call." My life included little that could be described as spiritual; it revolved around my classes, my job (waiting tables at a popular bar and restaurant near the Wayne State campus), and trying to get dates. Since I had been raised differently and was probably trying to suppress a lot of guilt about neglecting my faith, I think I was unusually open to the possibility that God might be trying to get my attention.

A few miles farther down the road, I saw a jet flying high above me, headed in exactly the same direction I was driving. I quickly realized that in the early morning sun, rising behind me, the jet's two perfectly straight contrails were creating shadows in the air, those two dark columns I had interpreted as God's sign that I should direct my thinking heavenward.

Well, who's to say that God can't use a jet to get someone's attention? What were the odds that everything would line up so perfectly, that the air would have just the right amount of humidity to create airborne shadows, and that I would be on that particular stretch of highway on that beautiful morning? I smiled at the fact that my ego had let me entertain, even for a moment, the thought that God might send a miraculous sign just for me, but even so, I kept thinking about God all the way to Grand Rapids.

* * *

Within the space of a few weeks, I met with the dean at Western Theological Seminary (no, I didn't tell him about the jet), withdrew from my classes at Wayne State, moved back home with my parents, and found a job (the one I mentioned before, working as a Cast Technician at St. Mary's Hospital in Grand Rapids). I was soon accepted for the fall semester of classes at Western, pending one thing: I had to take Summer Greek.

Summer Greek was an intense, seven-week crash course in the ancient language of the New Testament. Sessions met morning and afternoon, with plenty of homework in between and overnight. If you were successful, you moved directly into an exegesis course in the fall. If you did so-so in the class, you took remedial Greek. If you failed the class it was, "Are you sure God is calling you into ordained ministry?"

As I moved into the house where I would be living with other single male students, I was still looking for signs that I had made the right decision in leaving law school. Another jet would have been nice, but what God sent instead was even better: There were girls in the class.

In particular, my future wife, Leigh, was in the class. She was beautiful, she was smart, and she sat in front of me, which was very helpful for daydreaming through the tedious parts of the course. Missing the obvious, as I often do—I can imagine God saying, "I put the girl right in front of him; how much clearer could I make it?"—I briefly dated a different girl in the class. Yes, she dropped me too, but at least it wasn't because of my negativity. She had started seeing someone else (a really nice, but annoyingly good-looking guy).

As only God could have planned, my brief time dating this other student from late summer into fall actually allowed Leigh and me to become friends before we started going out. We were in classes together and often studied together, and late in the day, a group of us regularly got together to watch reruns of M*A*S*H. By the time the other girl told me that we would no longer be dating, I already knew a lot about Leigh. What I didn't know was whether she had any interest in dating a bland, self-centered, pessimistic law school dropout.

* * *

Turns out she did. Our first official date was in February, we were secretly engaged in April, we publicly announced that we were engaged in July, and we were married in December. At no point during this year did Leigh threaten to leave me due to my pessimism. In fact, she may have interpreted it as a sign of optimism when I originally asked her out on two dates at the same time (one was to hear the country group Pure Prairie League, the other was to the ballet; I figured I would cover the entertainment spectrum). She will tell you that I can still be a glass half empty kind of guy, but even I recognize that she has helped me to be much more positive than I used to be.

What set this relationship apart from all the others that had come before it can be summed up in a single word: Cherish. I cherished Leigh in a way that I had never cherished or cared for anyone before.

The word cherish has its roots in the French *cher* ("dear") and the Latin word *carus*, from which we also derive the word *charity*. Charity, of course, is the word that we find in the King James Version of I Corinthians 13: "*And now abideth faith, hope, charity, these three; but the greatest of these is charity*" (I Cor. 13:13 KJV). If you've been to a wedding in the last couple of decades, you already know that newer versions of the Bible translate that Greek word, *agape*, as "love."

Since Jesus drew such a clear connection between obedience and this same Greek term for love ("*If you love me, you will keep my commandments*" John 14:15 NRSV), I think it is fair to say that cherishing someone is all about obedience. In particular, it is all about that uncommon, Jericho-style obedience that so often seems to be just the opposite of our normal way of doing things.

This means that if we want love to last, we have to consider the unusual way that God teaches us to love. There are examples of this throughout the Bible, starting in Genesis with Adam and Eve and ending in Revelation with the new Jerusalem, *"... coming down out of heaven from God, prepared as a bride adorned for her husband"* (Rev. 21:2 NRSV). In the obedience which is required for God's covenant of marriage, we find the pattern for love which can renew an entire community of believers.

We've already considered Adam and Eve's disobedience, and how their decision to eat from the forbidden tree was a rejection of God's love. It was when their obedience failed that they became aware of their nakedness, and started to hide from God (in the bushes) and each other (behind fig leaves). A few chapters later, in Genesis 12, we discover Abraham and Sarah—still Abram and Sarai at this point—learning much the same lesson about obedience and trust.

A famine had struck the land of Canaan, Abram's new home, so he and his clan were headed down to Egypt to wait it out. On the way, Abram turned to Sarai and said, *"I know well that you are a woman beautiful in appearance"* (v. 11).

What a wonderful husband, complimenting his wife.

"When the Egyptians see you, they will say, 'This is his wife'" (v. 12a).

You can almost hear a hint of pride in his voice, can't you?

"Then they will kill me but they will let you live" (v. 12b).

Okay, now that could be a problem. Abram's solution was to tell Sarai to say that she was his sister, which she was, sort of; she was his half-sister. More importantly, she was his wife, and Abram didn't trust that God would honor their relationship when they arrived in Egypt.

It's hard to accuse Abram of acting selfishly—after all, it was not unreasonable to think that his life was on the line—yet that is exactly what he was doing. He was willing to sacrifice Sarai, to let her become a part of Pharaoh's harem, so that his own life would be spared. Not only that, but as the wealthy "brother" who had just delivered his beautiful sister to the palace, Abram was certain to be held in high esteem; and sure enough, we read that Abram was given *"sheep, oxen, male donkeys, male and female slaves, female donkeys, and camels"* (Gen. 12:16 NRSV).

Although Abram was willing to offer up his wife, God wasn't. God caused Pharaoh and his family to suffer serious diseases, after which the malady-stricken king figured out that Sarai was more than a sister Abram. He gave her back to him and sent them both on their way.

Not to be too simplistic about it, but like Abram, many people today—both husbands and wives—fail to trust in God's protection and love. When trouble comes, as it always will in a world corrupted by sin, they think the answer is to throw their mate under the chariot. Instead of choosing obedience to the sacred vows they made when they stood in front of God and God's people, they choose the more common—and today, I would even say readily accepted—path of disobedience.

This is when we might want to think about the Jericho effect—choosing obedience when everything and everyone else is encouraging us to act in what has become the conventional way. The commander of the Lord's army stood in front of Joshua on the road to his biggest obstacle, Jericho, and while Joshua wondered whose side this warrior would favor, the real question was whether Joshua was willing to prove that he was on God's side. Would he approach Jericho in the usual way or would he trust God enough to do things God's way? Will we demonstrate that same trust in our marriages?

* * *

You know how outsiders can sometimes see things more clearly than the people on the inside? In his time, the Apostle Paul, without personal experience in these matters, clearly understood marriage God's way. Rather than offering up their mates to despotic kings or making other self-serving choices,

Paul suggested that men should be willing to lay down their lives for their spouses, even as Jesus had given up his life for the church (Eph. 5:25). Similarly, he told women to be subject to their spouses, "as you are to the Lord" (Eph. 5:22 NRSV).

In other words, Paul was saying that both men and women could safely choose obedience to God's unconventional way of being in relationship, as demonstrated by Jesus. Being married is not about selfishness or putting ourselves first. It's about trusting so much in God's protection and love that we obediently put our partner's needs ahead of our own. It's about facing even the most difficult obstacles together, with confidence that God will see us through.

If you turn to the King James Version, in Ephesians 5:29 you will find one particular word Paul used to describe Jesus' relationship to the church, which is also the way we should be in relationship to our spouses. It's the Greek word *thalpei*, and the newer English translations render it as *cares for*. In this case, I think the KJV captures the deeper meaning: The word is *cherisheth*.

* * *

Before I met Leigh, I had never experienced this kind of self-sacrificing devotion in any of my relationships—but I had observed it. I saw it in my parents, who enjoyed 56 years of marriage before Alzheimer's disease and a broken hip took my father's life.

My first clear recollection that there was something weird about my parents—in a good way—was when I was still in grade school. This was before white flight and the suburban shopping mall craze, when downtown was the place to be; that's where my dad worked as an optician.

I remember him coming home from work one evening with a bag from Herpolsheimer's under his arm. Herp's (or Purplesheimer's, our other nickname for it) was one of downtown's finest department stores, and when my mom opened the bag, she was all smiles and kisses and some Dutch words that I didn't understand at the time. (Did I mention that we're immigrants? We came over from the Netherlands in 1956 when I was just about a year old).

I didn't think it was my mother's birthday, and I was pretty sure that Mother's Day was always on a Sunday, so I didn't know what was going on.

From that time on, I became aware of some other things that I didn't really understand until many years later. For example, how my mother would only serve pasta for dinner on the nights that my dad had to work late (I think I was in high school before I figured out that my dad didn't like pasta). When we went to Campau Lake on summer Saturday afternoons, my mom always offered to watch my brothers and me in the water so my Dad could lie on a beach towel with his eyes closed, a transistor radio near his ear, tuned to the Detroit Tigers. When my mom needed a car of her own to drive my brothers and me all over the place, my dad bought her a racy convertible (a 1959 Chevy Impala). When my dad couldn't decide which fragrance of bubble bath my mother would like best, he brought home six different bottles.

And there were more Herpolsheimer's bags, many more, and more Dutch words I didn't understand, every one of them a sign of how much my dad and mom cherished each other.

* * *

I assumed that everybody's parents were like this, and didn't really appreciate what a gift I had received growing up until my one of my friends was dating a girl who came from a very different set of parents. The father was the kind of guy who can only be described as a bully and the mother was the kind of woman for whom the term "longsuffering" was invented. I later dated a girl whose parents were like that, too; I couldn't believe the tension in her home. It seemed as if everybody's number one job was to make sure that they didn't do anything to set off His Royal Highness.

Let me say something here as clearly as I can, all kidding aside: I firmly believe that when these types of relationships cross the line into emotional or physical violence, or any other kind of abuse, it's important for the victims in the home to get out the door as quickly as possible. I do not believe, not for a second, that choosing obedience requires us to put up with abuse. We live in a sinful world, and sometimes all we have are choices that each seem to be sinful in their own way. God will forgive us if we've made a mistake, but he doesn't intend for us to live in fear or danger just so we can say that we are being obedient. That would be turning obedience into the worst kind of idolatry. 7.

I shouldn't have been surprised to encounter these very different kinds of marriages and families as I was growing up—the Bible shows us plenty of them.

For example, Abraham's son, Isaac, and his wife, Rebekah, certainly had some obedience issues. She was willing to help her son Jacob deceive his father in order to steal a blessing that rightly belonged to his brother, Esau. I'm pretty sure that falls outside the definition of cherishing.

Jacob, in turn, wasn't exactly an ideal husband or father either in the way that he played favorites with his wives and children. Maybe it isn't possible to cherish more than one wife at the same time, which is why God made monogamy the norm by the time of the New Testament. At least partly due to his father's favoritism, Jacob's son, Joseph, ended up being sold into slavery, something that might have been my fate, too, had any Midianites happened to pass through the south side of Grand Rapids when I was growing up (not because my parents played favorites, but because I could be such an annoying little brother).

King David also had trouble with obedience, not only in respect to his own wives, but in respecting his neighbor's wife; and God told the prophet Hosea to marry a prostitute, a lived-out illustration of the people's disobedience and faithlessness toward God.

But the family man I most want to consider is Achan, a name you might not even recall until I remind you that he's part of the Jericho story. Achan was the man who took some of the devoted plunder from Jericho and hid it under his tent.

Acan

* * *

Everything had been going extremely well for the people of Israel since they arrived near Jericho. Joshua had convinced his army to approach the city God's way, with marching and music instead of battering rams and siege works, and after a week the walls had miraculously collapsed. Obedience to God's commands was working.

To the west of Jericho lay the much less imposing city of Ai. Joshua's spies told him that he would not even need to send the entire army; just two or three thousand men would be sufficient. Joshua cautiously sent the larger number, but to his dismay, they were put to the chase by the men of Ai. Thirty-six were killed.

The significance of this defeat was clear to Joshua, and he complained about it to God. *"O Lord, what can I say, now that Israel has turned their backs to their enemies? The Canaanites and all the inhabitants of the land will hear of it, and surround us, and cut off our name from the earth. Then what will you do for your great name?"* (Joshua 7:8-9 NRSV).

As they had approached Jericho, fear of the Israelites had been growing amongst the people of Canaan. Rahab (more about her in chapter 8) had said to Joshua's advance men, *"I know that the Lord has given you the land, and that dread of you has fallen on us, and that all the inhabitants of the land melt in fear before you."* (Joshua 2:9 NRSV). She went on to tell them that her people had heard about the way the Red Sea had dried up for the Israelites and how they had defeated Sihon and Og, the two kings of the Amorites east of the Jordan.

Following the spectacular defeat of Jericho, the other cities of Canaan might have been willing to negotiate peace terms without so much as raising a weapon, but Ai had changed all that. Now the Canaanites knew that Israel could be defeated.

Joshua should have been able to figure out what went wrong on his own. Since obedience had been the key to defeating Jericho, it shouldn't have been hard to deduce that disobedience was the cause of the army's defeat at Ai.

God listened to Joshua's prayer and said, *"Stand up! Why have you fallen upon your face? Israel has sinned; they have transgressed my covenant that I imposed on them. They have taken some of the devoted things; they have stolen, they have acted deceitfully, and they have put them among their own belongings"* (Joshua 7:10-11 NRSV). He told Joshua about the theft of devoted items from Jericho and gave him a plan for revealing the guilty party. After narrowing down the possibilities by tribe, clan, and family, Achan was left standing in front of the assembled people.

Achan doesn't come across as a particularly evil person. In fact, it's hard not to feel some sympathy for what he did. He told Joshua that he had seen a beautiful robe from Babylonia, two hundred shekels of silver and a wedge of gold weighing fifty shekels. He coveted them, took them and hid them under his tent—no doubt planning to use every penny to pay his kids' college tuition.

The consequences were severe. Achan, along with the stolen goods, his sons and daughters, his cattle, donkeys and sheep, his tent and everything else he had were taken to the Valley of Achor where they were stoned, burned and buried under a large pile of rocks. In these dangerous circumstances, a strong example was necessary.

If my humorous comment about paying college tuition seems shockingly out of place just before the reminder that Achan's whole family was put to death, it's only because we have grown so accustomed to seemingly minor disobediences. We regularly make jokes about them and laugh them off. In the context of our disobedience-tolerating society, the punishment for Achan's sin appears to be all out of proportion to the crime.

It wasn't. This is why I wanted to take a closer look at Achan. Not only did he suffer for his disobedience, his entire family suffered. Thirty-six men died at Ai and their families suffered. Future battles for Israel were going to be much harder than they should have been, and the victims of all those future conflicts would suffer; and it was all because Achan had cherished a robe, some silver and a wedge of gold more than he cherished God, his family, or obedience.

* * *

You may have noticed that we aren't told if Achan had a wife. If he did, maybe she never would have let him bring home the stolen goods. "Not under my tent, mister. You bring those things right back to where you found them!"

He did have children, though, and I want to close this chapter by saying that one of the most important jobs God has given us is to pass along the wisdom of obedience to our children.

Cherishing our partner is an excellent way to begin teaching this lesson, but we also have to love our children enough to help them learn the connection between love and obedience. For example, in a recent trip to the grocery store, I observed a young boy, maybe four or five years old, asking his mother if he could have a piece of candy from the display in the checkout lane. She said, "No," but he put the candy on the conveyor with the rest of the groceries anyway. To my amazement, she didn't put it back, or in what might have been an even better lesson, she didn't make him put it back. Instead, she paid for it, he grabbed it, and off they went.

I know all about picking your battles, especially in the checkout lane of a busy store, but I think this one was worth fighting. If a direct parental "No" can be ignored without consequences, what other clear directives will this child choose to ignore?

Leigh and I weren't perfect with our three, but we worked hard at being consistent. If we said no, we meant no, and if we were faced with disobedience, there were appropriate consequences.

As much as possible, I tried to remember the things I appreciated about the way I had been raised. For example, if I didn't like what my mother had served for a meal, I didn't have to eat it, but neither was I allowed to leave the table or get anything else from the kitchen. If I asked, nicely, to stay up for an extra half hour past my bedtime, I would often get fifteen minutes. If I fought with my brothers and was sent to my room, my mother always came to talk to me before I could come out again.

In fact, as I remember those visits to my room, it makes me realize today how clearly my mother was binding love and obedience together for me.

My bedroom was pretty austere—it looked a lot like a small chamber in a monastery, only without the writing desk or the pot of ink. When Leigh sees pictures of it in our old family albums, she asks, "Where was all your stuff?" The truth is that my brothers and I didn't have a lot of stuff when we were growing up. I had an old, steel-framed bed, a rug on the floor and not much else (my clothes were on the left side of the second drawer in the tall dresser in my parents' room).

In other words, being sent to my room was real punishment; there wasn't much to do there but sit on the bed and think (although I did once discover that I could compound my crime by kicking the steel footboard of my bed, which apparently made a horrible noise in the living room directly below). After I had been in my room for the usual half hour, my mother would come in and sit next to me. Even though I tried to give every sign that I wasn't interested in talking—arms folded, head turned away, tight-lipped—she would ask me if I knew why I had been sent to my room. I would eventually grunt some version of "yes," and then after a few moments of silence my mother would ask, always in Dutch, "Houdt u van me nog?"

Do you still love me?

I couldn't have put it into words back then, but I knew I was cherished, and I've always tried to let my own children know the same thing.

When we cherish what God cherishes, obedience doesn't seem hard at all.

QUESTIONS FOR REFLECTION AND DISCUSSION

1. In your opinion, what gives a person a "cool factor?" Is it simply based on appearance? Are there any cool people in your family?

2. How did you meet your spouse (boyfriend/girlfriend)? Did it happen according to the plans that either of you had for finding a life partner? Was God's hand evident in your meeting?

3. Have you ever been cherished? What are some other words you would use to describe the feeling?

4. What are some of the ways disobedience makes itself known in partner relationships? What long terms effects can disobedience have?

 5. What did you learn about being in a relationship from your parents or grandparents? Can you cite some specific examples of where you saw them demonstrate obedience toward each other?

6. What effect does favoritism play in families? Is it ever a good idea for parents to single out one child for preferential treatment? What effect might this have on the obedience of all the children (including the one who is singled out)?

7. Why do you think Achan kept some of the devoted plunder from Jericho? Do you think he intended to harm his family through his disobedience?

8. How does choosing obedience teach us the real meaning of the word "cherish?"

9. How do we learn to cherish what God cherishes?

10. Before reading the next chapter, take a moment to think about your neighbors. What effect does your obedience have on them?

CHAPTER THREE: I RESPECT, GOD PROTECTS

Obedience with My Neighbor

Franklin Lakes, where I served my second settled pastorate in the late eighties and early nineties, is not what you would describe as a neighborly community, at least not in the sense of chatting with your neighbors over the backyard fence. It's not too big to be friendly—only a little over 10,000 residents—and I'm guessing that most of the people who lived there at the time would have been nice to know, if Leigh and I could have figured out a way to meet more of them. Unfortunately, one of the reasons people chose to live in the borough was to get away from neighbors (for example, it was reported that pop singer Michael Jackson lived there briefly in 2007). Although it is just a short drive from Manhattan, in the middle of densely populated northern New Jersey, much of the community is made up of estates rather than neighborhoods, so it's hard to even see your neighbors, much less get to know them.

A quick word about how our church came to be located there: Back in the mid 1960s, when Union Reformed Church was located on the north side of Paterson, many of the members had already moved north into communities like Prospect Park, Haledon and North Haledon. At about that same time, the people who were busily developing farm land a bit farther north yet, in Franklin Lakes, were looking for a church to anchor one end of a new subdivision.

I'm pretty sure the church leaders didn't know that this was going to become the seventeenth wealthiest community in the United States (with a population of at least 10,000). Minimum house size for this part of the borough was set at 3,500 square feet (most are much larger), no straight driveways were permitted, garages weren't allowed to face the road, and generous set back requirements resulted in lawns that looked like golf courses. This certainly didn't describe the kind of property owned by your typical, working class member of Union Reformed, many of whom were still living in closely spaced over-and-under duplexes.

As a result, the church came to be *in* the community but was not *of* the community, which is to say that only one of our member families had an actual Franklin Lakes address. Well, make that two; we moved into the parsonage located directly behind the church. Whenever other Bergen County people asked us where we lived, our answer would get us that not-so-subtle up- and-down look, as if to say, "Really? You don't look like you're made out of money. How did you manage to swing that?"

We didn't know any of this before we accepted the church's call, although it did seem odd to me that when I had asked in a phone interview, "Is there a parsonage, or will we be expected to buy our own home?" the search team chairperson laughed at me. He quickly recovered and said, "Oh no, you can't afford to live in Franklin Lakes. We provide you with a parsonage." In another phone conversation, it again seemed odd when a member of the church's leadership said, "I hope you're not thinking about trying to get Franklin Lakes people into the congregation; our last pastor tried that. You would be better off focusing on Haledon and North Haledon."

Once we settled in, I started to understand what these people were talking about. Leigh and I were regular visitors to the Franklin Lakes library, shopped at the Franklin Lakes market, ate in Franklin Lakes restaurants (our favorite at the time was the Windmill, which served Italian food—go figure), enrolled our children in Franklin Lakes schools, jogged up and down Franklin Lakes roads, and even managed to snag one invitation to a Franklin Lakes Country Club event. Yet no matter how much we tried to involve ourselves in the community, it was clear that these nice people were never going to be our neighbors, at least not in the, "Hey, could you watch the kids for an hour?" kind of way.

A perfect example was the family—at least I assume it was a family—who lived in the next home up our street. Our properties were separated by a narrow, densely-wooded buffer zone in which I once taught a troop of Franklin Lakes cub scouts how to build lean-to shelters, yet another attempt to get involved in community life; but it might just have well been an entire forest. In five years, I learned exactly two things about these mystery residents: They held a huge Kentucky Derby party each year in May, and they received packages via UPS, one of which had been left with us.

I can still remember my sense of anticipation, knowing that someone from next door would have to come over to pick up that parcel. Would it be a celebrity? A famous athlete? (I knew that several members of the Yankees and the Giants lived somewhere nearby). Would I finally get to be on a first name basis with someone who lived along my road?

When the doorbell finally rang, a rather normal sort of woman quietly asked if we had received a package for her. Leigh handed it to her, and then she was gone.

I didn't even have a chance to ask who she liked in the Derby.

* * *

If Franklin Lakes had remained an anomaly amongst American communities, I might not have even bothered to mention it here, but my experience in the years since we lived there is that more and more people are adopting that same kind of not-so-interested-in-being-your-neighbor lifestyle. Woods and water developments—sans sidewalks, of course—have risen out of the cornfields from coast-to-coast, and even in gentrifying, center-city neighborhoods, where buildings are only a few feet apart, the newly-arriving occupants seem far less inclined to be neighborly than in years past.

Does anyone still bring a plate of cookies over when they see a moving van pull up in front of a vacant house? Do people invite passers-by to join them on the porch for some lemony iced tea and juicy gossip? If I set a cooler of beer on the driveway and prop open my car's engine hood, will I still be able to attract half a dozen neighborhood gearheads, each with their own loudly-stated, but totally different opinion of what I ought to do next?

Here's another measure of how being neighbors has changed: Ask your minister if he or she feels comfortable just dropping in, unannounced, on church members today. Don't be surprised if the look you get makes it seem as if you are speaking Klingon.

That brings me to the key question: In the midst of all these changes in the way we live, or fail to live, in community with each other, what do I owe my neighbors in terms of obedience?

Answer: Everything. Even if the only thing I know for certain about my neighbors is that they would rather be at Churchill Downs in early May, I still need to be keenly aware of all the ways in which my obedience—or lack of it—can make a huge difference in their lives.

Once again, this is a Jericho thing. It's tempting to think that I don't owe my non-neighborly neighbors anything, but then I read God's Word and realize that God is repeatedly confronting us with a Jericho-style challenge: We can behave in the fashion that has become routine and predictable today and experience routine and predictable results, meaning that at best, we probably will never get to know our neighbors, or at worst, we might discover that our behavior causes disastrous consequences for them. Alternately, we can try things God's unusual way, anticipating that God will use our obedience to restore our communities, breaking down the walls that divide us.

Here's what I mean about behaving in a routine and predictable fashion (painful confession time): Our previous home was on a corner in an older downtown neighborhood, and other than the people who lived directly behind us and next door to us, I didn't really know anyone else. I used to see a special education bus pull up every morning and afternoon at a house that was across the corner, but I didn't know anything about the family that lived there. I knew that a house across the street to the west was a rental property—a vacancy sign went up periodically—but it was only when there was a drive-by shooting in the middle of the night that I learned that some of the teenagers there were caught up in gang activity. When a house across the street to the north unexpectedly went up for sale (it seemed as if there were renovations underway), I learned from my neighbor next door that the single man who lived there had committed suicide.

I could look into his front window from mine, and I didn't even know his name.

All of these things were going on within a few hundred yards of where we lived, and I didn't have a clue. I'm quite sure that my neighborhood wasn't unique, so the odds are pretty good that similar things are happening close to where you live.

In addition to being unaware of the ways in which we might be able to bless our neighbors, the usual way of doing things —by which I mean choosing to be deliberately ignorant about the people who live nearby—can contribute significantly to the deterioration of a community.

For example, I once worked at a neighborhood fast-food restaurant in which the manager sold illegal drugs. Many of my fellow employees, several of whom were still teenagers, took advantage of her special "service." She also sold over the counter to certain customers who knew how to ask. There were at least 25 or 30 of us who worked there, and not a one of us said or did anything about her sideline business.

At the time, my attitude was, "Not my problem." I figured that what she did on the side was no concern of mine, as long as I got my paycheck. Looking back now, especially as a parent whose children were once the age I was then, I'm appalled at my indifference. How many lives did we let her ruin by choosing to do nothing?

* * *

It's fairly easy to point at teenagers who get involved in gangs, or a woman who sells drugs, and say that these are the people who are ruining our neighborhoods. It's much harder to identify our own disobedience, acknowledging that even the smallest acts can have enormous consequences.

For example, if I indulge in too much alcohol and get behind the wheel, even once, I might endanger my neighbor's life. If I view pornography, even once, I'm contributing to the problem of violence against women. If I cheat on my taxes, even once, I'm stealing from all the people who do theirs honestly, and who will end up paying more because of my deceit.

In thousands of ways, my daily decisions about whether or not I will live God's way affects my neighbors. If I had simply walked across the street and shown some interest in how my neighbor was remodeling his house, even once, who knows whether or not things might have ended differently.

In the same way that small acts of disobedience can have far-reaching negative consequences, tiny acts of deliberate obedience can make a positive difference. I learned this lesson early in my ministry, when Leigh and I took our church youth group to Darien Lake, an amusement park in upstate New York.

We arrived at the park early in the day, set up a buddy system, set the time and place for checking in, and watched most of the kids run off to their favorite rides. Leigh and I shepherded some of the more timid kids around for a little while, but once they became comfortable finding their way through the park, they also took off.

Neither of us are big on rides, so we went to some of the singing and dancing shows, which proved to be typical theme park fare. We had some lunch, after which Leigh went off with a few of the girls, while I stayed in the picnic area to stretch out on a bench for a short nap (I had to be well-rested for the drive home, after all).

About fifteen minutes later, I was awakened by the voices of two older couples who were sitting nearby, complaining about the way many of the young people were dressed (note: this theme park had water rides). After a few minutes, they changed the subject to Las Vegas. One of the couples had recently been there on a trip and I heard them say that they enjoyed it tremendously.

At this point I sat up and said that I couldn't help overhearing the last part of their conversation. "When you were in Vegas," I asked, "did you by chance go to see any of the shows?"

"Oh, yes," they quickly replied. "They were wonderful."

"I've never been there, but if I understand Vegas correctly, weren't you seeing a lot more, um, revealing outfits there than you're seeing here at the park today?"

"Well yes," said the same woman who had started the original complaining. "But there, it's so tastefully done!"

At that point, I mentioned that I was a minister, trying for that sonorous tone of voice that would cause them to fear that worms might crawl through their Vegas-smitten eyeballs for all eternity. I then excused myself and went to find Leigh. We were planning on seeing one more afternoon show, a pirate-themed waterfront extravaganza, complete with trick water-skiing, swordplay, and invitations to purchase pirate-themed merchandise at the gift shop.

We took our seats in the amphitheater, the show got under-way, and all was just fine until it became evident that we were supposed to think that one of the pirates was gay. His man-nerisms became increasingly suggestive, the dialogue was full of unsubtle innuendos, and of course, the youthful audience (including many from our youth group) was laughing hysteric-ally.

All the while, "But there, it's so tastefully done," kept run-ning through my head. Should institutionalizing disobedi-ence make it acceptable?

When we got back home from the trip, I sat down in my study and composed a letter to the park director of Darien Lake. I began by telling him how much our group had enjoyed our day, complimenting him on the helpfulness of the staff, the cleanliness of the park, and their obvious efforts to make it a family-friendly venue. I said that we were looking forward to coming again the following year.

I then addressed my concern about the pirate show, telling him how hard we worked in our church to teach our young people to show respect for everyone, regardless of age, race, gender, religion or sexual orientation. "It's hard to convince young people that it's wrong to treat people as 'other,' espe-cially when they see it done as part of a professional show, with everyone around them laughing."

Less than two weeks later, I had a reply in my hands from the Director of Live Entertainment at the park. He said that his boss had given him my letter, after which they had gone together to watch the pirate show. They both agreed with my assessment of the show's content and he assured me that the show had been stopped immediately, and that the script was being revised. He closed with a sincere apology and thanked me for taking the time to let them know of my concern.

It probably took me less than half an hour to write and send that letter, and the result was that at least for one season in one theme park, there would be no more gay-bashing.

It seems like that's the way good neighbors should behave.

* * *

When it comes to this area of obedience, the Bible is filled with small challenges that can yield Jericho-sized results for us and our neighbors. Consider a few of the instructions from just one chapter, Leviticus 19.

In verse 9, God said, *"When you reap the harvest of your land, you shall not reap to the very edges of your field, or gather the gleanings of your harvest. You shall not strip your vineyard bare, or gather the fallen grapes of your vineyard; you shall leave them for the poor and the alien: I am the Lord your God."*

If you had fallen on hard times, wouldn't you be glad to know that there might be food for you in your neighbor's field? Naomi and Ruth certainly benefited from Boaz's obedience to this instruction (see Ruth 2). God didn't tell his people that they had to sacrifice everything in order to feed the entire world; he just said that they had to be mindful of their neighbors' needs.

Even though few of us live an agrarian lifestyle, this command still applies, and like the farmers of generations gone by, we'll discover that we hardly even miss the little bit that it takes for us to be mindful of our neighbor.

Let me give you an example from my table-waiting days in Detroit. I always tried to give good service, in exchange for which I hoped to receive a tip. You may not be aware of this, but servers can be paid less than minimum wage because of the expectation that they will receive tip income; so you can understand how important tips are.

After I had worked there a while, I came to the realization that my best nights, tip-wise, were not the nights when a few patrons left generous tips while others left nothing. Rather, the best nights were the ones when every table left something, even if it was just the customary 15%.

In the same way, God isn't asking any one of us to be the complete answer for a hungry world; he just wants each of us to do something. In addition to our church tithe, Leigh and I have chosen to support several causes that we care about; we give a little to each of them, and we hardly even miss it. If everyone did the same, imagine how many of these organizations would be fully funded.

We find another instruction in the second half of Leviticus 19:13: *"You shall not keep for yourself the wages of a laborer until morning."* Just as God hasn't commanded us to individually sacrifice everything until we solve world hunger, neither has he instructed us to single-handedly solve global poverty. What he has asked of us is to be fair and honest with our neighbors when it comes to money. If someone has done something for us to earn a day's wage, then we ought to give it to them that same day, or abide by whatever other payment arrangements we may have made with them.

As a seminary student, few things irritated me more than filling in for a Sunday at a local church and leaving without a check in my pocket. Leigh and I counted on that money to pay rent and buy groceries and gas up the car. If the deacons or the church treasurer decided that we could wait until the end of the month—or sometimes the month after that—it made things difficult for us.

Not only does the person who is owed the money suffer, every neighbor suffers when we fail to heed this instruction. One of the nurses I knew at my hospital job was a terrible money manager and rarely paid a bill until he got a second or third notice. All those extra mailings and late payments raise the cost of doing business, which gets passed on to every other customer.

Verse 16 of the same chapter has yet another small, but critical instruction: *"You shall not go around as a slanderer among your people."* It's amazing how even one little word, if it is false, can destroy our neighbor's reputation.

I've had a lot of experience with this because I used to write a weekly column for our city's daily newspaper, and if there's one thing people can't seem to remember, it's what I wrote in the paper. What they remember exceptionally well is what they *think* I wrote in the paper.

This kind of slander once cost me a job.

* * *

The incident began when Leigh and I were invited to the White House to attend the East Room welcoming reception for the President and First Lady of South Africa.

Ever since seeing the movie *The American President* on television, I had always wanted to attend an official White House function, so I looked up the name of then president Clinton's social secretary, wrote her directly, and said that if she ever found herself with some seats to fill at a White House event, we would love to be considered.

It wasn't much more than a month later that our invitation came in the mail. Leigh and I quickly booked a hotel room, debated what one wears to a welcoming reception (one's best suit, we decided), drove to D.C. and showed up the next day at the White House guest entrance with invitation in hand.

Let me tell you, there are few things cooler than showing up at the White House and having the guard glance at his clipboard and say, "You're expected; welcome to the White House."

The reception itself was impressive. The television cameras and media representatives were corralled in a roped-off area at the back of the East Room. All the cabinet secretaries were on hand, as well as a number of senators and representatives. The Marine Corps Band played and both presidents spoke, after which we got to shake their hands and share a greeting. I believe I said something along the lines of, "It's an honor to meet me ... I mean us ... no, I mean ...," at which point they had already moved on. I imagine that Presidents are used to greeting nervous people.

When the ceremony was completed and people were mingling and chatting, Leigh and I were approached by a woman we didn't recognize. She introduced herself as an assistant to the social secretary and then said, "You must be the Van Kempens."

That was even more amazing than being welcomed at the gate. To be in the White House at all as an invited guest, and then to have someone come over to us and call us by name— well, when I wrote about our whole experience in the newspaper, I closed my column by saying, "It was an honor to be invited to the White House, and an even greater honor to be reminded, once again, that yes, this is a great country."

Now, getting back to the biblical injunction against slandering our neighbor, it was just a short time later that I was sitting at a restaurant in Holland, meeting with some representatives from an area church which was looking for an associate pastor. I had submitted my résumé, and was pleased that I had been invited to the breakfast.

My pleasure quickly disappeared when one of the church representatives said, "You're that Clinton lover, aren't you?" That was pretty much the end of the meeting. I don't know that the man intended it as slander, but it certainly had that effect on the others at the table. It seemed like more effort than it was worth to try and explain to everyone that I hadn't written anything about my *opinion* of the president, just about my *experience* of being invited to a White House event. In the one man's mind, he remembered something different, and that was what he expressed.

As I said, I know people don't always remember what I've actually written, but rather what they think I've written, so if someone should ask you a question about something that I said in this book, all I ask is that you try to be a good neighbor, in the best biblical sense of the word.

* * *

Experiences like this disastrous breakfast meeting tend to stick with you, so several years later, when I got a phone call from an elder at Covenant Life Church (remember them? Grand Haven? Piano factory? Far too cutting edge for me?), my heart both rose and fell at the same time. I was thrilled to even be contacted by them, but at the same time, I was still absolutely convinced that they wouldn't want someone as bland as me.

The elder who contacted me said that they were eager to move quickly on a decision, since their current pastor would be leaving in less than a month. He told me that he and his committee had already spoken with two other interim candidates, but thought they should interview at least one more.

Since the pool of available interims at any given time is fairly limited, I was pretty sure that I knew who the two were, and I judged that one of them would be a much more attractive candidate than me (he wears much cooler glasses, and his hair has some actual style to it, not that a church would ever hire someone for such shallow reasons). At the same time, though, I remembered that he made his home in Grand Haven, which might not work in his favor. You see, interims often benefit from the peculiar notion, one which is held by many churches, that anyone who comes from more than thirty miles away must be an expert.

I allowed one molecule of hope to bubble up.

We spoke on the phone for quite a while, and everything I heard confirmed what I had seen on the church's web site. It was a congregation that was passionate about the arts, and that put a lot of resources and energy into worship. They had a large children's ministry, a creative approach to mission work (partnering with a church in Honduras), they had excellent programming for women and were preparing to do the same for men, they had an in-house coffee shop, plenty of room to expand—two whole floors of the factory hadn't been touched yet—and most importantly, they had recently hired an administrator to take care of day-to-day operations.

To an interim (to settled pastors, too), that last item is a phenomenal blessing. I always used to wonder why I needed a seminary degree if I was going to spend so much of my time on HVAC concerns (heating, ventilation, and air conditioning) and copier repair. As God is my witness, I once became so frustrated with an ancient copy machine that I cleaned the drum —the part you were never, ever supposed to touch—with Windex and a paper towel from the men's room. I thought that if I inadvertently wrecked the thing, maybe the deacons would finally decide to buy us a new one that actually made legible copies. Of course, it worked perfectly after my attempt at sabotage.

Apparently, I didn't sabotage myself over the phone either, because near the end of our conversation, the elder asked if it would be possible for someone to come hear me preach. I had only a couple of Sundays left at Hope Church in South Haven, and told the elder the times of our services. He said that he would see if he could get someone to make the trip down the following Sunday.

* * *

I decided that there was no way to make either Hope Church or myself cool in less than a week, so I did the only other thing I could think of in that situation: I tried to just be myself.

Surprisingly, unless you are afflicted with chronic anti-social tendencies, this is actually pretty good advice. I'm sure that I must have heard it from many people over the years, but the one time I recall hearing it clearly was when a group of my Hope College friends and I invited one of our favorite philosophy professors over to our dormitory for a round table discussion.

Toward the end of the evening, one young woman—who may have actually had stars in her eyes—asked the professor,

"If I wanted to be like you when I grow up, what would I have to do?" I'm sure she was expecting him to say that she had to read some ancient philosophers while yak-herding in the foothills of the Himalayas, but he just laughed and said, "You don't want to be like me, you want to be yourself." Just to make sure we understood him, he repeated it. "The best advice I can give you is to be true to yourself as much as you can be."

That seemed to be about my only choice as I thought about visitors from Covenant Life coming to hear me. My sermon was already done, and I resisted the urge to revise it. I also fought the urge to revise myself—no bleached hair tips, no leaving my shirt untucked, no preaching in sandals. I decided that I was who I was, and that was just going to have to do (except that I did decide to print out my sermon notes in a larger font so that I wouldn't have to use my reading glasses).

Since school was already out for the summer, worship services at Hope were packed with visitors, and there was no way for me to tell which of the many unfamiliar faces might belong to the guests from Covenant Life. The service went well; I've often found that people who choose to go to worship while they are on vacation bring good energy to a congregation. I think it's because they know that they don't have to teach Sunday School, greet, usher, make coffee, work in the nursery, or do anything else that they might do on a regular Sunday in their home church. They are free to simply worship, and from my own experience, I know how nice than can feel.

After the benediction, I went to the back of the sanctuary to shake hands and encourage people to stay for that coffee that they didn't have to make, and when nearly everyone had departed, I saw Bill Rockhold, one of my favorite senior members at Hope standing in a pew having an earnest conversation with an unfamiliar couple. Bill, a retired banker, was one of my biggest supporters, someone I had listed as a reference on my résumé. I walked over to where the conversation was going on, and Bill turned to me and said that these were visitors from Covenant Life Church who had come to hear me preach. "We used to work together," he said, and then, turning back to the couple he continued, "It was so good to see you again today. We'll have to get together soon."

A quiet "Thank you, Jesus," escaped my lips, and I allowed a second molecule of hope to bubble up.

* * *

I received a phone call the next day inviting me to a Friday morning meeting of the Covenant Life committee which was looking for an interim. Arriving a few minutes before my appointment at 9:00, I parked in front of what I thought was the front door, only to find a sign which said that the main entrance was on the opposite side of the building. As I was debating whether or not to move my car, someone opened the door and asked if they could be of help. I told him who I was there to see, and he said, "I know right where he is; let me take you there."

Walking through what I later learned was called Main Street, a gathering area which had been created to connect one of the old piano factory buildings with an adjacent warehouse (now the worship center), I saw a couple of dozen men who all seemed to be hard at work at various tasks—moving tables and chairs, cleaning windows, dusting off duct work, hanging things from the ceiling.

My expression must have given away my curiosity, because the man who was leading me to my meeting said, "This is the Friday Morning Crew. We get together every week for Bible study, and then we stick around to do whatever needs to be done around the church."

I was taken to the room where the interim committee was meeting, answered the usual "How did you get to be an interim?" questions, and spoke for a few minutes about the developmental tasks of the interim period. I talked about some of the congregational survey materials that I liked to use, how I used that information to shape a series of Pulse Nights (taking the pulse of the congregation), and spent a few more minutes on the search process itself.

It seemed like the interview was going well when one of the committee members suddenly said, "If you come to be our interim minister, you're not going to preach in a necktie, are you?" Up to that point, I hadn't realized that I was the only person in the room wearing one. I assured him that the tie could easily go the way of all mortal flesh.

It was at about this point, when I thought the interview was winding down, that another of the committee members sat back in his chair, and said, "You know, we aren't interested in just holding our own until a new minister comes. We want the church to continue to move forward while the search goes on. What are your thoughts about that?"

I didn't really know enough about the church to give anything like a specific answer to his question, and was about to say that, when suddenly I heard the word "Jericho" coming out of my mouth. I told the committee about this idea that I had been thinking about recently, a whole congregation committing to a study of God's Jericho-style challenge to obedience. It would culminate in a Jericho week and a Jericho Sunday, when the whole church, led by seven trumpets, would march around the building seven times, praying for God to tear down the walls that we build through our disobedience. I finished by saying, "From the little I've seen already, maybe this church is just unique enough—or crazy enough—to give the Jericho idea a try."

Driving home, I was afraid that I might have gone too far, and I didn't tell Leigh that I had brought up Jericho with the committee. I was surprised to get a phone call later that day, asking if I could come to a meeting of the full church council the following Monday night.

At that meeting (no necktie this time), I covered a lot of the same information again, and was determined that I was not going to go off on another Jericho bender. But one of the elders who had been present on Friday said, "Tell the council what you told us about Jericho last week."

So off I went again, providing a little more detail about the worship services which would lead up to the Jericho week, the six areas of obedience, the daily devotions, how we could commission a trumpet fanfare and march for seven trumpets, how we would carry the Bible as we marched around the church rather than the Ark of the Covenant, and how the final Jericho Sunday would give us the chance to experience God breaking down walls—between husbands and wives, parents and children, neighbors, co-workers and between each of us and God.

When I finished, it was quiet for a few moments. I answered a question about when I might be available to start and another about some contract details. Then the council president asked me to step out of the room for a few minutes.

When they invited me back in, they told me that they would like me to be their interim minister, starting one month after the current minister's farewell Sunday. As I was leaving, I turned to one of the elders who had been sitting near me and told him how thankful I was for the opportunity to serve Covenant Life.

"It was an easy decision," he said. "We could hear the trumpets."

QUESTIONS FOR REFLECTION AND DISCUSSION

1. Describe the community and neighborhood where you live. Do you judge that you are a part of the community or do you just live there? What difference does that make?

2. Is "neighborly" another way of saying "obedient?" Is it possible to be a good neighbor without also being an obedient neighbor?

3. What are some of the ways that a lack of knowledge about our neighbors can contribute to the deterioration of a neighborhood?

4. The couples who had been in Las Vegas said, "But there, it's so tastefully done." Does institutionalizing disobedience make it acceptable? Are the rules of obedience different depending on where you are? Should they be?

5. In biblical times, farmers were supposed to leave some grain in their fields and grapes on their vines for "the poor and the alien." What's the modern equivalent of this commandment? Does this apply to everyone in a community?

6. Am I responsible for feeding the entire world, or just seeing to it that my immediate neighbor has what he or she needs? How can I know if I am doing my part?

7. Is it possible to effectively retract a slanderous comment against our neighbor? Why or why not? What effect does slander or gossip have on the relationship between neighbors?

8. "Be yourself, as much as possible." When is that good advice? How can trying to be someone other than ourselves get us into trouble?

9. What characteristics would make a congregation into a good neighbor church?

10. The chapter title talks about respect and protection. How does respect for my neighbor result in protection for my entire community?

CHAPTER FOUR:
I WORK, GOD
PROVIDES

Obedience at Work

Deli counter clerk.
Stock boy.
Dry cleaning clerk.
Dry cleaning delivery driver.
Parks department playground assistant.
Pharmacy delivery driver.
Dishwasher.
Food service line cook.
Mailroom clerk.
Bottling plant line operator.
Pizza chef.
City Training Office assistant.
Bailiff.
Waiter.
Bartender.
House painter.
Legal office intern.
Nursing home aide.

Orderly.

Emergency room cast technician.

Library attendant.

Pastor.

To the best of my recollection, this is a complete list of all the paying jobs I've held since I was 16 years old, not including several stints with Manpower. There was one other job that I had briefly when I was 15, but I'll get to that one later.

As I look back over the list, I can think of specific examples of how I was disobedient at every single place I worked. I snitched Greek Kalamata olives when I was at the deli ("snitched" sounds so much more acceptable than "stole," doesn't it?) When the dry-cleaning manager asked if I knew how to drive a stick shift, I fibbed and said "Yes," even though I had never done any such thing (okay, it wasn't a "fib," it was a flat out "lie," and a new clutch can't be that expensive, can it?) When I was waiting tables, I joined in the kitchen banter about customers who gave special instructions with their orders (and "banter" sounds better than ... oh never mind, you get it already). When I was a food service line cook, well, let's just assume that you don't really want to know what happened to that one tray of sliced roast beef before it got served.

In spite of all the ways that I remember being disobedient at my various jobs, I am confident that every single boss I've ever had would say that I was a good employee. I arrived on time and didn't leave early. I wasn't taking money from the deli cash drawer or letting criminals sneak out the back door of the courthouse. I didn't water down people's drinks or open their mail. I was only guilty of the usual things, the kinds of minor disobedience that we take for granted in the workplace. We justify it by saying "everyone does it," and that's probably very close to the truth.

So, we should just move on then, right? Jump ahead to obedience in prayer, or maybe go back to partner obedience again? Why even bother to write about obedience in the workplace when we agree that a little casual disobedience is totally par for the course?

A number of reasons come to mind, not the least of which is the fact that God has something to say about our obedience at work. It doesn't really seem as if God is going to be okay with stuffing our pockets full of sticky notepads to take home, even though everyone else may be doing it. Throughout the Bible, God surprises us with some unconventional, Jericho-style instructions regarding work that might seem just as absurd to us as defeating a city by marching around it in circles.

* * *

Before we get to God's sticky note policy, let me just review some of the standard, and not necessarily biblical, reasons why disobedience at work is a bad idea.

First up, disobedience tends to grow. It may be just a few minutes of personal e-mail time today, but tomorrow you discover that you've spent half the day on non-work-related web sites.

For example, I had a manager at one of my pre-seminary, city jobs in Grand Rapids who called me at my desk early one morning to see if I could clear my schedule for the middle of the day—late morning, lunch, and the first part of the afternoon. He said that he wanted me to go with him to one of the city's other facilities so that I could meet some of the personnel there. That sounded good to me, so we met up a little after mid-morning, checked out a city car and hit the road.

We did stop, briefly, at the other facility which was located to the west of Grand Rapids, and there we spent not more than ten minutes with the people he wanted me to meet. We then continued on a little farther west to a community along the lakeshore for a leisurely lunch (this was one of those managers who loved to talk). After we had finished our coffee, we got back in the city car and drove to a nearby marina where —what a coincidence!—this manager slipped his boat. He told me that whenever work required him to be out in this direction, he always took a few minutes to check his dock lines. By mid-afternoon, when we finally got back to the office, there wasn't much time left for either of us to do any actual work.

I'm sure this manager didn't use a city car to run out and check his dock lines the very first day he was on the job. He probably started with just a few extra minutes of coffee break during which he may have made a quick phone call to the marina. But over time, his disobedience had become so brazen that he was willing to steal away for almost an entire day.

A second reason why routine disobedience at work is a bad idea is that it rarely stays at work. It has a way of spreading to other parts of our lives.

If you routinely lie to people on the phone about the progress of their orders, when in fact you haven't even gotten to them yet, it's that much easier to lie to your spouse when he or she asks why you were late coming home. I'm just guessing here, but I'll bet that former manager of mine didn't boast to his wife about how he had ripped off the city by spending nearly the entire day away from the office. It was probably more like, "I had *such* a busy day today, and then on top of that, I had to run out to the western office with that superb young man we hired. Oh, and as long I was out there, I took a second to check the boat. It's fine." Not completely a lie, but hardly the unvarnished truth, either.

A third consequence of being casually disobedient at work is that it forces us to tolerate other people's disobedience. There was a lot of alcohol being consumed in the back room of that pizza restaurant where I worked. Not surprisingly, this was against the rules (and I would think against the law, too; drinking beer while operating a 750-degree commercial pizza oven can't be a good idea). But since I was occasionally guilty of that particular indiscretion (which sounds so much better than "insanely illegal behavior"), I could hardly complain when another employee "accidentally" got an order wrong so that he would have something to eat on his dinner break.

I'm sure there are many other non-spiritual reasons why

even the smallest acts of disobedience at work should not be tolerated, but the bottom line is that it happens all the time. My oldest brother worked in the corporate office of a large chain of retail and grocery stores, and he told me that one of their biggest problems was employee theft. These weren't people who took the job so that they could make off with something significant and then disappear. No, these were people who thought it was okay to steal from the company and still show up for work the next day.

* * *

But clergy are immune from disobedience at work, right? Ha! Good one! If that was true, there would be better preaching (more of the time alleged to have been spent on sermon preparation would actually be spent on sermon preparation), more pastoral visitation (excuses like "I had a really busy week" would no longer refer to those two afternoons on the golf course), fewer pastoral terminations (dismissals for inappropriate sexual behavior are approaching epidemic levels), and possibly even less need for interim ministers, not that interims are immune from disobedience. If anything, we can get away with even more of it than a regularly installed pastor. Whenever someone can't find us for a few days, they just assume that we must be off doing whatever mysterious work it is that interims do.

It was when I was unpacking my 23 boxes of books at Covenant Life Church that I realized how easy it would be for me to get away with far less work than was expected of me. As I was scratching my head, trying to figure out how several volumes of classic *Bloom County* comics got in with my theology texts, one of the secretaries stuck her head in the door and welcomed me to the church. She said, "It will be nice to have someone around the office because our previous pastor was never here much. He did most of his work from home."

Before I continue, let me pause for a moment to express

my appreciation and amazement for what this previous pastor, Andy DeJong, had accomplished at the church. Andy had originally been called as a non-ordained, part-time pastor to work with a handful of families who had a dream of beginning a ministry in downtown Grand Haven. They began at the YMCA, and when that space became unavailable, they rented a leaky, drafty corner of an abandoned post-and-beam piano factory. Over the course of the next 17 years, they bought the factory and converted it into a wonderfully creative worship and ministry space; they started many unconventional programs for education, fellowship and outreach; they formed a close mission partnership with Vida Abundante, a church in Tegucigalpa, Honduras, sending dozens of adults and youth on work trips each year; and without ever advertising—or even putting a sign on the front of the building—they welcomed hundreds upon hundreds of new members. I was told that Pastor Andy had said, repeatedly, that if the church was going to grow, it was going to be by the personal invitation of those who already belonged to the congregation.

So even though the secretary had said that the previous pastor rarely worked from his study at the church, I'm not suggesting that he didn't work. In fact, it might have been the case that he was overworked, and that the increasing size and complexity of the ministry was one of the contributing factors in his decision to close his chapter at Covenant Life.

Still, when I heard that the church wasn't accustomed to having a pastor in the building, I realized how easy it would be for me to also "work from home," which in my case would mean *not* working from home, because when I'm home, I can always find something more interesting to do than work. This may be my biggest personal issue with disobedience in the workplace: I don't like to think of myself as lazy, but I sure can find a lot of things to do before I get around to what I'm supposed to be doing.

This is hardly a new problem, as evidenced by the fact that King Solomon had so much to say about it. A quick review of his Proverbs makes us realize that slackers have been irritating their bosses for thousands of years.

In fact, speaking of being irritating, Proverbs 10:26 (NRSV) says, *"Like vinegar to the teeth, and smoke to the eyes, so are the lazy to their employers."* Isn't that one of the important rules we learned as kids? If you really want to annoy your parents, do whatever they ask you to do, but do it as *slooooowly* as you possibly can? It's not so funny when that's the way you work as an adult.

Proverbs 20:4 (NRSV) says, *"The lazy person does not plow in season; harvest comes, and there is nothing to be found."* This doesn't sound like the person you want heading up your long-range planning committee. You really want to find someone who understands that it's today's work that yields tomorrow's results.

Proverbs 21:25 (NRSV) tells us, *"The craving of the lazy person is fatal, for lazy hands refuse to labor."* A young man whom I visited in prison was practically the embodiment of this verse. He desperately wanted to have lots and lots of money, but he didn't want to work in order to earn any. So he came up with a variety of boneheaded schemes by which he could amass his fortune, all of them against the law. "Fatal" in his case meant that life as he knew it was over.

Unfortunately, this kind of behavior isn't limited to foolish young sluggards (which is how the NIV refers to these lazy persons); quite a few well-educated corporate and political sluggards have been convicted for the same kinds of schemes, only on a much grander scale. It may not be the death of them, literally, but it sure is the death of their careers, their reputations, and quite often, their marriages and family relationships.

King Solomon had at least another half dozen things to say about lazy people in his Proverbs, but they all make pretty much the same point: If you choose to be disobedient through laziness, you are very likely to end up with exactly what you deserve: nothing.

* * *

I want to say just a quick word about the bookshelves in my study at Covenant Life, because they illustrate how much the members there cared about the way even the littlest things were done.

Since the previous pastor kept his library at home, I saw only a tiny shelving unit in the study when I first toured the building. I mentioned this to one of the elders who said that he would take care of it. By the time I was moving in a couple of weeks later, the Friday Morning Crew had taken a couple of massive wooden posts (rescued from a part of the building that had been torn down in the renovation), sandblasted them to remove the old paint, ripped them into two-inch thick planks, sanded and stained them, and then installed them along one complete wall in the study. They were gorgeous; you would have thought they had been in the building for a century.

Now, back to obedience. When my books were finally in place, the church administrator came by to ask if I wanted to have my office furniture rearranged. He was thinking about whether or not I wanted to be able to see out a window while I was working, while my first thought was about which way my computer screen would be facing. In particular, would it be visible to people coming in the door?

You see, I know myself all too well, and it is important for me to always have my screen situated in such a way that anyone can sneak up behind me—or just walk past my open door —and at least have an idea of what I'm working on. I need for that possibility to exist, because not only am I tempted to spend way too much time playing spider solitaire (which is ridiculously addictive; in fact, let me just pause here ... oh well, I lost), but it is also far too easy to click a few keys and suddenly be staring at something inappropriate. In this case, "something inappropriate" is the polite euphemism for adult content.

A lot of disobedience at work is about sex. Whether it's the Internet, the person in the next cubicle or the cute copier repair guy, we may try to pretend that it's harmless, but we know that it isn't. We typically spend eight hours a day at work, which is likely to be more time than we spend awake with our husbands or wives. That's a lot of time for temptation to work on us, and even the smallest compromises in our obedience can have devastating consequences.

I first learned about the combination of work, disobedience and sex when I was 15, filling in for one of my older friends at a place called Phone-a-Maid. A few weeks earlier, he had told me about this great new job he had gotten. It was just a couple of hours each afternoon, and all he had to do was restock cleaning supplies and check the equipment trays that the maids turned in when they came back from their jobs.

When he went away with his family for a couple of weeks of vacation, I quickly discovered why he liked this job so much: Most of the cleaning supplies came back untouched. I occasionally had to replace a few rags or put a new bag in a vacuum, but the majority of the trays came back without so much as a sponge out of place. This being my very first experience with employment, I was afraid that maybe I had misunderstood what I was supposed to be doing, so I went to speak to the boss. He just smiled and told me that I was doing a great job.

It suddenly occurred to me that maybe Phone-a-Maid wasn't all about the dusting, if you know what I mean. I never found out for sure if my suspicions were correct (I never even got to meet any of the maids!) and they went out of business pretty quickly, but in my 15-year-old brain, it was the first time I had ever thought about the connection between sex and disobedience on the job.

* * *

I don't know what my expression looked like when the possible truth about Phone-a-Maid dawned on me, but I'm pretty sure I saw something like it on the face of one of my seminary classmates when our Old Testament professor, Dr. Piet, taught us about the role of Rahab in the Jericho story.

We were covering the early part of the Israelite conquest of Canaan, and had gotten to the part of the story where Joshua had sent two spies into Jericho to check it out. As I recall, Dr. Piet was saying something about the providence of God in keeping the spies safe when one of my very conservative friends raised his hand and asked an innocent question along the lines of, "How do you think the spies found Rahab?"

The professor paused for a moment. Then he said, "Well," and then paused again as if he wasn't quite sure what he wanted to say next. In that precise moment, it appeared that my friend suddenly remembered the contemporary meaning of the label which almost always follows the name Rahab: "The harlot." Lo, his face turned exceedingly red, and yea verily, for a moment he was stricken dumb. He finally stammered something about how that couldn't possibly be right, while Dr. Piet quickly moved on, reminding the class about the way that Rahab would have known to keep secrets, how she might have had information about the city's leadership and army officers, and how her house was perfectly situated in the city wall so that the spies could escape.

We never did have any further discussion about how the spies happened to be staying at her place.

* * *

In Rahab's case, it was obedience to a God she only knew by reputation that made all the difference for the spies. She was willing to put not just her livelihood, but her life itself at risk for the sake of doing what she believed the God of the Israelites would want (Joshua 2:8-21).

I'm certainly not suggesting that what God wants of us today is to find an illegal, immoral, or unethical line of employment, and then use it for a godly purpose; Rahab is not a "Go thou and do likewise" story, at least not in that way. What I am saying, in the same way that Jesus used the example of the reluctant judge (Luke 18:1-8) or the crooked steward (Luke 16:1-9), is that if even Rahab knew enough to use her work as an opportunity to achieve a godly end, how much more shouldn't we use our daily work to obediently accomplish God's purposes?

This is the Jericho challenge when it comes to our jobs. The conventional attitude toward work is that it is a necessary evil that we endure in order to make enough money to support ourselves and our families, with maybe a wee bit to spare for charity. A few people truly enjoy their employment (my own dad kept working as an optician until he was 79), while at the other extreme, a few people actively despise going to work every day. But the majority of the wage slaves in between seem to just put up with work as something that they have to do in order to pay for their real lives, which begin at quitting time—which may explain why disobedience at work is so rampant. If I don't love, cherish or honor my job, why would I put any special effort into being obedient while I'm at it?

God suggests a completely different attitude when it comes to the way we work. Like Joshua standing on the road to Jericho, considering a radically different way of dealing with the city, God's approach to work also requires a leap of faith and obedience that defies conventional wisdom.

To begin with, God definitely expects us to work. I would even say we were made to work, and I fully expect that we will still have jobs in the life to come. Adam had work to do in paradise—"*The Lord God took the man and put him in the Garden of Eden to till it and keep it*" (Genesis 2:15 NRSV)—so it's entirely reasonable to conclude that work has always been a part of God's plan for humanity, and that it will still be a part of God's plan when Jesus returns in his glory.

Secondly, there is a direct connection between our daily

work and our daily bread. When Paul was writing to the church at Thessalonica, he said, "For we hear that some of you are living in idleness, mere busybodies, not doing any work. Now such persons we command and exhort in the Lord Jesus Christ to do their work quietly and to earn their own living" (II Thessalonians 3:11-12 NRSV). A verse earlier, he had been even more direct: *"Anyone unwilling to work should not eat."*

I was once at a restaurant south of the church I served in Oostburg, Wisconsin, the walls of which were covered with Delft tiles, all of which had popular Dutch sayings painted on them. While I was waiting for my food, I walked around and read several of them, only one of which I remember: "God feeds all the birds of the air, but he doesn't throw the worms into the nest." That's not a bad summary of what the Apostle Paul was saying to the Thessalonian Christians. Obtaining the basic necessities of life is supposed to get us up and going in the morning.

But that's not the most important reason that God gives us work to do. We may be made for work, and our need for daily bread may be our immediate motivation, but we experience the Jericho effect when we choose to work God's way, remembering that work itself was once as good and perfect as anything else in creation.

Clearly, God didn't need to give us jobs in order to provide for us. When I was a very young child, I thought that the big red breadbox on our kitchen counter was magic. Not only did fresh loaves of bread show up in there, but sometimes there were cookies! God could have created the world in such a way that our bread boxes actually did refill themselves. I'm not exactly sure what Adam was doing when he was tending the Garden of Eden, but he certainly didn't need to do it for food. I imagine that whatever the work was, it gave him perfect satisfaction and joy to know that he was cooperating with God in caring for creation.

After Adam and Eve sinned however, the earth no longer

gave up its bounty so easily. The joyful work of gardening became the painful toil of tilling the ground. Everything in creation was corrupted by sin, work included (Genesis 3:17-19).

As anyone who hits their Monday morning snooze alarm six times or more can tell you, we're still dealing with the consequences of sin every time we have to go to work. But this doesn't mean that our work can't reveal the glory of God. When we choose to do it God's way, we can begin to experience what Adam felt in the Garden, not to mention what Joshua felt when the walls of Jericho fell down.

To put it very plainly, the Jericho approach to work means that we have to completely abandon the idea that we are working for ourselves.

* * *

As I sit here working today, there is a classic, 85 foot, 1929 Hoffar-Beeching Motor Yacht for sale at a marina in Port Orchard, Washington. It is a gorgeous boat, beautifully restored and maintained, and I would love to be its next owner.

If I made that my primary reason for going to work every day, I could afford to buy the boat. Of course, Leigh would have to give up her car, our children would have to pay us to babysit our grandchildren, our charitable giving would be reduced to zero, and there's a chance we would fall behind on our mortgage payment (good thing the boat is big enough to live aboard). The point is that I could make my work all about me and my own wants, thinking that this is the way that I will experience joy in my labors. But in the long run, I know that my joy would be fleeting.

Even so, this is more or less the conventional way of thinking about why we work—so we can get more stuff. Obviously, we take care of our families and pay for things like food and tuition and the electric bill and so on, but after that we start eyeing the big screen TVs, the stainless steel gas grills, and yes, the Hoffar-Beeching Motor Yachts. Now, tell me if you agree with this: Our joy at owning any of these things is temporary, right? These fruits of our efforts may give us a short burst of joy, but when the plasma screen goes dim, the gas jets clog up and the boat sinks (what did you expect? It was built in 1929!), we realize that there must be a better way to find lasting joy.

There is, and there's nothing hard about it. It's just that it's the opposite of the way that we usually think about work.

Consider what the Apostle Paul said when he was writing to the slaves who were part of the Colossian church: "Slaves, obey your earthly masters in everything, not only while being watched and in order to please them, but wholeheartedly, fearing the Lord. Whatever your task, put yourselves into it, as done for the Lord and not for your masters, since you know that from the Lord you will receive the inheritance as your reward; you serve the Lord Christ" (Colossians 3:22-24 NRSV). Paul had a word for the masters, too: "Masters, treat your slaves justly and fairly for you know that you also have a Master in heaven" (Colossians 4:1 NRSV).

There are two things I want to point out here. The first is that whether we are slaves or employees, masters or bosses, the same principle applies: It is the Lord Jesus Christ we are serving. The way we do our work says something about our relationship with God. If we present ourselves as Christians, disobedience in the way we work gives God a bad name.

Secondly, Paul holds out the promise of a reward for those who remember that they are working for the Lord. He calls it an inheritance, which may cause us to think about eternal life, but even if that is what he had in mind rather than something more immediate, we know that the promise of the life to come already has benefits in this life.

For example, when I was about eight, and my parents told my brothers and me that our summer vacation was going to be at Niagara Falls, just knowing that I could go up and down the street and brag to all my friends that we were going someplace special was a reward in itself. That's probably not a good approach to evangelism, but you get the idea; the future promise has tangible benefits today. Remembering that we work for the Lord and that he has promised us a reward is a first step in changing our attitude toward the way we work.

Now consider what Paul wrote to the Ephesians: *"Thieves must give up stealing; rather let them labor and work honestly with their own hands, so as to have something to share with the needy"* (Ephesians 4:28 NRSV).

Doesn't the last part of that verse seem like a non-sequitur? (Yeah, I had to look it up, too. A non-sequitur is "a conclusion or inference that does not follow from the premise.") Paul tells the thieves to get to work, not so that they can eat or take care of their families or stay out of jail, all the reasons we might expect him to cite, but so that they can join the ranks of charitable donors. It's unexpected, but it clearly reveals Paul's understanding of why we work: It's so we'll have something to give away.

I've been robbed twice in my life, once when I was 11, by a gang of violent terrorists (okay, they were maybe 13 or 14, but they poked me really hard and threatened to push me down), and again when I was 17, working at the drycleaners. In that case, I really was the victim of violence, having been clubbed over the head with a baseball bat. In both cases, the thieves didn't care to work; they just wanted to take what belonged to someone else and keep it for themselves.

Working obediently produces exactly the opposite result. God challenges us to work diligently, and then to give away some of what we earn so that those who are in need will have daily bread of their own; and that will give us lasting joy in a way that stealing—or even just working hard but keeping everything for ourselves—will never provide.

Just in case you think Paul's comment in his letter to the Ephesians was a fluke, he said much the same thing when he was with them in person. *"You know for yourselves that I worked with my own hands to support myself and my companions. In all this I have given you an example that by such work we must support the weak, remembering the words of the Lord Jesus, for he himself said, 'It is more blessed to give than to receive'"* (Acts 20:34-35 NRSV). Although that's a saying of Jesus not found in the gospels, it is consistent with everything else he said.

Leigh and I have certainly found it to be true.

* * *

When it comes to the way we work and what we choose to do with our income, Leigh and I have always tried to live according to what Paul was teaching. Okay, "always" might be an exaggeration; there was that time that I test drove a vintage Porsche when Leigh thought we should probably be looking at something with a roomy back seat. But most of the time, we have tried to keep in mind the opportunity for blessing others with a significant part of what we earn.

In more than 37 years together, there's nothing we've done with our money that has made us richer, or given us more joy. The Jericho effect of being obedient in how we work and in what we do with our income continues to astonish us.

When we first got married, we decided that we would live by the principle taught in Malachi 3. The Israelites had been unfaithful to God and were asking how they could return when God told them that they had been acting like thieves. *"How are we robbing you?"* they asked.

"In your tithes and offerings," God answered. *"Bring the full tithe into the storehouse, so that there may be food in my house, and thus put me to the test, says the Lord of hosts; see if I will not open the windows of heaven for you and pour down for you an overflowing blessing"* (Malachi 3:8b, 10).

At first, I was much more legalistic about this than Leigh. I would regularly work out the percentages to make sure we were tithing, but just barely. She, on the other hand, was so eager to give away our income that when she got her first paycheck as an ordained minister, she tried to tithe 110% of it. She had such a long list of people and ministries that she wanted to support, she was ready to give away more than she had earned.

Over time, Leigh's joyful embrace of God's promise has changed the way I think about my obedience at work. I used to think that if I could just get a better position at a bigger church that paid more money, then all our financial concerns would disappear forever. But that didn't happen.

So I tried buying a lottery ticket. That didn't give me any joy (and I keep it in my wallet as a reminder to never buy another one).

I even thought for a while that perhaps I was supposed to look for secular employment, but no one wanted to hire me. Most of the time, I couldn't even get anyone to respond to a letter of inquiry.

It was Leigh who said, "Maybe we just need to be more generous in our contributions." Hmmm ... give away more of our money in order to feel more financially secure? That made about as much sense as marching in circles around Jericho.

It was biblical, though. When Paul was writing to the Corinthians about their over-and-above gift for the church in Jerusalem, he said, *"You will be enriched in every way for your great generosity, which will produce thanksgiving to God through us; for the rendering of this ministry not only supplies the needs of the saints but also overflows with many thanksgivings to God. Through the testing of this ministry you glorify God by your obedience to the confession of the gospel of Christ and by the generosity of your sharing with them and with all others"* (II Corinthians 9:11-13 NRSV).

All the key words for approaching our daily work in a Jericho manner are there: generosity, obedience and sharing, resulting in overflowing expressions of thanksgiving. As we've tried to live by these words, Leigh and I have never been more content in our work or more secure in our finances.

Do you suppose that's what God meant when he said, "Put me to the test?"

QUESTIONS FOR REFLECTION AND DISCUSSION

1. What was the best job you ever had? What made it such a good job?

2. What are some examples of disobedience that you have witnessed in your workplace? Are they treated as disobedience or just accepted as routine? What effect do you think this has on the way people do their jobs?

3. Do you think you would like to work with people whom you know to be disobedient? Why or why not?

4. Would it be hard for you to get away with being disobedient at work? If not, what's stopping you?

5. Why do you think King Solomon had so many things to say about lazy people? Is it true that lazy people don't get ahead in the workplace?

6. What are some examples of disobedience related to sex that you have observed in the workplace? Is it possible for women and men to work together without this becoming a problem? What does each person need to do?

7. How can our obedience in the workplace advance God's kingdom?

8. For whom do you work? More specifically, who benefits from your work? Does your list include God?

9. What does the way you work say about your relationship to Jesus Christ? Does the way you work give him a good name?

10. If you made a list of the reasons why you work, would "So I can give money away" be on your list? Should it be? How can generosity in giving affect our attitude toward our work?

CHAPTER FIVE: I ASK, GOD ANSWERS

Obedience in Prayer

I can still remember the first time I knelt beside my bed to pray. I was probably seven or eight years old, and I must have seen a picture of someone praying this way, or else I may have heard our minister say something about kneeling in prayer, because this wasn't something that Van Kempens did.

Almost all of our family's praying was associated with eating, so our prayers were of the sitting variety—heads bowed, hands folded, and no peeking to see if my two older brothers were peeking back (which they always were). At breakfast and lunch, we were taught to recite a brief set prayer together before a bite of food passed our lips, typically, "God is great, God is good, let us thank him for our food. Amen." We never used the second half, "By his hands we are fed, give us, Lord, our daily bread," which might have been a little too wordy for us. At the end of the meal we always prayed again, this time a silent free prayer "in our heads," before leaving the table. At suppertime, my father prayed aloud before we began, and when we finished, he would read from the Bible and a devotional book, and we would take turns reading the closing prayer.

In other words, like so many things in the Van Kempen

household, prayer was part of a comfortable, carefully observed routine. For a long time, it never occurred to me that it might be possible to pray in a different way.

But then at some point, I had either seen or heard about this business of kneeling to pray. Being middle-of-the road Protestants, we never did this at church and I had never observed anyone in my family doing it—and would have been mortified if my brothers had caught me at it—but I decided that I should give it a try. So, one night, shortly after turning off my light and waiting until I didn't hear any noise from the room my brothers shared across the hall (I had a room to myself; it pays to be the youngest), I slipped out from beneath the covers and knelt beside my bed.

Curiously, I felt both pious and disobedient at the same time. I didn't think I would be punished if my mom or dad caught me kneeling by my bed, but it certainly seemed as if I would have to explain why I was doing it. I was afraid they would think I had committed some major sin for which I was seeking forgiveness, which really wouldn't have been a bad guess. So I made sure that I was very quiet, avoiding the one squeaky floorboard which was about two feet away from the edge of my bed. (If you're going to sneak downstairs in the middle of the night to snitch candy, you have to know where all the potential trouble spots are.)

I wasn't sure if this posture required me to pray out loud, or if "in my head" would still work. I think the fear of being discovered convinced me that speaking very, very softly would be acceptable.

Now that I was in this position, I wasn't sure what I should pray for. It seemed as if this might be my opportunity to ask for something special, since God was undoubtedly pleased that I had gone to all the trouble of getting down on my knees. But nothing came to mind. I specifically remember thinking that if I had wanted a pony, this would be my chance to ask for one—but I didn't really want a pony. What would I do with a pony? I lived in the city for Pete's sake, and it wasn't like my dad was going to let me keep it in the garage.

That was the way my thoughts wandered for a few minutes, punctuated with the repeated salutation, "Dear Lord," as I tried starting over several times. I can't recall much more about the prayer; I think I probably ended it by simply listing the things for which I was grateful, which was my usual bed-time routine.

What I do remember though, very clearly, is the warm feeling that I had as I crawled back under my covers. The words of my prayer certainly hadn't been anything memorable or noteworthy, but now I understood why some people chose to kneel before God. I don't know if I would have been able to put it into words then, but the feeling that I had as I settled back into my bed was that God was right there, tucking me in.

* * *

A little over four decades later, I was trying to decide where my praying would take place at Covenant Life Church. I don't get on my knees every time I pray, but I do it often enough that I don't want to have to think about where I'm going to do it each time. Also, I still don't want to be caught at it, because, well, I'm not sure why. I guess it still feels like something I would prefer to keep private.

Covenant Life had a beautiful prayer room at the base of what had once been the shaft for the piano factory's old freight elevator. I could have gone in there for prayer every day, but leaving the study for half an hour or more meant that I might have to tell the secretary where I was going, and that just seemed like I was trying to be holier-than-thou; and also, there was comfortable furniture in the prayer room, which meant that my prayer time ran the risk of becoming nap time.

Other options included walking a few blocks to the Grand Haven waterfront for some open-air praying (except that there would be no kneeling, and in season, I would be easily distracted by boats), or going into the worship center (concrete floor, and in the opposite season, unheated during the week). I ended up doing what I've done in most of the churches I've served: I just slipped down off my desk chair, turned around and knelt in front of it, with my feet back under the kneehole of my desk. If anyone came in unexpectedly, I was looking for something I dropped.

Although I had the place for kneeling in prayer figured out, I have to admit that there were many days when I still didn't know exactly what I was supposed to say while I was down there—so I didn't say anything. I just listened. I might begin by confessing my sins, and I still made lists of the things for which I was grateful, but after that, I tried to let God speak. I was often tempted to fill the silence with a laundry list of everything I wanted God to do for me, but that didn't seem consistent with the whole idea of kneeling in humility before God.

In properly pious terms, I guess you might call it "waiting on the Lord." Some days, God spoke clearly, some days God brought a verse to mind, other days it was a song, a memory or a face and a name. But every time—every single time—I still had that warm, in-the-presence-of-God feeling when I got back up again.

* * *

I'm not sure Joshua would have said that he had that same feeling, but it's clear that he was struggling with the same question—what am I supposed to say down here?—when he fell to the ground in prayer following the defeat of the Israelite army at the battle of Ai.

After Jericho, Ai was supposed to be little more than a speed bump on the way to complete victory over the land of Canaan. Nevertheless, Joshua had dealt with it cautiously, sending spies again, just as he had done before approaching Jericho. The spies returned with a favorable report: *"Not all the people need go up; about two or three thousand men should go up and attack Ai. Since they are so few, do not make the whole people toil up there"* (Joshua 7:3 NRSV). Even though it appeared that it was going to be a conventional battle this time, it seemed as if God was still watching out for the Israelites.

Joshua decided to send the larger number that the spies had recommended, but Ai proved to be a much stronger foe than they had anticipated. The Israelite army was quickly forced to retreat and thirty-six of Joshua's men were killed. He knew that word of this defeat would spread faster than a plague of locusts, and would be more welcome, too. To everyone who heard it, it would mean that the mighty Israelites, the miraculous victors at Jericho, were vulnerable after all.

Joshua tore his clothes and fell to the ground in front of the ark of the Lord. He stayed there until evening, when he finally began to give voice to his prayers.

"Ah, Lord God! Why have you brought this people across the Jordan at all, to hand us over to the Amorites so as to destroy us? Would that we had been content to settle beyond the Jordan! O Lord, what can I say, now that Israel has turned their backs to their enemies! The Canaanites and all the inhabitants of the land will hear of it, and surround us, and cut off our name from the earth. Then what will you do for your great name?" (Joshua 7:7-9 NRSV).

Doesn't this sound a lot like our prayers? Okay, it doesn't actually sound anything like our prayers, but the general outline is certainly familiar: State the problem, carefully hinting that it might be God's fault; demonstrate sincere distress; express uncertainty about what to do next; and then try to put the whole mess into God's hands, hoping that God will deal with it and quickly reveal an answer.

For example, here's a prayer I recall from my freshman year in college: "Oh dear Lord, why did you ever let me sign up for Calculus 101? If only I had been content to take Pre-Calc, I wouldn't be in over my head right now. In fact, I'm facing an enormous test tomorrow, and if I flunk it, I might flunk the class, and then what would I do? What will my parents say? Please help me pass this test!"

Or this one from when my children were little: "Father in

heaven, why did you ever let Leigh and me think that we could take care of three children? Why didn't you stop us at one or two? Can't you see that they have us outnumbered? We want to do a good job raising them but we confess that sometimes it seems as if we don't know what we're doing. Please help us!"

Even if our prayers don't follow Joshua's outline at all, if they are well-considered prayers of praise, confession, gratitude and intercession, a close examination will often reveal that they still include one or two phrases which suggest that we either believe a situation is beyond our control, that we've done all we can do, or that we are just plain stumped about what we should do next. "Please bring peace to the Middle East. Please feed the starving children in Africa. Please protect all the refugees." In a thousand different ways, we are essentially saying to God, "This is in your hands; it's up to you to fix this."

I don't think that's how God intends for us to pray, which might explain why so many people are frustrated with their prayer life. It might also explain why so many of us spend such an insignificant amount of time in prayer. Sincere people tell me all the time that they don't hear God speaking to them when they pray, so it's no surprise that they don't keep at it for very long. If I'm on the phone and it doesn't seem as if there's anyone on the other end, why would I keep talking?

But I think these people are wrong. Not only do I believe God is speaking to them when they pray, I think God is practically shouting at them. Unfortunately, we've become so accustomed to routine disobedience in our lives that we may no longer know how to listen for God's voice.

There have been many times in my life when a preference for disobedience meant that I didn't really want to hear God. For example, when I was 16, I almost lost my driver's license. In Michigan, you can get up to 12 points on your record before the state revokes your driving privileges; I had 11—one red light, one accident, and three speeding tickets. "Dear God, please don't let me lose my license!" I fervently prayed. Never mind that the answer to this prayer was under my own right foot; I didn't want to hear that. Instead, I complained about how unfair it was that I got caught even though everyone runs red lights, and everyone speeds, and that accident? That wasn't my fault. I'm sure the brake lights on the car in front of me weren't working even before I smashed into them. I didn't want to hear anything about changing my behavior; I just wanted God to make sure that the police were far, far away whenever I was behind the wheel.

Do we really think we're going to hear God speak when we offer that kind of prayer?

Obviously, that's an extreme example of not wanting to listen to God, but it's not all that different from many of the prayers that we offer. "Dear God, I don't really want to be a faithful steward with my money, but will you provide food, shelter and clothing for my family anyway? Also, I don't want to cut back on fats or sweets, but would you keep me healthy just the same? Oh, and I don't have a lot of time for the kids this week, but will you see to it that they grow up to be responsible, faithful adults?"

You know what I think? Even though I said before that God is practically shouting at us when we pray—through his Word, his church and his servants, and especially through the Holy Spirit—I think our prayers sometimes leave God speechless.

* * *

When it comes to prayer, the Jericho effect suggests that just as there was a different way for Joshua and his army to approach the impenetrable city, so too, there is a different way for us to pray. Instead of prayer being an overture to God which we initiate, in which we assume that we can hand something off to God, or that we're going to persuade God to do things our way, perhaps prayer is supposed to be our response to God's overture in which we say that we are willing to do things his way.

97

Here's what that difference looks like: Let's imagine that I'm visiting my daughter in Chicago and I see a homeless person in Lincoln Park (which is the neighborhood where she used to live). I don't speak to him or give him anything, but simply pass him by. Later that evening, when I'm offering my prayers, I remember seeing him and I say to God, "Please bless all the homeless, and also the staff at the Lincoln Park Community Shelter" (which is housed in the basement of my daughter's former church, Lincoln Park Presbyterian).

In this scenario, I am initiating a conversation with God, asking him to respond to a need I observed as I went through my day. Result? Not much happens, I don't hear God say anything, and I wonder if God loves homeless people.

Now consider this alternative: When I see the homeless person in Lincoln Park, I recognize it as an overture from God, an invitation for me to do something God's way. Remembering the story of the Good Samaritan (Luke 10:25-37), and Jesus' statement, "Freely you have received, freely give" (Matthew 10:8 NIV), as well as many similar passages, I stop and ask the man if he needs a place to eat or sleep and I tell him that there is a shelter in Lincoln Park. Maybe I even offer to show him where it is, and if I'm truly channeling the spirit of the Good Samaritan, maybe I even give the shelter a donation to help take care of the man.

Clearly, we're not going to do all these things every time we encounter a person in need, but if we're attentive, we'll notice that there are particular times when the Holy Spirit prompts us—the overture—offering us a chance to respond.

That night, in my prayers, I tell God about what happened and express my gratitude for the opportunity to be a messenger of God's grace. I pray for still more grace to be revealed in the homeless person's life, and ask the Spirit to make me aware of more chances to be useful.

In this scenario, I am responding in obedience to God's initiative. Result? A homeless person may choose to take advantage of an opportunity to fed and sheltered. I had a chance to encourage and maybe even support the good people who staff the community shelter. I hear God say, "Well done," and I have no doubt that God loves homeless people.

* * *

God's response to Joshua's prayer of woe may be one of my favorite lines in the entire Bible: *"Stand up! What are you doing down on your face?* (Joshua 7:10 NIV)" As soon as something went wrong at Ai, Joshua should have known that it wasn't God who was at fault, but rather that someone had disobeyed God's commands about keeping their mitts off the devoted plunder from Jericho.

It's not as if God was vague in his instructions; Joshua himself had relayed them to the people: *"As for you, keep away from the things devoted to destruction, so as not to covet and take any of the devoted things and make the camp of Israel an object for destruction, bringing trouble upon it.* (Joshua 6:18 NRSV).

Lying on his face in prayer before God wasn't going to solve this problem. If Joshua had thought about it for a few minutes, he probably could have figured this out on his own. Instead, he jumped to all kinds of erroneous conclusions—that God was delivering Israel to the Amorites; that Israel should have stayed on the other side of the Jordan; that Israel was going to be wiped out by the Canaanites—and Joshua was ready to hold God responsible for all of this.

Joshua isn't alone. I can't count how many times I've heard people praying like Joshua, trying to hold God responsible for all kinds of things that were never God's intent. I've done it myself. In nearly every instance, the issue at hand was something that God clearly warns us about in the Bible. When we choose to ignore those warnings, is it fair to blame God when the wheels come off?

I've heard people trying to blame God for their spouse's infidelity, for the loss of their job, for the pregnancies of their teenage children, for their financial crises, for the fact that their adult children have chosen not to be involved in the church, and for many other things. Over and over, it's, "Oh God, why did you deliver us into the hands of this trouble?" That's not the way they actually word it, of course. You have to listen carefully to some of the other things they say before you get the "Aha!" moment, realizing that they are pinning their problems on God. They may say things like, "If God got us into this, God can get us out," or "When God closes a door, he opens a window," or "I believe that God never gives us more than we can bear." Then they tell me how much they've prayed about whatever the situation is, but that they haven't gotten an answer yet from God.

So far, I've managed to resist saying, "Stand up! What are you doing down on your face?" That's God's line.

* * *

What we learn from Joshua is that prayer cannot be an instrument that we use to avoid responsibility, either our own, or as was the case in the defeat at Ai, someone else's. We can't expect God to quickly answer us if all we're trying to do is dump our self-made or self-solvable problems on heaven's doorstep. I find no biblical justification for that approach. What I do find in God's Word, repeatedly, is that prayer is most effective when it is offered as an obedient response to something God has said or done. By effective, I mean a prayer that reveals that our will is aligned with God's will, and that we are willing to obey whatever God tells us in order to accomplish God's purposes.

For example, after God had freed the Israelites from Egypt and brought them into the wilderness—leading them by a pillar of cloud by day and a pillar of fire by night, giving them manna to eat and water to drink, and generally taking care of all their needs—they began to complain bitterly. So God sent a little fire to singe the outskirts of their camp. The people got the point and cried out to Moses. He prayed on their behalf, and God extinguished the fire (Numbers 11:1-3). It was a warning shot across the bow, as if God was saying, "Knock it off; you can trust me."

A few verses later however, the people were complaining again, this time because they were tired of manna and craved some meat. Moses prayed again, but this time, his prayer was similar to the one Joshua would offer forty years later: "*Why have you treated your servant so badly? Why have I not found favor in your sight, that you lay the burden of all this people on me? Did I conceive all this people? Did I give birth to them, that you should say to me, 'Carry them in your bosom, as a nurse carries a sucking child, to the land that you promised on oath to their ancestors'?*" (Numbers 11:11-12 NRSV). Moses went on to question where he could get meat for so many people, and said that he would rather die than continue on as Israel's leader.

It's clear to those of us reading the story that God had been nothing but good and gracious to Moses and the Israelites. But Moses' prayer made it sound as if God was to be blamed rather than praised for bringing the people out of Egypt.

As with Joshua, God wasn't going to accept responsibility for Moses' complaint. God wasn't a genie in a lamp who just needed a vigorous rubbing to suddenly appear and solve everything. Instead, Moses and the people would have to learn that God could be trusted, and that if they obeyed God's Word, taking responsibility for their own actions and doing things God's way, they would be blessed. But since God was still nation-building in dangerous surroundings, they also needed to learn that disobedience would have serious consequences.

God promised the people that meat was on the way, but as a consequence of their disobedience, God told the people that so much meat was coming that it would rain meat for a month, "*until it comes out of your nostrils*" (Numbers 11:20). With the quail came a severe plague, and many of the people died.

When they were obedient, as when they were still in Egypt and had carefully observed God's requirements for the Passover, Israel had experienced miraculous blessings—escaping Egypt through the Red Sea, finding water, eating manna. But when they were disobedient, they suffered severe losses—first fire, then plague, and eventually, forty years of wandering in the in the wilderness.

Someone should have remembered this when Israel, in obedience, defeated Jericho, but in disobedience lost the battle to Ai. That someone was Joshua, because in the middle of the story about Israel's complaining and Moses' prayer and all the quail, we read that Joshua, the son of Nun, *"had been Moses' aide since youth"* (Numbers 11:28 NIV). Maybe Moses never told his young aide about his prayer, because it seems as if Joshua had to learn the connection between obedience and prayer for himself.

* * *

If we were to methodically examine every prayer recorded in God's Word, we would find that obedience and prayer are nearly always in close proximity to each other. When we choose to do things God's way and then pray in that spirit of obedience, prayer becomes a marvelous act of communion and cooperation with God. But when we choose disobedience, prayer becomes a frustrating attempt at manipulation that brings no results.

When Hannah prayed to God for a male child, she made a promise, saying, *"I will set him before you as a nazirite until the day of his death"* (I Samuel 1:11 NRSV). When the child, Samuel, was born, Hannah did exactly as she had promised, which led Eli, the priest, to pray for Elkanah, Hannah's husband, saying, *"May the Lord repay you with children by this woman for the gift she made to the Lord"* (I Samuel 2:20 NRSV). The next verse says, *"And the Lord took note of Hannah; she conceived and bore three sons and two daughters."* Do you suppose any of that would have happened if she had chosen to be disobedient to her promise?

When God called Jonah to preach to the Ninevites, and Jonah tried to flee, his disobedience landed him in the belly of a great fish. Jonah 2 begins, *"Then Jonah prayed to the Lord his God from the belly of the fish"* (what does it say about me that this is another of my favorite verses?) In his prayer, he recognized that it was God who had thrown him overboard: *"You cast me into the deep"* (vs. 3). He thanked God for providing the fish: *"... yet you brought up my life from the pit"* (vs. 6); and he promised that he would now be obedient to God: *"What I have vowed I will pay"* (vs. 9). Would God have given Jonah a second chance to go to Nineveh if he had tried to renege on his promise? (Cue the fish again, perhaps this time with sharp teeth).

Then there's the New Testament story of Cornelius and Peter, which has so many examples of listening to God and being obedient that I hardly know where to begin. Cornelius was a centurion who didn't know Jesus, and yet we are told, *"He was a devout man who feared God with all his household; he gave alms generously to the people and prayed constantly to God"* (Acts 10:2 NRSV). He was being obedient to God before he even knew the whole story of salvation. As a result, he received a vision in which an angel said to him, *"Your prayers and your alms have ascended as a memorial before God"* (vs. 4).

Cornelius was told to send servants to find and bring back Simon Peter, who was staying in the home of Simon the tanner, who lived near the sea in Joppa.

At noon the next day, as the servants were making their way to Joppa, Peter decided to go up on the roof to pray (now there's a place I never considered at Covenant Life). He also received a vision, one in which he saw something like a sheet coming down from heaven filled with all kinds of four-footed creatures, reptiles, and birds. Then a voice said to Peter, *"Get up Peter; kill and eat"* (vs. 13).

Peter resisted, saying *"By no means Lord"* (vs. 14), because to do so would have been disobedient, just as under Jewish law, mingling with the likes of Cornelius would have been considered a sin. The voice told Peter not to call profane anything that God had made clean. All of this was repeated three times, after which the sheet was whisked back into heaven.

At just that moment, the Spirit told Peter that three men were looking for him, and that he was to go with them. He went downstairs, invited the men to stay the night, heard all about Cornelius and his angelic vision, and set off with them the next day.

When Peter arrived in Caesarea, Cornelius met him, *"and falling at his feet, worshiped him"* (vs. 25). Peter said, *"Stand up,"* (where have we heard that before?) and he assured Cornelius that he was only a mortal.

Peter then began to tell Cornelius and his household that as they knew, Jews did not normally associate with Gentiles, but since God had told him not to call anyone profane or unclean, here he was, and what could he do for them?

A wonderful account of obedience upon obedience follows, as Cornelius relates his vision, Peter teaches about the good news of peace through Jesus Christ, everyone in the household receives the Holy Spirit and begins to speak in tongues, and Peter finally says, *"Can anyone withhold the water for baptizing these people who have received the Holy Spirit just as we have?"* (vs. 47). In the next chapter of Acts, Peter had to defend his actions before the Apostles in Jerusalem, until they, too, praised God for sending salvation to the Gentiles.

God spoke to Peter and Cornelius through visions; we hear him through his Word, the church, other believers, and the Holy Spirit (and also, I believe, through the occasional vision). Peter and Cornelius both were obedient to what they had heard, and as a result, not only were Cornelius, his relatives and friends baptized in the name of Jesus, but the leadership of the young Christian church was put on notice that God also wanted Gentiles to hear the good news about Jesus.

It was outrageous, unheard of, and completely the opposite of everything Peter had known his entire life. It was as crazy as marching in circles to defeat a fortified city. But this was the unexpected way God had chosen to use prayer and obedience to bring salvation to the Gentiles.

* * *

Not surprisingly, prayer was a common topic of discussion at Covenant Life Church. There was one woman in the congregation, Trudie Kok, who was deemed especially faithful in prayer, but she, oddly enough, was deliberately trying to eliminate the church's need for a designated prayer ministry. It was Trudie's belief that if prayers for specific concerns were regularly assigned to a prayer team, other groups and individuals in the church might assume that they were relieved of that responsibility, and wouldn't come before God for their own time of seeking God's will.

With Jericho regularly on my mind—in particular, a way to prepare the congregation for the Jericho series I had been thinking about since before I arrived at Covenant Life —Trudie's unconventional way of thinking about prayer seemed right on target. She was suggesting precisely the opposite of what might be considered a congregation's normal approach to prayer. It had certainly never occurred to me that dismantling an existing prayer ministry might be an important first step in getting a congregation to be much more serious about prayer. It was definitely a Jericho kind of idea, and also a wonderful example of how God had already put Jericho-minded people in place at Covenant Life.

As a result, I was always on the lookout for ways to get the congregation more actively involved in prayer. A perfect opportunity arose on a late winter day (about six months into my tenure), when Steve Caton, the Director of Worship, stuck his head in my study door and told me that in a couple of months, he and most of the musicians were going to be away for a weekend of training. Did I have any ideas about how we might hold a worship service that Sunday with no music?

God gave me an answer almost as quickly as I had experienced the Jericho idea. "What about a prayer walk?" I suggested. We had just started a series of worship experiences on the subject of Vertical Habits, all the different ways that we communicate with God in prayer, and this seemed like an ideal chance to put what we were learning into practice. I said that I would run the idea past the Leadership Coordinating Team (Covenant Life's version of an executive committee), and if they approved, I would get to work on it.

Several rounds of e-mail later, with the idea approved and fine-tuned, I began work on implementing the details. We would combine both morning services into one; we would divide into seven walking groups, each led by an elder, plus a group for non-walkers who would stay at the church and pray; each group would follow a 30-45 minute path I had mapped out, sort of like the outline of flower petals—really irregular and uneven petals—beginning and ending at the church; and we would return to the church for a light lunch when the walk was completed.

Steve designed an eye-catching, oversized postcard to go out to the community, inviting people to join us or to send in prayer requests for the day of the walk. We received about a dozen responses, including one from a bank manager who sent us the first names of every one of her employees!

My own prayer as the day of the walk approached, more fervent with each passing day, was about the one thing that I couldn't control: "Dear God, please don't let it rain!" I was afraid that it wouldn't take much of an excuse for the members of the church to decide that this was a good week to catch up on their sleep.

* * *

Of course, the day of the walk dawned under a steady light rain, and I was in a sour mood as Leigh and I drove the half hour to church. Yet by the time the walk was ready to begin, the ministry center was filled with a large crowd of worshipers, all with umbrellas in hand, practical shoes underfoot, ready to walk.

We sang a song (we had managed to find a piano player), I spoke briefly about how to be mindful while walking (toys in the yard meant kids in the house; broken down cars might mean transportation issues; a ramp or an oxygen sign on the door might indicate a health concern), and I handed out the community prayer requests to the elders leading groups on the appropriate routes. We joined in a brief prayer and the walk was underway.

As soon as Leigh and I joined our group outside and opened our umbrellas, I realized that I was learning once again that God's ways are always better than mine. In this case, it was God's rain: It was perfect. It wasn't a hard rain or a cold rain, and it wasn't blowing at all. It was just enough to keep all of us under our own umbrellas, like walking under private prayer tents. It discouraged us from talking to each other when we were supposed to be walking and praying, and we were much more visible as we went through the neighborhoods surrounding the church. Many other people had come to the same conclusion, and told me afterwards how glad they were that God had sent such a perfect, gentle rain.

I hoped that they would remember that thought if it happened to rain during the week that we were reliving Jericho.

QUESTIONS FOR REFLECTION AND DISCUSSION

1. What is your normal posture for prayer? When was the last time you prayed on your knees? Do you think the place or manner in which we pray makes any difference? Why or why not?

2. If you had to describe your typical prayer in a single word, what would it be? Is there a different word you would prefer it to be?

3. What is your reaction to the phrase "I'm putting this in God's hands?" How would you react if your own children tried to put their every problem into your hands? What would you prefer that they do?

4. Why don't we pray more often than we do? Is the problem with us, with God, or with our understanding about why we pray?

5. Would the world be a better place if God did everything we asked for in prayer? Why or why not? Can you give some examples?

6. What's the relationship between obedience and prayer? Can we say that we are being obedient in prayer if all we are doing is praying? What else does obedience in prayer require?

7. What are some of the ways that we use prayer to avoid responsibility? How do we know what part of responsibility belongs to us and what part belongs to God?

8. Would you say that your prayers are effective? What does that mean to you?

9. The members of Covenant Life participated in a prayer walk through the neighborhoods around the church. How might a walk of this kind inform your prayers?

10. In the Lord's Prayer, Jesus teaches us to say, "Thy will be done." Do we really mean that? How would our obedience change if we did?

CHAPTER SIX: I EXAMINE, GOD REVEALS

Obedience in Private

This is the chapter that I really don't care to write, because it's about all the things we do when we think that no one is looking. As we're going to see, a less conventional, Jericho-style approach to our private behavior can make an incredible difference in the way we experience God's blessings, but only if we first acknowledge our personal, no-one-here-but-me activities.

Obviously, and let me say this right up front, we know that God is aware of what we're up to all the time, but we certainly don't act as if that's uppermost in our minds. If we did, this chapter wouldn't be necessary; but we don't and it is, so here goes.

I have a long history of thinking that I can get away with things that I do in private. I've already alluded to my middle of the night candy dish raids, so let me begin there and ease my way up to some of the more egregious examples of secret behavior that have taken place more recently, which is to say, when I definitely should have known better.

To begin with, I blame it all on Brach's candy corn. Has there ever been a more perfect food? Those little tri-color cones are such delectable morsels that I find everything about them completely irresistible. They have that waxy exterior that won't stain your hands or your clothes; they're sweet, but don't make your teeth ache like caramels or toffees; you can experiment with delayed gratification by holding one in your mouth for as long as possible before you finally give in and bite down; and the perfect size always leaves you wanting one more. Best of all, unlike M&M's, if people see you with candy corn, they rarely ask you to share.

I don't know when candy corn first appeared in my parents' house—it was before I can remember—but it made regular appearances in our candy dish rotation. Jelly beans were pretty good, gum drops made me suspicious (you never knew if you were going to bite into one of the gross, spicy ones), and anything with a wrapper meant that you were only going to get one piece at a time. I definitely kept an eye out for the candy corn, and whenever it appeared, I knew that I had a mission to carry out that night.

At the time, I was convinced that my mom and dad had no idea that I was sneaking past their open bedroom door and making my way downstairs to raid the candy dish. In retrospect, I think they were playing a game with me, kind of the way the British have made a hobby out of seeing how hard they can make it for squirrels to get onto their bird feeders.

Our candy dish was kept on the middle shelf of the dining room china cupboard—which had a lock on its door. In my earliest recollections, the key was simply left in the door and I could take whatever I wanted. As I got a little older however, I discovered that the cupboard would often be locked, and I would have to go in search of the key.

At first, it was just on top of the china cupboard, which meant that I had to drag over a dining room chair, climb on it, get the key, unlock the door, move the chair out of the way, get the candy, lock the door, move the chair again, put the key back on top and put the chair back by the table. Mind you, I believed that I was doing this in perfect silence, that no one could hear the furniture moving or the clinking of the dishes and the glassware except me.

When the key disappeared from the top of the china cupboard, I had to think about where else my parents might be hiding it. The first place I found it was in a kitchen cabinet alongside the everyday dishes. Then it was in the cabinet on the other side of the sink, next to the cookie tin. (Were they testing me to see if I could be distracted from my goal? Why didn't they put it in the refrigerator next to the leftover cooked carrots that I had refused to eat the night before?) Another time, I found the key above the stove, in the cupboard with the chips and the breakfast cereals (that time, I did indulge in a handful of Chicken-in-a-Biskit crackers, my favorite amongst the savory snacks). They almost stumped me the night that the key was tucked behind the cinnamon jar in the spice rack.

Whenever I scored my double handful of candy—never more than twenty pieces—I took it back to my room, closed the door and turned on my overhead light. (Did I mention that my parents never closed their bedroom door? How could I have thought that they wouldn't notice the light streaming from underneath mine?) To extend my pleasure, I broke each kernel into three pieces—white tips, orange middles and yellow bottoms—arranging them next to me on the bed. I then picked up whatever book I was reading at the time, and utterly enjoyed my secret sin.

* * *

Maybe it would have been better if my parents had made it clear that I wasn't actually fooling them with my midnight sorties, because as I grew older, I continued to behave as if there were things I could get away with when no one was looking. For example, there were those Playboy pictures that

I found in the woods—and hid in my oldest brother's closet (I'm not completely stupid); there were the early attempts at smoking (*haaack, cough, cough*); and then there was the Rolling Stones incident.

My middle brother had gotten the Stones' *Flowers* record album as a gift, and immediately issued clear and direct orders that no one was to touch it, under threat of severe punishment. I, of course, did not presume that meant me, so one morning when I was home alone, I took the album out of its sleeve and placed it on my brother's turntable.

Younger readers have probably never played an actual record, and might not know that gently lowering the stylus onto the vinyl was always a delicate proposition. I did, and was trying to be exceptionally careful as I held the needle above the grooves for *Ruby Tuesday*. To this day, I don't know what happened; it was either a muscle spasm or the Holy Spirit jostled my elbow. Whatever it was, I sent the needle skidding over the entire track, so that Mick was now singing, "Goodbye, Ruby (click) Tuesday, Who could hang (click) a name on you? When you (click) change with every new day, (click) Still I'm gonna miss (click) you."

By the way, this is the first time my brother is hearing about this, so, um, hey there, brother; sorry about that. Can I download a digital copy for you?

This incident introduced two new elements into my secret behavior: Lying and shame. Of course, I had previously lied to my brothers and my parents, probably hundreds or even thousands of times, but for some reason, none of those seemed to weigh as heavily on my conscience as the blatant lie I told my brother when he asked if I knew anything about the scratch on his Rolling Stones LP. Even years later, I would wake up in the middle of the night and feel horribly guilty about what I had done.

But that didn't cure me of sinning when I thought no one was looking. As a teenager, I managed to find all the naughty bits in the adult non-fiction section of the Grand Rapids Public Library; as a young adult in college, I kept a bottle of wine hidden in my dormitory room (the drinking age at that time was 18, but we weren't supposed to have alcohol on campus); and as a full grown adult, not long after it was invented, I discovered the seamy side of the Internet.

* * *

In the early 1990s, my faithful Apple II had finally given way to a Packard Bell PC with online capability (and the hard drive had almost one full gigabyte of memory!) It took a lot of fiddling with something called HyperTerminal, but I finally got our dial up connection working. It was text-only, and Leigh and I used it almost exclusively for e-mail. Since we didn't know many other people who had e-mail yet, neither of us spent more than a few minutes a week at the computer, at least not online (we did compete for high score on some of the games that had come bundled with our machine).

It must have been about a year later when someone at the church I was serving decided that we needed a web site. Thankfully, I didn't have to do anything but sign off on the design of the pages—which were loaded with pictures! With our text-only connection at home, I had no idea that the Internet had become so image-friendly, even if it did take an eternity for each individual picture to appear (remember those agonizing, line-by-line downloads?)

When the church's web site went live, so did my office desktop computer, which up to that point had been little more than a glorified typewriter and file cabinet. I can't remember the exact sequence of events, but it went something like this: First, I looked at our church web site. Second, I looked at some other church web sites. Third, and predictably, I decided to see if I could find some pictures of Ferraris, and entered *Ferrari, model 348ts* (one of my favorites at the time), into the search field of the browser.

A list of search responses popped up, and I saw that the

browser had not only keyed onto the word *Ferrari*, but also the word *model*, which is to say a female-type model, the kind that you associate with fashion designers, only I quickly discovered that some of these weren't wearing any fashions, if you know what I mean.

I think my heart rate jumped to about a thousand, and I remember feeling jittery as it suddenly dawned on me that my office computer had become like an instant Playboy magazine that was never more than a couple of clicks away. When I turned off the computer a few minutes later, I had the exact same guilty feeling that I so often had in the middle of the night when I thought about my brother's Rolling Stones album, only about 100 times worse.

Over the next few months, even though I was sincerely determined that I would not give in to using my computer for anything other than godly purposes, my resolve occasionally weakened, and I ended up clicking through to inappropriate sites. I tried rationalizing my behavior by saying to myself that I had to "know what was out there," or by remembering that even the Apostle Paul said, *"For I do not do the good I want, but the evil I do not want is what I do"* (Romans 7:19 NRSV). But the nauseous feeling in the pit of my stomach told me that trying to deceive myself wasn't going to erase my feelings of shame.

In all of this, my only comfort was that no one else knew what I was doing. I was convinced that this was a perfectly private activity, and I kept on believing that right up to the moment on an early Saturday morning when my Internet connection failed.

I don't remember all the technical details, but I knew that the PC in my study was connected through the church secretary's computer. If her connection went down, so everybody else's at church. So I went to the outer office and rebooted her machine, and when it still refused to connect, I started clicking around on it to see if I could figure out the problem (mind you, this was like giving a toddler a wrench and telling him to go balance the Weber carburetors on that Ferrari over there). What I discovered in my poking around was that the secretary's computer maintained a list of the users who were connected through her machine. Following each name was a window that listed every web site visited by that user.

Every single one.

Now my heart rate went to ten thousand. Did anyone else know about this? Had the secretary been keeping track of what I was doing online? Had she told anyone else, and were they just waiting for just the right moment to nail me with the evidence? If there was a list of my web activity on this machine, did that mean that there were similar lists on other machines farther up the line? Was it possible that the people who ran our local Internet service provider knew what I had been doing?

Never mind that this would have meant that they were sifting through the online records of thousands of users with hundreds of thousands of web searches, nearly all of which were totally benign. Guilt makes your brain do funny things.

I discovered that there was a way to erase my browsing history on the secretary's machine; just to be safe, I erased everyone else's lists, too. If this caused a problem, I figured I could always play dumb and say that I didn't know what had happened, that I just rebooted the secretary's computer when the connection went down. So now I was planning public lies to cover up my self-deceptions, and I was on the verge of tears. What a phenomenal idiot I had been to think that I would be able to keep my sins secret!

* * *

That's the problem with doing things our own way when we think no one is looking. God is still there, and God isn't all that easily fooled or amused by our feeble attempts at secrecy. Tell me these verses from the Apostle Paul's letter to the Ephesians aren't spot on, as those British squirrel watchers might say: "*Take no part in the unfruitful works of darkness, but instead expose them. For it is shameful even to mention what such people do secretly; but everything exposed by the light becomes visible, for everything that becomes visible is light.* (Ephesians 5:11-14 NRSV). The Apostle John agreed with Paul, and in his first letter, which is all about obedience, he tells us that "*God is light*" (I John 1:5 NRSV). So guess what? Nothing we do is going to stay in the dark.

I saw this repeatedly when I worked as a bailiff for the 61st District Court in Grand Rapids. It was amazing to observe all the defendants who thought that they had been doing a perfect job of concealing their drug use, their crooked business dealings, or their anonymous relationships. But there they were, in front of a judge, forced to deal with their supposedly secret sins.

The same was true in the hospital emergency room. Many of our secret behaviors can have health or safety consequences, and the ER docs were pretty good at figuring out what had been going on in the moments before the ambulance was called.

I don't want to create the impression that this is a "gotcha" game that God is playing with us, because that makes God seem like that crotchety neighbor who peeks through the drapes so that he can suddenly jump out the door and yell, "I told you kids to keep off my grass!" God doesn't expose our sins just to prove that omniscience is a thing (and it really is—trust me on this one), but rather so that we can deal with our sins and experience the joy of God's forgiveness.

Now, having said that, it's going to seem a bit awkward when I go back to the story of Achan's secret sin at Jericho, because after his theft was exposed, he ended up, well, dead rather than forgiven or joyful. In fact, his whole family died with him as a consequence of what he thought was a well-concealed sin. Was it a severe punishment? Undoubtedly. But it wasn't the last word when it comes to the way that God deals with our sins. What it illustrates for us is just one early step in the incredible story of grace that God that has been unfolding for us since Adam and Eve's first sin in the Garden of Eden.

* * *

If we stopped reading after the story of Jericho, we would have a very incomplete idea about God's grace. Achan may have died, but King David got to keep his job as king after his infidelity with Bathsheba. Jonah got a second chance to go to Nineveh. The Ethiopian eunuch (not that he was guilty of any secret sin) was baptized even though God had earlier said that no one of his kind would be welcome in the assembly of the Lord (Deuteronomy 23:1). By the time Paul wrote his letter to the Galatians, he understood that grace had completely set us free from the law: *"Now before faith came, we were imprisoned and guarded under the law until faith would be revealed. Therefore the law was our disciplinarian until Christ came, so that we might be justified by faith. But now that faith has come, we are no longer subject to a disciplinarian"* (Galatians 3:23-25 NRSV).

Israel's experience of God's grace as they were crossing the Jordan may have seemed to be about little more than the need for strict obedience and discipline, but God wasn't being petty or cruel. Instead, God was demonstrating that the land of Canaan could be conquered with a minimum of suffering and bloodshed (on the Israelite side; more about that later), if the people were willing to do things according to the divine will, rather than everyone going their own way. If Achan had received nothing more than a slap on the wrist for his secret sin, the immediate result would have been anarchy, and the long-term consequence might have been the total defeat of the Israelites.

Even though our experience of God's grace today doesn't include the threat of death by stoning if we are caught in our secret sins (unless your older brother catches you in the act of playing his *Rolling Stones* record), the underlying principle of God's grace hasn't changed at all: God still desires to bless all people, but God won't be played for a fool. For the sake of Jesus, God spares us the ultimate punishment we deserve, but we can't expect God to shower us with earthly blessings if we choose to continue in our secret sins. If we persist in our disobedience, we will have to deal with the consequences of turning our backs on God's grace.

* * *

We don't know a lot about Achan, but what we read about him in the Jericho account makes him seem like a pretty ordinary guy. He had a good Jewish family lineage, he had sons and daughters, and he owned cattle, donkeys, sheep and a tent. So it seems as if he was about as middle class as you could be in a nomadic tribe. He probably went to his kids' soccer games and joined the other dads in yelling that there was no way that that player was offsides.

When the walls of Jericho fell, Achan saw a beautiful Babylonian robe, two hundred shekels of silver (about five pounds) and a wedge of gold weighing 50 shekels (about a pound and a quarter). By his own account, he coveted them, but he didn't stop there. He also took them and hid them in the ground underneath his tent (Joshua 7:21).

Maybe the most extraordinary thing about Achan's story is that he was apparently the only person in all of Israel who took any of the devoted plunder. Joshua must have made it abundantly clear that none of the Jericho stuff was to be touched, and the fact that Achan concealed the items under his tent is all the evidence we need to prove that he knew the instructions as well as anyone else.

At Ai, God drew a clear connection between Achan's secret sin and its consequences. Because one person had secretly disobeyed, the whole nation suffered. Now, it's not like Achan was going around boasting about what he had done; he wasn't trying to get other people to do the same thing. But eventually, if the missus had shown off the robe to her knitting club (if Achan had a wife; she isn't mentioned in the story), or if Achan had shown up in the market flashing his wedge of gold, people would have known that he had gotten away with disobeying God's word, and they would have been inclined to do the same. Instead, we know that Joshua, with God's help, revealed Achan's sin, and established the link between what he had done and what all Israel had suffered: *Why did you bring trouble on us? The Lord is bringing trouble on you today"* (Joshua 7:25 NRSV).

It seems as if we have lost that connection. We aren't likely to think about what our secret sins mean in terms of the health and well-being of our families, much less our whole society. For example, I once had a parishioner who had a secret gambling habit. His work frequently took him to a city that is known for its casinos, and whenever he was there, he spent some of his hard-earned money playing games of chance. It was just an amusement at first, but then it became a compulsion, and eventually an addiction. He got himself so far into debt—still unbeknownst to anyone—that he saw continued gambling as his only hope for redemption.

This guy wasn't trying to destroy his family the first time he sat down at a Blackjack table. Neither was he trying to single-handedly destroy the American work ethic, replacing it with the belief that we are entitled to get something for nothing. He was just a lonely guy, many miles from home, passing the time with what he initially believed was a little harmless gambling.

If it wasn't for this kind of secret sin, casinos might not exist. I've been in a few of them (one time in Atlantic City for *Jeopardy!* tryouts, another time in northern Michigan to use the bathroom), and I never saw that glamorous group of people that they show on all the television ads; you know, the whole twenty-something crowd, laughing and having a fabulous time? They're not there. Their seats are occupied by sad, solitary figures who don't seem to be having a good time at all. Many have a look of desperation about them, which isn't surprising, since my parishioner certainly wasn't the only person to ever find himself drowning in debt because of gambling.

If you wander a few blocks away from the casinos, you'll discover evidence of what gambling does to society. There you find the run-down hotels that have become home to the gamblers who haven't got any other home to go to anymore. They're right next to the pawn shops and the big signs that say "Sell your jewelry here."

No one thinks about this when they secretly buy a few lottery tickets and decide not to tell their wife or husband. I mean, how bad can it be? They're being sold by the government! It's no wonder that so few people make the connection between secret sin and the deterioration of our society.

Secret drinking has similar consequences. It may begin with just a shot or two when no one is around, but pretty soon there's a pint hidden behind the toilet tank, another hidden in the trunk under the spare tire, and that meeting with the boss tomorrow is probably about getting fired. All of a sudden, that secret sin isn't as harmless as it seemed.

Secret e-mails, secret lies, secret meetings, secret deals, secret fill-in-the-blank—all of these have a way of not staying secret. Cain secretly killed Abel in the field and tried to deny it, saying, *"Am I my brother's keeper?"* (Genesis 4:9 NRSV). In a joint effort at secrecy, Joseph's brothers sold him to the Midianites and attempted a cover up with a bloody robe and a tale about wild animals (Genesis 37:31). Judas sold out Jesus for thirty pieces of silver and tried to conceal it with an affectionate greeting (Luke 22:48). But Abel's blood revealed Cain's sin, Joseph himself turned up alive in Egypt, and even as Judas greeted Jesus with that friendly kiss in the garden, Jesus said, *"Judas, is it with a kiss that you are betraying the Son of Man?"*

* * *

Based on both scripture and our own personal experiences, it should be clear to us that there is no such thing as a secret sin. If, at the very least, we are willing to acknowledge that God knows what we are up to in every circumstance, then we also have to acknowledge that God can use this knowledge of our sins to get us to deal with them.

But before God does that, we should take note of the fact that we are always given a chance not to commit the sin in the first place. In his first letter to the Corinthian church, Paul wrote, *"No testing has overtaken you that is not common to every-one. God is faithful, and he will not let you be tested beyond your strength, but with the testing he will also provide the way out so that you may be able to endure it"* (I Corinthians 10:13 NRSV). If you pay close attention to what is going on in the moments just before you are about to commit a secret sin, you will see that this verse is true, every time.

During my seminary training, when I was filling the pulpit at a small congregation in Ontario for a twelve-week summer assignment, I quickly realized that the Canadians allowed some "art house" movies on television that probably wouldn't get by the network censors south of the border (this was before premium cable channels or even video rentals had become common). On a Tuesday morning, I saw one of these movies listed in the paper, and since I had nothing on my schedule for that evening, I was fully expecting to be in front of my TV at 8:00 p.m., a patron of the arts.

At precisely 7:59—really—my doorbell rang. It was one of the elders from the church, and he just thought he would drop by to see how things were going, and did I have time to visit? Clearly, I could have thanked him for stopping, made up some story about how busy I was, and gone back to my attempt at viewing half-naked Canadians (in retrospect, it doesn't sound nearly as interesting as it did at the time). But instead, I invited him in, we talked for exactly two hours, and when he left, the movie was over.

Because of countless incidents like this, you'll never convince me that God doesn't provide a way out when we are facing temptation; I've seen God do it again and again. The phone rings, the web site won't load, something goes wrong with the car, the mail is delayed, the meeting gets cancelled, the check doesn't show up in the mail, the appointment has to be rescheduled, and on and on. If it only happened once or twice, I might be tempted to say that it was just a coincidence, but it happens all the time! As I said, if you play close attention to what's going on just before you try to indulge in that secret sin, you will notice that God is giving you a chance to not to do it.

But it's also true that if we are bound and determined to continue with the sin, we can. God may give us a way out, but we aren't forced to take it. If we choose the path of sin, God's Holy Spirit turns from prevention to a campaign of reclamation and restoration. It's a much more difficult and often painful process, but one for which we can be eternally grateful.

* * *

For the sake of self-preservation, but even more importantly, to protect the reputations of other people who were involved, the final part of this chapter is thoroughly falsified. At the same time, it is also completely true. In other words, I want to say something about the way we can make unconventional, Jericho-style choices about private behavior, and I want to use a personal example to make my point, but I don't have the right to drag other people's personal behavior into it. So when I say that this account is completely true, I mean that in the same way that we might consider the lessons of Jesus' parables to be completely true. We don't know if there ever was, in fact, a Prodigal Son who took his inheritance and squandered it in a foreign country, but we certainly know that we have a heavenly Father who welcomes us home with open arms.

When I arrived at Covenant Life Church, I was in the middle of dealing with a secret sin that I thought I had conquered more than two decades earlier. In the late 1970s, I expected that I would forever be able to say that I *used* to have a problem with illegal drugs, but unfortunately, shortly after the turn of the century, that past tense had once again become a present reality.

Ironically, I had first been introduced to smoking marijuana when I was a law student in Detroit. A huge beginning-of-the-school-year bash, hosted by a 2L student and attended by one of our professors, had featured several circles of people who appeared to be passing around smallish, hand-rolled cigarettes. I was curious to know what all the fuss was about, but chose not to participate in such a public venue.

At just about the same time, I heard that one of my fellow servers at the restaurant where I worked was growing her own cannabis, but I never gave that much thought, at least not until a few months later when she asked if I could watch her house (and her two evil cats) while she and her husband went away on a three-week business trip out west.

When I arrived at her home to get my instructions for taking care of things, she introduced me to the cats (they were about as thrilled as I was), she told me where she kept the cat food and the kitty litter, and then she showed me where she kept her stash. She even told me that I could find a couple dozen pre-rolled joints in the freezer. "Help yourself," she said, as if she was leaving a plate of cookies on the counter.

Well, I did. On a Saturday night, with the drapes closed and no one knowing where I was or what I was doing, I lit up a joint and inhaled deeply. I won't lie to you—this isn't part of the falsification of the story—I liked it. I liked it a lot. By the time my co-worker returned at the end of her three weeks away, I was just starting think that maybe this was going to be a problem.

I was right. It became a problem rather quickly. Just when I thought I was going to be able to handle it, I frightened myself by driving to Burger King and discovering that I was unable to order. I just kept staring up at the oddly amusing menu and eventually left without getting any food. Maybe the scariest part was that I was driving.

Rather than learning the correct lesson, which would have been something along the lines of, "Hey, you moron, stop doing this," I simply became a better manager of my secret behavior. I didn't indulge before going to class or if I had to work, and definitely not if I had to drive anywhere. With these minor adjustments, no one had to know how I spent my personal time. Not only that, but the fact that I was getting my supply from a home-grown source even allowed me to pretend that I wasn't contributing to any drug lords or gang members.

I continued pretending when God called me away from Detroit. What I said to myself was that I had successfully dealt with this particular problem when I left law school for the seminary. God was moving me away from my supply, so that was the end of it. As long as I didn't go looking for a new dealer, I didn't think that I had to do anything else. Problem solved, right?

Wrong. Since I had never so much as confessed this sin, much less asked God to help me conquer it, it was just waiting to rear its aromatic head. When a non-church relationship in west Michigan suddenly made a new supply available, I went off the deep end again, and picked up right where I had left off.

As I said before, most of what you've just been reading has been obfuscation. All I will say is that I wasn't a drug addict when I went to Covenant Life Church—that wasn't the problem—but I was definitely dealing with an unconfessed sin which had been a few years in the making and which I thought had been resolved by distance. Moving to Covenant Life Church made it clear to me that I hadn't actually dealt with it at all.

God spoke very clearly when I had been at CLC for a few months. As excited as I was about getting going on with the Jericho project, I couldn't seem to make any progress. Other people were ready to start working on it, and were just waiting for me to provide some direction, but I was having one of the weirdest experiences in my life. Every time I tried to do something with Jericho, it was if my brain took a leave of absence. I couldn't manage to get two words down on paper.

Finally, exasperated, in one of my prayer times, I heard this from God, clearly: "I won't let you teach about obedience if you aren't being obedient." I knew exactly what God was talking about, and I knew what I had to do.

It took a couple more months before I finally surrendered to God. It was one of the most painful and one of the most meaningful experiences in my life. If you have ever been through a similar struggle, you know exactly what I mean. Now, finally, I can say that I have dealt with my secret sin (but read chapter twelve), and that day-by-day, God is giving me the strength I need to remain obedient.

* * *

Conventional wisdom says that we can keep our private and public lives separate. A conventional attitude toward secret sins is to say that they don't matter, as long as no one is getting hurt. The conventional way of dealing with secret sins is to do everything in our power to keep them secret. What no one talks about much is the conventional outcome of secret sins: ruined lives, ruined marriages, ruined families, even a ruined society.

God's Word suggests an unconventional approach to secret behavior: Tell someone. Confide in someone. Say it out loud. Say it to God. Say it to someone who knows God and will talk to God on your behalf. Just stop keeping the secret.

Proverbs says, *"No one who conceals transgressions will prosper, but one who confesses and forsakes them will obtain mercy"* (Proverbs 28:13 NRSV). As long as we hang on to our secrets—which we already know are no secrets to God—everything will be a struggle. John said, *"If we say that we have no sin, we deceive ourselves, and the truth is not in us"* (I John 1:8 NRSV). Secret behavior is the ultimate self-deception, because we are constantly pretending to be something other than what we really are.

Achan's secret sin in stealing some of the devoted plunder from Jericho is the counterpoint to Joshua's obedience in approaching the city in God's unconventional way. Joshua obeyed God and succeeded in bringing down an impossible wall. Achan disobeyed, and brought down 36 soldiers, his family, and nearly the entire nation of Israel.

Which would we rather accomplish? Until we change the way we live when we think no one is looking, we won't see many walls come tumbling down. That's what the second half of this book is all about—bringing down the walls.

QUESTIONS FOR REFLECTION AND DISCUSSION

1. What kinds of things did you think you were keeping secret when you were a child?

2. Do you think God is always watching over us? If so, why do we so often act as if he isn't? Do we forget or do we simply not care if he sees what we are doing?

3. What are some ways that the Internet makes seemingly secret sins possible? (If in a group, see how complete a list you can make, and discuss ways that these "opportunities" might be avoided).

4. When a secret sin is exposed we often say that "it came to light." What's the biblical connection between light/dark and obedience? What does it mean for our obedience that Jesus described himself as the light of the world?

5. Why did Achan have to die for his secret sin? Why do you think God ordered his whole family to be put to death with him? If this was a deterrent, don't we still need deterrents today?

6. Have we lost the connection between our secret sins and their societal consequences today? Give an example of a secret sin and how it might have a broader effect than we first realize.

7. Is it true that God will not let us be tempted beyond what we can bear? Does God always provide a way out?

8. Many secret sins have to do with addictions—gambling, drinking, drugs, etc. Why are so many people drawn to these behaviors? Do they stay hidden? Can you think of people who have conquered these sins? If so, how did they do it?

9. Is it possible to manage our secret sins in a way that allows us to continue indulging in them? Why or why not?

10. Why wouldn't God let me write about obedience if I wasn't making an effort to be obedient? Can only perfect people write books about some aspect of God's Word?

PART TWO: WALLS TUMBLING DOWN

CHAPTER SEVEN: KNOWLEDGE

*Bringing Down Walls Between
Me and God's Word*

"Case, did you take a look at what the guys are doing over there?" It would have been hard to miss the group to whom Leigh was referring. There were nearly a dozen of them—and several girls, too—all bunched around a TV, watching one young person flying through the various stages of a video game.

I had just walked into the basement fellowship hall of our church in Franklin Lakes where our young people and their sponsors were enjoying a Saturday game night. The checkers, chess and Monopoly tables had been mostly abandoned when one of the youth group leaders arrived with a brand-new Nintendo Entertainment System (the original NES), and the young people were all eagerly waiting their turns to see if they could help Mario save Princess Toadstool.

It was obvious that one of the boys—the one we were all watching—was already familiar with the game. In fact, he was truly amazing; I had never seen anyone demonstrate such mastery of a video game before. I had played my share of Pac-Man and Frogger and had even gotten a decent score on Missile Command a few times, but none of those games required the memory or skills that were necessary to do well at Super Mario Bros.

As I watched from the back of the crowd, I saw Mario leaping up in seemingly random places to reveal dozens of hidden coins. He then jumped down certain green tubes to discover still more treasure underground and to win extra lives. When he slowed down and even paused in certain spots, it quickly became apparent that he was just waiting for other creatures to get out of his way. He then hopped onto floating platforms and clouds in the air and rode elevators to just the right levels. Finally, with the castle in sight, he dodged flaming swords, raced underneath the last guard, and moved one step closer to rescuing the princess.

As our young player cleared each level (to wild applause; he was having a good night), it occurred to me that in a very short period of time, he had accumulated a vast body of knowledge about this video game. Not only did he remember the hundreds of secret locations, hidden traps and special moves necessary to win each stage, he also knew the complete back story about the two plumbers, Mario and Luigi (who had apparently started out as carpenters in another game, Donkey Kong). He spoke so knowledgeably about the eight "worlds" of Super Mario Bros. and all the characters that inhabited them that you would have thought that he had studied them in his Geography and Social Studies classes.

Later that evening, when Leigh and I were getting ready for bed, I turned to her and said, "Weren't you impressed by how much our little Nintendo whiz had to learn in order to play that game as well as he did? And yet when I'm teaching him and his friends in Sunday School tomorrow, I guarantee that one of them is going to ask me, 'Where do I find Genesis?' or 'Did Moses come before Jesus or after?'"

I paused for a moment. "You know what I think? I think somebody needs to turn the Bible into a video game."

"I know what you mean," Leigh answered, "but it's not just

the kids who can learn a lot of information if they're truly interested in something." A smile crossed her face, and then she asked, "How many cylinders did that Ferrari have again?"

"Ah, that would be the 1962 Ferrari 250GT Lusso to which you are referring," a car I had been raving about earlier after reading about it in one of my car books. "It had twelve cylinders for a total displacement of just under three liters, producing approximately 250 horsepower. The body design was by Pininfarina, and only about 330 of them were made."

"You are such a nerd," Leigh responded, "But you're my nerd."

"And I also know how to find Genesis."

* * *

You find Genesis by opening the Bible and starting at the beginning, a step fewer and fewer people seem willing to take today. It's clear that our problem with Biblical knowledge isn't due to an inability to learn or remember anymore than Joshua would have had a hard time remembering the angel's instructions at Jericho ("Wait, is that march seven times, then one long trumpet blast, or trumpets first and then march?") There just seems to be something intimidating about the Bible, almost as if there's a barrier around it that discourages people from picking it up and discovering what it has to say.

It hasn't always been this way. My first church had a number of old-fashioned farmer-theologians amongst its members, both men and women who seemed to spend as much time with their Bibles as they did with their *Hoard's Dairyman* or the *Ladies Home Journal*. Even though many of them had only completed an eighth-grade education, they were able to quote long passages of scripture from memory, and they regularly surprised me with the depth of their understanding about Reformed doctrine.

It's not that these scripture-quoting farmers were all exceptionally gifted and talented as children; they just didn't know that there was any alternative to learning their Bible lessons. When their generation was coming of age, long before video games and computers—or even before radio and television in some cases—it was widely assumed that for a happy and successful life, you needed to know your Bible and your catechism just as much as you did your reading, writing, and arithmetic. The church at that time was serious about teaching the content and meaning of scripture; you don't find a lot of sermons from the early 20th century about things like how to be a better co-worker or how to manage your leisure time.

The same was true in the Netherlands, where my mother had to memorize the entire Heidelberg Catechism—all 129 questions and answers—before she was allowed to make her profession of faith and become a full member of the church. Before she passed away, she still remembered a lot of it (although I couldn't really quiz her; my Dutch is more of the conversational variety, and I don't know the words for things like sanctification or propitiation).

When I tell my junior or senior high Sunday School classes today about what my mother had to learn, they seem utterly stunned, as if no one could possibly be expected to accomplish a feat like that today. Yet, at the time, on both sides of the Atlantic, this kind of learning was considered perfectly normal—a minimum accomplishment rather than some kind of extraordinary feat of scholarship.

During my own childhood years in the 1960s, the emphasis on scripture memorization had started to decline, but attendance in Sunday School and catechism classes was still considered mandatory. I can clearly remember the year when my brothers and I had to go to catechism class on Tuesday afternoons, because that was the only time that we ever got to ride our bikes to church. Even though the class was right in the middle of prime after-school play time with our friends, it never would have occurred to us to ask our parents if we really had to go. We knew that answer to that question.

That brings us to today, when hardly a month goes by without someone telling me that their family won't be in church or Sunday School because they have to take their children to an out-of-town soccer game. "You know how it is," they will say, with a slight shrug of their shoulders. They're hoping that I will absolve them of the twinge of guilt they are feeling for helping their children choose sports over church involvement; and of course, I do, because they are what we consider "good families." They still come to church more than half the time; they may even serve on committees or sing with the choir.

But don't ask their kids where to find Genesis.

* * *

It would be nice if we could identify just one thing that has caused our contemporary lack of familiarity with the Bible—and then fix it. For example, if it was just the advent of Sunday sports leagues, we might be able to convince families that the life-long value of a biblical education is greater than the lessons learned on a traveling soccer club. Or if we thought that the archaic language of the Bible made it seem irrelevant to today's world, we could commission a new translation and get people back to reading again.

But Sunday sports leagues are a symptom, not a cause. If learning the Bible was still a significant family value, no coach ever would have suggested putting soccer onto the Lord's Day calendar. Neither is the language of the Bible a problem. We've seen an explosion of easy-to-read Bible translations over the last couple of decades. New editions of the Bible come onto the market almost every year, many of them with excellent reading guides and margin notes targeted for specific groups; there's probably even a Soccer Player's Bible. Not only that, but the Bible is consistently the best-selling book in America, which seems to suggest that the problem isn't with the translation.

How about television then? Whenever I ask church groups to speculate on the reasons for our declining knowledge about the Bible, this is usually the first thing someone says, after which there is often a competition amongst the older adults to see who can claim to watch it the least.

"We only watch the news and a couple of game shows after dinner."

"I only turn on a few nature programs."

"Except for the weather, we almost never have the thing on."

No one ever says, "I *love* TV! I watch it all the time!" even though national viewing statistics suggest that this would be closer to the truth, especially since the advent of streaming video, and the possibility of binge-watching one's favorite shows.

In spite of the undeniable influence of television, I think it's too convenient to say that it is the primary reason for our biblical illiteracy. It has certainly contributed to the decline (and I'll get back to this in a moment), but not for the reason many people think, which is the "Who reads anymore?" hypothesis. The advent of social media has proven that people will still read, if only to find out what their peers think about the latest episode of their favorite TV program.

Our home had only one screen when I was growing up, but I loved watching *Leave it to Beaver* on that old black and white set just as much as today's kids love watching their shows on their phones, tablets and multiple flat-screen TVs. In fact, I don't think there's a child living who could plead more persuasively than I did for an extra few minutes of TV time before bed. Most successful ploy: Asking to stay up to watch just the first contestant on *I've Got a Secret* (I had a thing for Bess Myerson).

But my love for television didn't mean that I stopped doing everything else in my life, and that's still true of today's families. The TV may be on hour after hour (more than eight hours a day per household according to recent surveys) but that doesn't mean people are watching it to the exclusion of doing anything else. It's on in the kitchen while people are cooking; it's on in the dining room while families are eating; it's on in the bedroom while people are going to sleep or getting up in the morning. But people still go to work, they play sports, they attend concerts and plays, and they even read books. So TV may be one factor in the decline of Bible knowledge, but I'm not at all convinced that it's the most significant reason.

Here are a few other possibilities:

1 Conjecture: We're just busier than we used to be, and spending time learning about the Bible got squeezed out. Objection: Go talk to some of those farmer-theologian families, and ask how busy they were when they were planting a hundred acres, milking fifty cows, and raising seven or eight kids, all without the benefit of modern conveniences like four-wheel drive tractors, milking machines, barn cleaners, or GPS-enabled combines with air-conditioning and ten-speaker stereos. Neither did they have automatic washers and dryers, microwave ovens, Teflon cookware, wrinkle-free fabrics or instant anything, yet they still found time to study the Good Book.

2 Conjecture: We expect that science is going to solve our problems today, and turning to the Bible for answers seems inconsistent with scientific inquiry. Objection: Well, of course it does, if you try to treat it as a science text book, but I don't think there are many people who do that. The vast majority of people, upwards of 90%, say that they believe in God, a Being whose existence has never been scientifically proven. If they can make that leap of faith, I think it is safe to say that they also know that God's Word, the Bible, isn't going to provide the same kind of direction that we expect from scientific inquiry.

3 Conjecture: We're living in the early years of an information revolution every bit as transformative as the one which followed the invention of the Gutenberg printing press in the fifteenth century, and print-only texts like the Bible are going the way of the dinosaur. Objection: Yes, we are witnessing an

information revolution, and I think that in a few years we will see some amazing new scripture versions that take full advantage of all the multi-media options that are available. But in the meantime, print isn't going away. Soothsayers have been predicting the demise of the paper-and-ink book for years, but it stubbornly refuses to disappear. In fact, with the latest print-on-demand technology, no book ever has to go out of print again.

Conjecture: We're just too sophisticated today to believe that a cobbled-together book written thousands of years ago by dozens of different authors, the final content of which wasn't settled until a series of synods in the fourth century, can possibly make a difference in our lives. Objection: And yet a modern-era First Lady of the United States was known to consult an astrologer for guidance, so how sophisticated can we really claim to be?

Every objection that serious people might raise about the way in which the Bible came into existence can be turned around and viewed as a miraculous act of God in creating and preserving a written Word through which the existence of God and God's will for our lives could be revealed. Those fourth century bishops weren't arguing about the historicity of the Torah; they weren't debating whether the prophets pointed toward Jesus or someone else; they weren't trying to decide if they needed to do some drastic editing, or if they should write a few more books to make the whole canon of scripture hang together better. No, what they had in front of them was a collection of texts which the church had already come to consider as the authoritative Word of God. Different branches of Christendom disagreed on the inclusion of a few books (some of which have come to be known as the Apocrypha), but the amazing thing was that over the course of hundreds of years, most of the church had come to recognize 66 books as the Word of God.

I'm convinced that anyone who says that we are too sophisticated for the Bible hasn't actually studied it in depth. I can't think of any book that is more sophisticated in terms of its recurring themes, its ethical considerations, its progressive revelation, its interpretation of world events, and even its literary qualities, and yet is able to convey the essential message of salvation in language and images that a grade school child can understand. The full range of human experience is found within its covers, and to suggest that we are somehow too advanced, too intelligent, or too urbane to take its teachings seriously is nothing short of absurd.

* * *

We could spend a lot more time thinking about why people are so reluctant to pick up their Bibles today, but I believe that all the different possibilities boil down to one thing:

Disobedience.

If we suspect, even the slightest bit, that we are regularly disobeying God in any or all of the six areas of life that we've already considered in Part I, how quick are we going to be to pick up a Bible in order to confirm that suspicion? How insistent are we going to be that our children learn more than just the simplest Bible stories? Do we really want them questioning the inconsistencies in our lives?

It is almost as if every act of disobedience that we commit adds a brick to the wall of separation between us and God's Word. As we've already observed, we live in a culture in which there is widespread tolerance—and in many cases, even support and encouragement—for low-level disobedience, which means that by the time we're adults, we're probably looking up at a pretty impressive wall. It's hard to get excited about making the effort to go over or through this obstacle in order to get to our Bibles, because we already suspect that that there is no such thing as an acceptable level of disobedience. Subconsciously, I think we choose to leave our Bibles untouched because it is easier to suspect that something may be disobedient, but not to really know for sure, than it is to open our

Bibles and have all doubts removed.

Let's go back to television again, and another show that I loved when I wasn't yet in charge of the remote control (figuratively speaking, since this was in the era when you actually had to *go to the TV* to do things like change the channel or adjust the volume).

In the late 1960s, Rowan and Martin's *Laugh In* had become a huge hit with its mix of stand-up comedy, musical numbers, political satire, and go-go girls, the most famous of whom was Goldie Hawn, dancing in a skimpy—for the time—bikini with assorted words and phrases painted all over her body. I was thirteen when the show debuted; do you think I was interested in watching Ms. Hawn? This was hardly the first show to combine sexual innuendo with sexual imagery, but it was the first one I remember being allowed to see.

If my father had been home, that wouldn't have been the case. I'm pretty sure the channel would have been changed— and quickly, too. But he worked until 9:00 p.m. on Monday evenings, and my mother, bless her heart, always had an amazing ability to tune out whatever was on the TV, even if she was reading or knitting in the same room. So my brothers (especially my middle brother) and I could tune in to *Laugh In*, crack up at all the naughty jokes, ogle Goldie Hawn, and then go to school the next day knowing that we would be able to say "Of course" when someone asked, "Hey, did you catch *Laugh In* last night?"

Was watching *Laugh In* disobedient? (Hint: Now would be a good time to say, "Of course.") It's tempting to think that *Laugh In* was a harmless show from a more innocent time, because "You bet your sweet bippie" pales in comparison to "You bet your sweet [expletive deleted]," a saying that we're likely to hear on many current programs. But just because *Laugh In* cleared the network censors doesn't mean that watching it was acceptable, any more than stealing a dime is acceptable because it's so much less than a hundred dollars. Theft is theft and wrong is wrong.

Watching *Laugh In* in our household was wrong, and my brothers and I knew it. Had he been home, my father would have been completely justified in turning off the TV, because laughing at the sexual jokes and drooling over Goldie Hawn wasn't exactly teaching us respect for women or preparing us for the appropriate place of sexual activity within marriage (see Jesus' comment about lust and adultery in Matthew 5:28). We knew that we were getting away with something, something that we considered to be a very low-level offense, but an offense nonetheless.

Believe me, I know how silly it sounds today to declare that watching *Laugh In* was an act of disobedience. But this is precisely how TV has contributed to our biblical ignorance. Not because it's taking up all our reading time, not because it's taking away time from religious activities, not because its programs are so blatantly pornographic (even though many of them are), but because it overwhelms us with such a perpetual flow of disobedience-as-normal that it all begins to seem acceptable. We know that the Bible will tell us that many TV programs are no good for us, but who wants to be the first one to say, "Shouldn't we turn this off?" Who wants to go to work and say, "No, I didn't watch that show last night because I don't agree with what it teaches." So instead, we've stopped taking the Bible seriously in this area of our lives—and many others.

Because really, if we're not going to be serious about what it teaches, why study it at all?

* * *

Joshua could have tried taking on Jericho the old-fashioned way; he didn't have to take what the commander of the Lord's army said seriously. Had he gone with the conventional approach, it seems pretty clear that he and his army would have been on their own, but he could have made that choice. In the same way, we can just keep on doing things the usual way too, adding bricks to that wall that separates us from God's Word, but we have to acknowledge that this will leave us to fend for ourselves more and more of the time.

Why would we do that? Listen to Psalm 81: *"O that my people would listen to me, that Israel would walk in my ways! Then I would quickly subdue their enemies, and turn my hand against their foes"* (Psalm 81:13-14 NRSV). I have never caught God in a lie, so when God makes a promise like this, I am inclined to believe it. God's ways are always going to be better than our own, but we have to know what they are before we can follow them.

Consider this slightly longer passage from Isaiah 55:6-11 (NRSV):

Seek the Lord while he may be found,
*   call upon him while he is near;*
let the wicked forsake their way,
*   and the unrighteous their thoughts;*
let them return to the Lord, that he may have mercy on them,
*   and to our God, for he will abundantly pardon.*
For my thoughts are not your thoughts,
*   nor are your ways my ways, says the Lord.*
For as the heavens are higher than the earth,
so are my ways higher than your ways
and my thoughts than your thoughts.

For as the rain and the snow come down from heaven,
*   and do not return there until they have watered the earth,*
making it bring forth and sprout,
*   giving seed to the sower and bread to the eater,*
so shall my word be that goes out from my mouth;
*   it shall not return to me empty,*
but it shall accomplish that which I purpose,
*   and succeed in the thing for which I sent it.*

This makes it pretty simple: God is near; God wants us to acknowledge that doing things our own way leads to sin; God will freely pardon us for the sins we've committed; following God's way will prove to be better than our own way; and if we choose God's way, God's Word will accomplish the purpose for which he sent it.

We could pick just about any book in the Bible—in fact, we could pick practically any page in the Bible—and find an example of how God's thoughts and God's ways are better than our own. Go ahead and try it; I just did it myself, and here are a few of the pages I opened to at random (truly; I just stuck my thumb in the pages and opened it up).

I Samuel 16: Samuel is sent to anoint a successor to King Saul, and he thinks he's supposed to choose Eliab, one of Jesse's strapping young sons. God responded, *"Mortals ... look on the outward appearance, but the Lord looks on the heart."* God then directed Samuel to choose David instead.

Daniel 3: King Nebuchadnezzar throws Shadrach, Meshach and Abednego into the fiery furnace, where they are joined by a fourth figure, and they emerge unharmed. Nebuchadnezzar responds, *"Blessed be the God of Shadrach, Meshach, and Abednego, who has sent his angel and delivered his servants who trusted in him. They disobeyed the king's command and yielded up their bodies rather than serve and worship any god except their own God."* Daniel's friends could have bowed down to the king's giant statue, just like everyone else was doing, but they trusted God and God protected them.

I Peter 1: Peter writes,*"If you invoke as Father the one who judges all people impartially according to their deeds, live in reverent fear during the time of your exile."* This is a particularly good example of how living according to God's will is going to be different than the world's usual way of doing things. It will be as if we are exiles in this current world, people who don't even know the routine—and disobedient—way of doing things.

I could keep this up for a long time (my Bible has 2,335 pages), but I think the message is clear: On nearly every page, the Bible shows us that us that when we put the conventional way of doing things alongside God's way, God's way will prove to be better every time. God's Word will not return to him empty if we are willing to learn what it says and live by it.

* * *

If every act of disobedience adds a brick to the wall that separates us from the Word, then every act of obedience takes one away. As each brick comes down, it becomes that much easier for us to choose God's way the next time we are confronted with a world's-way-versus-God's-way decision.

When I began planning the Jericho series at Covenant Life Church—especially when I was thinking about the Jericho Week itself, with its emphasis on deliberately bringing down walls by choosing to do things God's way—I realized that I would have to prepare the members of the congregation with some kind of immersion in God's Word. My sense was that this congregation, for all its energy and creativity, didn't necessarily have a better than average knowledge of the Bible; so asking them to commit to a solid week of radical obedience was going to take some preparation. Plus, it wouldn't hurt to see if we could get people into the habit of reading their Bibles every day.

I had already thought that we would need at least six weeks to get ready for Jericho Sunday, so after several discussions with the Wednesday morning worship planning team, we settled on a schedule: For six weeks, our Sunday services would each focus on one of the areas of obedience. Between Sundays, we would challenge the congregation to commit to a daily scripture reading and devotion, along with consideration of some reflection questions on the week's subject; these would all be available in booklet form and also on the church's web site.

During the sixth, Jericho week, we would invite the congregation to give obedience a serious try—no inappropriate TV, movies or Internet, no foul language, no cutting corners at work, no going along with something just because everyone else was doing it. For encouragement, we would have six evening meetings during this week, each one an in-depth study on one of the areas of obedience. Particular emphasis would be given to how obedience in that area could bring down walls, and each would end with a single walk around the church.

Finally, we would come to Jericho Sunday, when we would be marching around the church seven times, praying for God to bring down all the different walls that divide us from God and from each other.

Our goal was to keep it simple, so that the members of the church would be able to focus on the meaning rather than the mechanics of what we were doing. Unfortunately, the one thing that would prove not to be simple was finding a time to put this seven-Sunday series on the church calendar.

I had arrived at the church in mid-summer, and as excited as I was about Jericho, my first priority was to get the usual interim work underway. This meant forming a transition team, facilitating a self-study procedure, moderating several congregational meetings to assess the results of the self-study, convening a search team, drafting a church profile, and initiating the nationwide search process. All of this took until nearly the end of the year.

No problem, I thought; I'll still have from January to at least the following July—when my interim term was supposed to be finished—to fit in the Jericho series. But when I met with Steve Caton, our Worship Arts Director, and actually tried to find seven consecutive Sundays on the calendar, we kept running into obstacles. For example, we had received a grant from the Calvin Institute of Christian Worship to create a Lenten series on the theme of Vertical Habits, all the different ways that we communicate with God. During another block of time, we had a large number of adults going to visit our sister church, *Vida Abundante* in Tegucigalpa, Honduras. Shortly after their return, we had committed to a pulpit exchange with one of *Vida's* pastors (I was unable to keep up my end of the exchange due to emergency back surgery—yet another obstacle in this whole process). Several weeks later, we had invited the Youth Praise Team from *Vida Abundante* to lead our worship.

I didn't want to cancel any of these commitments, but the longer we went without getting Jericho onto the calendar, the more fearful I became that the whole series might not happen. It had seemed so clear to me, riding in the car all those months earlier, that God wanted me to give this project a try, and then he had even provided a perfect place for it. There had been so much initial enthusiasm for the idea at Covenant Life, but now it seemed as if we were going to let a series of obstacles —all of them perfectly reasonable—prevent us from even getting Jericho onto the calendar.

Could anything be more conventional than that? We allow perfectly reasonable obstacles to stop us all the time, and I didn't want the Jericho series to become another casualty of perfectly reasonable thinking.

The more frustrated I became with trying to get Jericho onto the church calendar, the more I found myself thinking about an earlier episode at another church in which I had allowed reasonable thinking to convince me that we shouldn't start a second Sunday morning worship service. The neighborhood around this church was changing rapidly, and while we were seeing a lot of community people at our Wednesday evening suppers and family activities, they weren't joining us for worship on Sundays. So I had suggested that we begin a second service which would be designed to meet the needs of these newcomers.

After presenting a six-month preparation and roll out plan for the new service, the board had signed on to the idea, and I began to get excited about the first trial run. But before we ever got that far, people started raising "reasonable" objections: How would we pay for the musicians leading this new service? Since the multipurpose room, the proposed venue for the new service, was often used for Saturday activities, when would we set it up for worship? What would happen to the existing coffee and fellowship hour which took place in—you guessed it—the multipurpose room? What would be the impact on the Adult Sunday School classes, especially if those people currently attending now needed to get ready for a second service?

The most important question, one which was asked over and over again, seemed to be: What would happen to the existing, traditional worship service if all the young families decided to join the newcomers at the new, second service?

If all the objections had been coming from the usual curmudgeons and back-benchers, it might have been easy to persuade the board to stay the course and give the new service a try. But they weren't; they were coming from many of our perfectly reasonable members, which eventually made it perfectly reasonable for me to give up. I allowed the board to reverse itself and kill the new service before it even got started.

I didn't want this to happen to Jericho. So in an unusually bold move for me (I've always been Mr. Reasonable), I told the Wednesday worship team that we were going to set aside seven Sundays in June and July for the project.

Not surprisingly, when word about the worship schedule started to circulate, many reasonable people let me know that early-to-mid summer, especially in a resort community like Grand Haven, was the worst possible time to try a special series of worship services. Everyone would either be gone on vacation or would be focused on serving vacationers. Musicians would be hard to come by. The visual artists would be in the middle of their busiest season. Summer visitors wouldn't know what was going on. No one would want to give up a whole week of summer evenings for meetings on the subject of obedience.

I listened politely to everyone, but I had had enough of being reasonable. For once, I just wanted to be obedient to God, and Jericho stayed on the calendar.

QUESTIONS FOR REFLECTION AND DISCUSSION

1. Is the Bible intimidating? To everyone?

2. The Bible is the number one best-selling book in America year after year. Do you think it is also the most read book in the country? Why or why not?

3. What would happen to church membership if we required people to memorize the Heidelberg Catechism or long passages of scripture before they were allowed to join? Are you sure?

4. What would you say to parents who are considering a Sunday sports team for their children? What will you say to them ten years from now if their children no longer have any relationship with the church?

5. What effect do you think television viewing has had on biblical knowledge? Is it fair to blame TV for the seeming increase in biblical illiteracy?

6. True or false: Sophisticated people don't talk about the Bible. If this is true, where do these people turn for their guidance in daily living?

7. How does the Bible bring inconsistencies in our lives to the surface?

8. Was it a sin to watch a show like Rowan and Martin's "Laugh In" in the 1960s? Is it possible to watch any prime-time TV show today and not add bricks to our wall of disobedience?

9. We're not serious about what the Bible teaches. Agree or disagree?

10. Open your Bible at random to any page. Can you find something there that convinces you that God's way is better than your own way?

11. How does "reasonable" get in the way of "obedient?"

CHAPTER EIGHT:
COVENANT

*Bringing Down Walls Between
Family Members*

When I get to heaven, I need to look up Rahab and apologize for waiting nearly 23 years before preaching a sermon about her. Not only is her story a critical part of the Jericho account, but Matthew mentions her in the genealogy of Jesus, the author of Hebrews includes her as one of his heroes of the Old Testament, and James lifts her up as an example of how our actions should be prompted by our faith. In other words, it certainly seems as if I should have gotten around to sharing her story in worship long before I arrived at Covenant Life Church.

I will readily admit that I avoided her because of the whole "oldest profession" thing, and how uncomfortable it makes me to have to deal with something so earthy and immoral in worship (and now I'm probably going to have to apologize to her for being judgmental, too). My fear was that if I used the "P" word—or even just read it in the scripture passage—the kids would go home and ask, "Mom, what's a prostitute?" She would look at Dad for help, but he would suddenly be very engrossed in his Sunday paper, and I would almost certainly hear about it later. (This was not a completely unfounded fear: I once got lectured for inadvertently using the word "gee" in a sermon, because "... pastor, don't you know that 'gee' is short for 'gee whiz,' which is just a substitute for Jesus, and do you really want to be teaching our young children to use God's name in vain? From the pulpit? Well?")

When I was growing up, we didn't have prostitutes in the Bible, only harlots, and no one at Seymour Christian Elementary School ever taught us what a harlot was (eunuchs either). I think my friends and I figured out that the term harlot had something to do with women who misbehaved around men, but it never would have occurred to us that money was involved.

Cooties, possibly, but not money.

* * *

Before I continue with Rahab's story, this might be a good time to address the nature of Jericho itself and why it was subject to destruction. Like Noah and his family at the time of the flood, or Lot and his kin in the city of Sodom, it's possible that Rahab was the only righteous person in the entire city.

Righteous, in this circumstance, does not necessarily mean someone who has chosen to worship the one true God (although Rahab appears to have made that decision—more below), but a person who, in the manner of Romans 1, has discerned the existence of a Divine Being, as well as something of the divine nature, from creation itself: *"Ever since the creation of the world his eternal power and divine nature, invisible though they are, have been understood and seen through the things he has made. So they are without excuse"* (Romans 1:20 NRSV).

I've always operated on the assumption that Jericho was as thoroughly corrupt as Sodom or Gomorrah, because it would seem to be inconsistent with God's nature to order the destruction of innocent people. At Sodom, God was willing to spare everyone—the entire wicked city—if Abraham could

149

find as few as ten righteous people there (Genesis 18:32), and in Ezekiel, God said, *"As I live, says the Lord God, I have no pleasure in the death of the wicked, but that the wicked turn from their ways and live"* (Ezekiel 33:11 NRSV). So when God ordered that nothing of Jericho be allowed to survive, I always took it to mean that there were no righteous people there, or even people whom God knew might turn from evil to righteousness.

I find my assumption about Jericho's evil nature confirmed in the curse that Joshua pronounced as he stood before the ashes of the ruined city: *"Cursed before the Lord be anyone who tries to build this city—this Jericho! At the cost of his firstborn he shall lay its foundation, and at the cost of his youngest he shall set up its gates!"* (Joshua 6:26 NRSV). Joshua wanted the debris to remain as a warning to anyone who was crossing the Jordan: Do you see what happened to Jericho? Know that the God of the Israelites will not tolerate wickedness.

If the curse itself doesn't confirm that Jericho was a sinful city, the fulfillment of it certainly does. We find this in the book of I Kings, during the reign of King Ahab. We are told that *"Ahab son of Omri did evil in the sight of the Lord more than all who were before him,"* and again, after a list of his sinful activities, *"Ahab did more to provoke the anger of the Lord, the God of Israel, than had all the kings of Israel who were before him"* (I Kings 16:30, 33 NRSV).

In the context of this evil king's story, we suddenly find this note dropped in: *"In his days Hiel of Bethel built Jericho; he laid its foundation at the cost of Abiram his firstborn, and set up its gates at the cost of his youngest son Segub, according to the word of the Lord, which he spoke by Joshua son of Nun"* (I Kings 16:34 NRSV). I'm pretty sure that what we are supposed to take away from this is that during the reign of a thoroughly evil king, a thoroughly evil city was being rebuilt.

* * *

It is in this unholy place that we find a harlot whose name was Rahab. If we knew nothing else about her, her profession wouldn't surprise us in the least—in a sinful place, you expect to find people doing sinful things. Such was the case when I worked in the emergency room at St. Mary's Hospital in Grand Rapids. Ours was the hospital closest to South Division Avenue, a notoriously crime-ridden corridor running through the heart of the city's south side, and when people were beaten up, knifed or shot, or if they just fell on their heads because they were too drunk to stay on their feet, they generally ended up at our facility.

I remember one particularly sad night when a drunken man came staggering through the ER doors, yelling at the top of his lungs, "SUPER DUPER EMERGENCY! I'VE BEEN SHOT!" He had been, just moments earlier, and he died of blood loss less than half an hour later. None of us were surprised to learn that the shooting had taken place on South Division.

What surprises us about Rahab of Jericho then isn't her choice of profession, but her course of action in spite of her profession. When two foreign spies came to her house (presumably also her place of business), it would have been an easy decision for her to do the expected thing, which would be to report their visit to someone in an official capacity—a soldier, a guard, a gatekeeper—who in turn could get word to the king that spies had entered the city. Rahab might have been rewarded for ratting out the spies; at the very least, she would have been protecting herself from any accusations of aiding and abetting foreign invaders.

But instead, Rahab did a completely unexpected, unconventional thing: She trusted in a God she only knew by reputation. Word of the Israelites' approach had already reached Jericho, including the stories of how their God had dried up the waters of the Red Sea, and how the fleeing refugees had defeated the two kings of the Amorites. Rahab said, "As soon as we heard it, our hearts melted, and there was no courage left in any *of us because of you. The Lord your God is indeed God in heaven above and on earth below"* (Joshua 2:11 NRSV).

Rahab's decision to trust God was very similar to the one Joshua would soon make when he was confronted by the commander of the Lord's army. Like Joshua, she could have chosen to do the usual thing, expecting the usual results, which in her case almost certainly would have meant momentary praise, the death of the spies, the possible defeat of the Israelites, and then continued employment as a harlot. Or she could choose to trust in a God who seemed to delight in doing the unexpected, which in this case meant sending his spies straight to her doorstep.

If she chose to do the outrageously risky thing, would the God of these Israelites be merciful to her, a—cover the kids' ears—prostitute?

* * *

When Rahab decided to trust God, she hid the spies under some stalks of flax that were drying on the roof of her house, told a couple of impressive lies (for which she is never criticized in scripture, by the way; that would have been helpful to know when I was younger), sent the king's men off on a wild goose chase, and then did one other completely unexpected thing: She made the spies swear an oath that in exchange for their lives, they would save her family. Finally, we get to the subject of this chapter: Family!

Even in a place as sinful as Jericho, it's hard to imagine that Rahab was considered a model daughter or sister by the other members of her clan. I'm pretty sure that even thoroughly wicked people don't want their children or siblings to sell their bodies to strangers. As any good mobster movie will illustrate, evil people like to use others for their own purposes, but they don't typically want themselves or their family members to be used.

We don't know anything about Rahab's family other than

that she had a complete set—father, mother, brothers, sisters —and we know that there were others who belonged to some of these; nieces and nephews, perhaps. But even though we don't know what any of them thought of her, or if they even thought about her at all, we definitely know that she thought about them. She wanted all their lives saved when Jericho was attacked.

It's sometimes easy for us to forget that notoriously sinful people have families. When I was beaten and robbed by a drug-addled 17-year-old (more about that in the next chapter), and had to testify against him in court, I think I did an actual double-take when the judge determined that he should be released to the custody of his parents. Parents? It had never occurred to me that someone as antisocial as this teenage thug might have a family of origin that cared for him.

I was reminded of this again during my bailiff days at the 61st District Court. I was always surprised by the family members—especially the mothers—who would show up in the courtroom, wailing about the innocence of their little lambs, even if their particular lamb happened to be caught on surveillance video looking a whole lot like a wolf, carrying a sack of money in one hand and a Glock 30 in the other. None of that mattered, of course; incontrovertible evidence is no match for a mother's love.

Family ties are arguably some of the strongest relationships we will ever have in our lives, which is why it is so painful when disobedience builds walls between us and our family members. Every sinful act, no matter how small, adds a brick. If we deal with it quickly, the brick can be removed just as quickly, but if we never address the sin, that brick remains, and many others are likely to be added on top of it.

* * *

Several years ago, I observed an almost literal wall under construction between a man and a woman who were thinking of getting married. He had proposed, but she wasn't sure if she wanted to say yes, so they asked if I would meet with them to talk it through.

When I arrived at the man's home, it quickly became evident that they were living together, which is a kind of mutually agreed upon sin that almost always proves to be the beginning of a significant dividing wall. I was tempted to dive right in and start talking about how difficult it is to build a faithful marriage relationship on a foundation of shared dis-obedience, but thinking that there might be other issues as well, I began with a little small talk, chatting about some mutual acquaintances. When there was a lull in the conversation, I casually asked the young woman if she had any thoughts about why she was reluctant to say yes to her boyfriend's proposal.

Not surprisingly, it had to do with money. As soon as I saw their spartan living arrangements, I had suspected that her hesitancy might be related to their finances.

"He always spends his paycheck on toys," she said.

"Collectibles," he corrected. "They're going to be worth a lot of money some day."

"But they really cost a lot and we could use that money to do a lot of other things," She persisted.

"But they're going to be worth a lot of money some day," he repeated, and then added, "Especially if I have a complete set."

I was curious to find out what this guy had been buying (and sincerely hoped that it wasn't Beanie Babies), so I asked him if I could see his collection. While she rolled her eyes, he invited me to follow him into the next room, where I saw an enormous wall of authorized miniature NASCAR racing cars and helmets, all in their original boxes. I had no idea what these cost, but guessed that they weren't cheap, and he had what appeared to be many dozens of items.

The smile on his face as he gazed lovingly at his die-cast nest egg made me realize how clueless he was about what these, um, collectibles, were doing to his relationship with his girlfriend. Every time he bought another one and added it to the stack, he was also putting a brick on the wall that was coming between the two of them.

Now, in and of itself, buying collectibles isn't a sin (although when it comes to some of the stuff they sell online, it ought to be). The disobedience in this nascent relationship —beyond the fact that they were living together without the benefit of marriage—was in the disagreement they were having about how they would spend their money. He had repeatedly promised to be more responsible with his paycheck, but every time another car appeared, she realized that he had no intention of keeping his word. The wall of distrust over this one issue was preventing her from seeing any of his other qualities.

Note: They never got married. She moved out shortly after our meeting. Also, NASCAR miniatures have yet to make an appearance on the commodities exchange.

* * *

Once we become aware of how each act of disobedience adds a brick to the wall of separation that divides us from our spouse, or when we see similar walls growing between us and our children, our parents, or other family members, it's easier to name them for what they are. It's also easier to see how our current culture encourages us to leave the walls intact, rather than doing whatever is necessary to remove them.

Older television programs like *Leave it to Beaver* (a traditional family), *My Three Sons* (a single parent family), *The Brady Bunch* (a blended family), or *Gilligan's Island* (people acting like a family), would often begin with someone committing an act of disobedience. Beaver would tell a lie at school, or would take something that belonged to Wally. Chip or Marcia would have a misunderstanding with a sibling. Gilligan would destroy a piece of valuable equipment that could have gotten all his shipmates off the island. In each case, you could immediately see how the disobedience, whatever it was, began building a wall between the family members. Further misbehaviors often added to the wall or created new ones as the plot unfolded.

Within thirty minutes however, the wall was removed. The whole point of most programs during this era was to uncover the disobedience, deal with the consequences, and restore harmony within the family.

Later shows, especially those that were targeted at the young people who came of age during the Gilligan era, followed a more disturbing formula. Rather than dealing with misbehavior, these programs tried to normalize it. There was one popular show about another group of people who were living almost like a family in New York City—we'll call them friends—who, week after week, engaged in all kinds of wall-building disobedience. But they rarely identified it as such. In fact, because they were all such good friends, they were supposed to tell each other how okay it was to just keep on doing whatever they felt like doing, no matter how big a wall they were building.

In the world of fiction, people can pretend that walls don't exist or don't matter, but in the real world, where we live with our real spouses, parents, children and siblings, the walls are real, too, and they matter a lot. If we try to ignore them, or expect other people to simply accept them as inevitable, we will eventually find ourselves completely estranged from the people with whom we should have our closest relationships. If, on the other hand, we accept responsibility for our actions and choose to follow a new course of deliberate obedience, we can begin to take those walls down, brick by brick.

Can't you almost hear the Skipper calling Gilligan "Little Buddy" again at the end of the half hour?

* * *

I don't think it is a coincidence that the Jericho account in scripture is framed by two very different family relationships. At the beginning of the story, we find the harlot Rahab, whom we would normally assume to be a model of disobedience; yet she chose to believe in God's power even though her belief was based solely on what she had heard about God from others. She made the unexpected choice to save the spies, and honored her family by getting the spies to swear that they would save all of her close relatives.

At the other end of the story, after Jericho was defeated, we find family man Achan, whom we would normally assume to be a paragon of obedience. Wouldn't you be, if you had just witnessed God's power in destroying Jericho's walls, first hand? Even so, Achan chose not to obey what God had commanded about Jericho and made the disastrous decision to steal some of the devoted goods. The result of his disobedience was that he and his entire family were destroyed.

Both Rahab and Achan teach us that choosing the way of unconventional obedience is exactly what God wants us to do, because it requires us to put our trust in God. Leigh and I have experienced God's trustworthiness many times, one example of which was when we bought our boat.

We were still living in a parsonage at the time; our children were in their early teens and I had convinced Leigh that we should invest in a sailboat as something that our family could enjoy together. I had sailed a 29 foot e-scow in college (a flat bottom, twin keel board racer), and had gotten some experience with displacement keel boats on my brother-and-sister-in-law's Pearson 33. Leigh said that she was willing to give it a try—have I mentioned that I have the best wife in the world?—and so we purchased a Columbia 34 MkII (don't forget the MkII if you want to see one online). It was a great boat: plenty of room for our whole family and guests, easy to sail, and at 12,000 pounds of displacement, unlikely to capsize in anything less than hurricane force winds.

Postlude (our new name for her; the previous name was *Easy Rider*), went into the water on April 12. By mid-May, Leigh and

I were taking long day trips north or south on Lake Michigan, whichever way the wind was blowing. When school let out for the year in early June, our children joined us for some of these longer trips, but of the three, only our youngest ever showed any enthusiasm for it.

By the middle of the summer, it was clear that sailing was separating us from our children at just the time when we needed to be most available, even if only to monitor their comings and goings. We certainly didn't want to force them to join us onboard, so our outings became shorter and less frequent than they might have been otherwise (although according to my logbook, we still managed to get out 39 times). By late August, it was clear that Leigh and I had a decision to make: keep sailing, knowing that it would continue to take us away from our children, or try to sell the boat, a dubious proposition just as the Michigan sailing season was drawing to a close.

Obedience to the needs of our family seemed to call for the latter, so I reluctantly called our yacht broker and asked if he would put *Postlude* back on the market. Not wanting to make things too easy for God, I actually named a selling price that was nearly twenty percent higher than what we had paid just half a year earlier.

Within three weeks, we were watching *Postlude* sail away with her new owner.

I don't think that owning the boat for that summer was a sin, and I'm not sure that keeping it would have been either. That would have been the easier decision, but Leigh and I both had a strong sense that God was challenging us to make the more difficult, and more obedient choice of letting the boat go. God blessed that decision, and has continually blessed our relationship with our children. Had we kept *Postlude*, we knew that every outing could have become another brick in a steadily growing wall between us and at least two of our kids.

You know, we named our boat *Postlude* because the post-lude is what comes when everything else in the worship service is finished. Perhaps when our current family commitments subside, we'll look for another boat. There's always the chance that some our grandchildren might take to sailing.

* * *

"Hey! What was that?" I had just flinched and ducked my head under something that had caught my eye at the last second, and in precisely that same moment, I realized what a perfect plan the Impact Team had implemented for the Jericho series.

Covenant Life's Impact Team, an artistic group of out-of-the-church-box thinkers, was responsible for the visual presentation of whatever our current worship or ministry theme happened to be. When I had first arrived at CLC, just a month after the farewell for their founding pastor, there were hundreds—maybe even thousands—of colorful paper cranes hanging in long strands from the high ceiling in Main Street (part of the ministry center). Several weeks later, these were replaced with intricate mobiles made of curved copper tubing and wire, and carefully cut pieces of copper sheeting. My sermon series was on restoring balance in our lives and the mobiles were a perfect reminder of how getting all the little pieces right makes it easier to get the big things in balance.

A short while later, a Sunday service on how we make the most of our time found the worship center filled with enormous clock faces, as well as a live image of the National Atomic Clock—with every fraction of a second flashing away —displayed on both of the video screens throughout the entire service (we also had a group of singers join the band for *Seasons of Love,* the "525,600 minutes" song from the musical *Rent*; they had practiced for weeks, and absolutely nailed it). Near the end of the calendar year, when my Advent theme was Faces of Christmas, the Impact Team did a phenomenal job of hanging four huge floor-to-ceiling muslin scrims in the worship center, with a black-and-white image of a face rear-projected on each one. The faces changed every week; some were gorgeous, some were hard to look at. All of them were incredible.

I could hardly wait to see what the Impact Team was going to do for the Jericho series. I assumed, logically enough, that it would involve bricks—probably a lot of bricks. I was a little worried about any walls that they might decide to build in the worship center, because for the final Jericho Sunday, we were going to need that space completely free of obstacles—but I assumed we would take care of that when the day came.

Silly me. Using bricks for a series of messages on Jericho, all about walls tumbling down? Whatever was I thinking?

Clearly, I wasn't thinking the way the Impact Team was thinking. I'm going assume that the Holy Spirit had a lot to do with their planning, because everything about their design was exactly the opposite of what most people—by which I mean me—would expect for a series on Jericho. Since the whole idea of the project was to get us to think about choosing to be obedient to God's unconventional way of doing things, the team had also chosen an unconventional design.

For starters, they didn't use any actual bricks, blocks or stones; not one. Secondly, nothing was stacked up on the floor; all the elements of the design were hung from the ceiling. Third, unlike most walls that prevent you from seeing what's happening on the other side, this design was perfectly transparent. Finally, unlike most of the art installations that the team had done over the course of my year with them, all of which had an immediate "wow" factor, this installation was subtle. The wow hit you later—and repeatedly—when you least expected it.

* * *

To help you picture what the team had done, let me describe the Covenant Life facility in a little more detail. When CLC bought the former Story and Clark piano factory in Grand

Haven, they had to tie two very different buildings together. The one to the west was an ancient post-and-beam structure, three stories tall, the ground level of which the congregation had converted into a variety of offices, classrooms, a library, and the Loading Dock coffee shop. It also housed a large multi-purpose ministry center with tables, chairs, and a large video screen with live feed from the main worship space. The upper two floors had been cleaned out, and were available for future expansion.

To the east was a newer, single story warehouse. It was essentially a giant rectangular box which had been converted into a technologically-sophisticated, flexible worship space. Upstreet, the children's ministry area, was built to the north of the worship center, and the open space where railroad tracks used to run between the two buildings became the church's Main Street.

Once enclosed, Main Street was used as a spacious, high-ceilinged gathering area that I would describe as visually energetic. As soon as you walked into either the north or south entrances, there were lots of details to catch your eye: parts of the brick face and the massive wooden beams of the original factory, exposed heating and cooling ducts, the tables and chairs of the coffee shop, the TV monitors and video screen in the ministry center, and the gleam of theatre lighting coming through the doors that opened into the worship area. First time visitors often walked a few steps forward through one of the entrances, and then just stopped as they looked around and took it all in.

In keeping with the church's desire to engage all the senses, the facility was also a delight to the ears (like the meshing of chains and gears when the large, overhead, garage-style doors into Upstreet were opened), the nose (the old wood; also, wonderful coffee aromas), the tongue (the Loading Dock coffee tasted pretty good, too), and the sense of touch (there were different textures everywhere; I would often see people just running their hand over a time-weathered beam, or across a fabric wall hanging).

I've never seen another church with a facility like Covenant Life's. As I've already said, Steve, our Worship director, used to remind us, "We only have 52 chances a year to worship God together," and he made sure that worship began not just when the music started playing or when the pastor said, "Welcome," but as soon as people walked through the door.

* * *

On the first Sunday of the Jericho series, worshipers entering through either end of Main Street were confronted with a single large Plexiglas panel hanging directly in front of them, just about a dozen feet past the inner doors. Along the base of these panels, the Impact Team had glued several courses of Styrofoam blocks that they had painted to look like bricks (they didn't use any real bricks; I guess they couldn't figure out how to get them to stay in place). There were about three or four rows of these amazingly realistic Styrofoam bricks at the bottom, and then fewer in the next row, and fewer still above that. Beyond the bottom third of the panel, the rest of it was perfectly clear.

The idea was to get people thinking about walls, but not in the usual way, because throughout the rest of Main Street and the worship center, the team had hung dozens of clear panels in many different rectangular shapes and sizes, all hanging in either an east/west or north/south orientation, and all suspended at different levels. Many of them were just a few feet above head level, and as people walked through Main Street or entered the worship space, they would find themselves flinching as the glint of light reflecting off a panel suddenly made them think they were about to run into something.

If you actually stopped to consider the clear panels, they were kind of pretty—the way the light reflected off them, their slight motion in the moving air—but it wasn't as if the Impact Team had tried to recreate Superman's Fortress of Solitude. There wasn't anything about the panels that would keep your eye on them for very long, which is precisely why they were such an effective reminder of the invisible walls that we build through our disobedience. Every now and then, one of the Plexiglas panels would unexpectedly catch your attention. In the same way, unexpected events can suddenly make us become aware of the walls that interfere with our family relationships.

* * *

Although the Impact Team chose not to use real bricks for their part of the Jericho worship services, the Drama Team found a way to incorporate both bricks and a Plexiglas divider into the drama that they presented for the week that we were focusing on obedience in families. *Walls* was written and directed by Ruth Saukus, a member of Covenant Life Church, and is reprinted here with her permission.

WALLS

(Wife, in a bathrobe, enters, stretches and yawns and goes to the breakfast table, which has several bricks on it. On either side of the table is a wheelbarrow full of bricks. She fusses a bit with the silverware, dropping a spoon. She glances over her shoulder, wipes the spoon on her robe and puts it on the table.)

She (mostly to herself): Five-second rule. (Slips a brick onto the table)

(Husband enters)

She: Good morning, sweetie, how did you sleep?

He: Lousy, if you're really interested.

(Both pick up a brick and put it on the table between them)

He: Those new sheets you got are too slick.

(Puts up a brick)

She: (in a haughty tone) Those are very high-quality sheets, they have a thread count of 600, but maybe you can't count that high.

(Puts up a brick)

He: What did you pay for those "high-quality" sheets? Whatever it was, you got taken.

(Puts up a brick)

She: I didn't pay that much; I got a bargain. We needed new sheets; the old ones were all full of pills and you couldn't stand them.

(Takes down a brick)

He: You're right, I couldn't stand them. So where did you get your bargain sheets?

(Takes down a brick)

She: (In a small voice) T.J. Maxx.

He: Oh great! (Puts up a brick) What else did you buy? (More bricks) I told you you've got to stay out of that place, you have no resistance. (Stacking bricks all the time)

She: (defensively) I only went in to look for sheets, and that's all I purchased. (Sneakily puts up several more bricks)

He: All right, whatever. (Takes down one brick) By the way, I might be a little late tonight. I wanted to get out to the driving range and hit a few balls. (Tries to take down bricks, but she immediately puts them back up.)

She: You played golf twice this week already and I was hoping you'd make dinner tonight.

He: How about if I bring home dinner to the kids when I'm finished at the driving range? Would that help?

(They both take down some bricks)

She: That would be great, but please, not McDonalds. Scott just finished some kind of study in Health class at school and he's all paranoid about eating their food.

He: No, no. I'll get something better than that, Wendy's or KFC.

She: Honey, that's no better; it's the same thing. (Putting up bricks) Put a little more thought into it. What are you thinking?

He: Fine, maybe you should bring home dinner. (Putting up bricks) You should put a little thought into it.

She: (putting up bricks furiously) I put thought into it EVERY day, EVERY time I cook.

(Young teen boy and younger sister enter)

Girl: Mom, are you mad at Dad?

Mom: (trying to take down bricks, but instead just puts them in a neater order) No, honey, we were just having a little difference of opinion. Sit down and eat your Cream of Wheat.

Boy: Cream of Wheat? I hate Cream of Wheat!, It's like eating cement. (Puts up a brick)

Dad: (under his breath) Tell me about it (then in regular voice) Eat it up son; it'll put hair on your chest ... or your tongue ...

Girl: I'm going to eat it! Thank you VERY MUCH, Mother. I love your Cream of Wheat. (Looks smugly at brother and puts up a brick)

Mom: That's my good girl. (Both putting up bricks in front of boy)

Boy: Mama's "little angel"; you're a pain! (Slams a brick on the table)

Girl: Nyahhh! (Sticks out her tongue)

Mom: Kids, please ...

Dad: Hey, look at the time! Come on you two, get going. You're running late.

(Dad and Mom go to kiss each other but the bricks get in the way, they fumble and manage something. Boy starts stuffing his backpack full of bricks.)

Mom: (To her daughter) Let me help you with your back-pack, honey. (Puts a couple of bricks in it)

Dad: Can I help you with that, son?

Boy: No! (Slams a brick on the floor)

Mom: (Kisses girl) Bye, honey, I love you. (In a hopeless voice to her son) I love you, too. (Kids exit; boy staggers deter-minedly, dragging the fully-laden backpack)

(Both parents turn back to the table)

He: That wasn't a very good start to our day. (Starts taking down bricks and she joins in)

She: No. It wasn't. I'm sorry.

He: Me, too.

She: (wistfully) I need a hug.

(They walk around to the front of the table and go to em-brace and run into a piece of Plexiglas. Only slightly taken aback, they put their hands up to the glass.)

She: What the heck? (She shrugs)

She: Gimme a kiss. (She puts her cheek against the glass and he kisses it firmly and then turns to go)

She: Do you have everything you need for work? (He picks up his wheelbarrow and wheels it off.)

(She stays at the glass and wistfully puts her hand on it. The phone starts to ring; she looks at the caller ID)

She: Oh great. (Sits down and starts lethargically stacking bricks) Hi, Mom ... yep, it's my day off. So how have you been feeling? Uh huh ... uh huh ... (aside) I don't know if I have enough of these. Uh huh ...

(Lights fade)

QUESTIONS FOR REFLECTION AND DISCUSSION

1. At what age should we teach our children about some of the earthier characters in the Bible? Until then, what should we say to them about a person like Rahab?

2. Do you agree that Rahab might have been the only righteous person in all of Jericho? Would God have ordered the destruction of the city otherwise?

3. "In a sinful place, you expect to find people doing sinful things." What are some sinful places today, and what effect would it have on our obedience if we avoided them?

4. Why should it matter to us that even notoriously sinful people have families (especially children)?

5. Give some examples of how the big three—time, sex, and money—lead to disobedience in marriage. Can you think of any common disobedience that isn't related to one of these three?

6. Rather than showing disobediences being resolved, many modern TV shows try to normalize disobedience. Are they simply being more realistic than the shows of years gone by?

7. What are some of the ways that parents build walls between themselves and their children? Are these walls ever justified? Are they acceptable as long as they are temporary?

8. What is the relationship between selfish behavior in families and walls? Who is more likely to be selfish, parents or children? Does this change as either children or adults get older?

9. The clear Plexiglas barriers in the Covenant Life worship space often made us flinch when we suddenly realized they were there. Do the walls in our family relationships sometimes make us flinch, or have we become so accustomed to them that they never surprise us anymore?

10. The *Walls* drama shows walls going up and down quickly. Do our walls of disobedience really appear and disappear with such speed?

CHAPTER NINE:
EQUALITY

Bringing Down Walls Between Neighbors

As I mentioned earlier, I have been robbed twice in my life, once was when I was about eleven years old and another time when I was sixteen. Even though the second assailant stole almost exactly one hundred times as much money as the first, my feelings of anger and frustration each time were amazingly similar.

At the time of the first incident, my father was working as an optician in downtown Grand Rapids. On Saturdays, when the Optical House was only open until 1:00 o'clock, my brothers and I would often ride into town with him, and then spend the rest of the morning playing. We considered downtown our playground.

As we made our way west on Fulton Street toward the heart of downtown, we passed Smeelink Optical, a competitor of the Optical House whose name just begged for mispronunciation. That kept us giggling at least as far as Jacobson's, a clothing store that gave no thought to the needs of children who were trying to entertain themselves on a Saturday morning. Instead, we went a little farther and crossed the street toward

Herpolsheimer's, a classic downtown department store with creative window displays (especially at the holidays), escalators (always good for ten minutes of fun), and a well-stocked toy department in the basement. One of the coolest things at Herp's was the elevated train that ran around the lower level of the store. As I recall, it only operated around Christmas time, and it either took you to see Santa or else Santa was the engineer; I'm not sure which.

After we had carefully examined and critiqued the toy inventory, we exited the store onto Monroe, and made our way up the street to Wurzburg's, another department store that could have come right out of *Miracle on 34th Street*. If Herpolsheimer's was our version of Macy's, Wurzburg's was Gimbels: almost as good, but not quite. What it did have was elevators, and with the toy department up on one of the highest floors, we had a lot of time to practice things like balancing on one foot, guessing which floor the car would stop at next, and arguing about whether a well-timed jump would save your life if all the cables broke at the same time.

Wurzburg's stock of toys never seemed to change as quickly as Herpolsheimer's, so within fifteen minutes or so, we were usually ready to move on to the intellectual and historic parts of our Saturday morning activities. This involved a stop at the Grand Rapids Public Library, which had lots of good car magazines that you could just sit and read as long as you wanted; the East Building of the Public Museum, with its full-sized Gaslight Village display of what a city street would have looked like during the horse and buggy era; and finally, the main building of the Grand Rapids Public Museum itself, with all its lifelike mounted animals, kitschy dioramas, and the enormous whale skeleton suspended overhead.

These were pre-ironic times (not to mention pre-environmentalist), and I loved the museum, at least until the Saturday when I got robbed. I had gone downtown by myself that day, but had generally followed our regular routine. By late morning, I was headed down the front stairwell of the museum, thinking of going back to the Optical House a little early to play with the magnifying glasses and the electric adding machine.

I heard what sounded like a large group of teenagers coming up from the lower level, and when we met on the landing halfway between floors, they quickly surrounded me and asked me if I had any money. One of them, clearly the leader of the group, started shoving me around, and with the others egging him on, he started to get angrier and more aggressive. I didn't want to get pushed down the steps, so I reached in my front pocket and gave him all my money—a dollar bill and some change.

It wasn't a fortune, but he seemed satisfied with it, and within a few seconds, all of them had run down the steps and disappeared. I could hear them laughing until the door at the bottom of the stairwell closed behind them.

At some point while all of this was going on, I had started crying, but I didn't move for a minute or two, embarrassed about the way I had just stood there but also afraid that they might be waiting for me outside the building. I finally got up the courage to slowly make my way down the steps. When I got to the main entrance of the museum and didn't see them anywhere around, I ran back to the Optical House as fast as I could.

When I told my dad what had happened, he called the police and a very kind officer came and took a complete report —where did it happen, what time was it, how many of them were there, how much money did they take? The one question I remember most clearly was the obvious one, "What did they look like?" but I could only come up with one detail about their appearance:

"They were black."

* * *

Up until that morning, I don't think that I had ever spoken

more than a word or two to an African-American. There weren't any at Seymour Christian School, there weren't any in my church, and there weren't any living in my neighborhood. I saw quite a few of them at Garfield Park, which is where we rode our bikes to go swimming during the summer months, but they played with their friends and we played with ours. I'm sure I saw them in stores, restaurants and other places too, but I had never had any interaction with one that I can remember.

Because of that single act of disobedience in the museum, a huge wall of anger, distrust and resentment had instantly gone up, not just between just me and the half dozen youths who had taken my money, but between me and an entire race. It only took that one sin for me to quickly respond with my own disobedience: holding all members of the African-American community responsible for the actions of a few young people. Even at eleven years old, I think I knew better than that, but it seemed as if I couldn't suppress my feelings of fear and anger whenever my path crossed that of a black person.

As a result, I just chose to keep my distance as much as I could. I managed to get through junior high school (seventh through ninth grades) without any incidents, and even my sophomore and junior years at Ottawa Hills High School were mostly fine. I once accidentally bumped the elbow of a black student who was carrying a portable record player down the hallway—while it was playing—and he yelled at me, but before I knew if he was going to put the thing down to come after me, I was long gone.

I'm ashamed to admit it, but all I wanted was to get through my last year of high school in one piece. I had zero sympathy for the concerns of the African-American community, and other than the occasional twinge of conscience in church, it never would have occurred to me that I was supposed to think of these people as my neighbors.

That's probably one of the worst consequences of the neighbor walls that we build through our disobedience: We choose not to have any dealings with the people on the other side of the wall. We'll quickly make assumptions about them without ever getting firsthand evidence to see if our assumptions are true, or we'll choose to believe the anecdotes we hear from other people, but we won't make any effort to find out if their stories have any basis in fact. As a result, the people we think of as our real neighbors are mostly those people who are just like us. We're content to let the walls remain standing between us and everyone else.

That was my approach to African-Americans. I tried not to tell ethnic jokes (unless there was a Dutch person involved), and I didn't complain about "blacks always this" or "blacks always that." But in my private thoughts, I believed that the African-American community was dangerous and to be avoided if at all possible.

* * *

Near the end of my junior year, a high school counselor approached me to ask if I was looking for a summer job. He knew someone who ran a chain of dry-cleaning establishments, and he was looking for someone who could clerk at one of his stores part time during the summer, and then work late afternoons when the school year began in the fall. That sounded like a pretty good deal to me, so I said yes, and arranged to meet with the dry-cleaning tycoon at his main store near downtown Grand Rapids.

Once he satisfied himself that I was qualified to do the job and filled me in on what he considered to be the most important details ("Now remember, it's your job to brush the lint out of the pockets and cuffs,") he told me which branch needed help: The Franklin Street store.

I knew the neighborhood, and it wasn't good. Our family had lived in that area for a couple years when we first came to America, and the one story I had heard several times was about a knife-wielding thief who had broken into our house and threatened my mother. I briefly considered turning down the job, but the money was good, the job was all during daylight hours, and when I had asked the owner if I was supposed to mop and dust the store between customers ("time to lean, time to clean" is how I was raised), he emphatically said no, that I was simply supposed to be available whenever a customer walked in the door.

So I met him again the following week, this time at the Franklin Street location, and I was pleased to see that there were vertical security bars from countertop to ceiling which stretched the full width of the store, dividing the customer and employee areas. They were spaced four or five inches apart—you could easily pass hanging clothes between them—and there was also a good-sized horizontal pass-through just above the central part of the counter where the customer could hand over the clothes that needed to be cleaned.

Knowing that I would be working in a safe area put me at ease, as did the kindly older woman who normally worked the day shift. After showing me how to log in and tag the clothes —and brush the lint out of the pockets and the cuffs—she assured me that it was a nice place to work, and also that she would leave behind her stack of tabloid magazines so that I would have something to read between customers (favorite headline: "Baby Singing in Womb; Mother Thought it Was Radio").

Over the next month and a half, I settled into a comfortable routine at the store and got to know a few of the regular customers, nearly all of whom were African-Americans. Whenever my friends would hear where I was working and expressed concern about the neighborhood, I responded with a casually superior, "Oh, it's not that bad," as if they were deeply prejudiced while I was Mr. Equality. I even sort of believed it myself. One, maybe two bricks were starting to come down from the wall I had so carefully maintained for the previous five years.

Until another fateful Saturday, that is. It was just about one in the afternoon, and it had been a slow day: exactly $125.71 in the till. I'm not sure what I was doing—probably reading one of the magazines, or trying to copy the picture of that little dog to prove that I could be an artist—when a young adult, an African-American, came into the store.

He wasn't anyone I had seen before, but that wasn't uncommon. What was unusual was the glassy-eyed look on his face; that and the fact that I couldn't find any clothes under the name he had given me. I had run through the entire rack several times, trying several different spellings of the last name and even the first name, but no luck. I asked him if he was sure he had dropped off the clothes at this store, and he mumbled back to me that he had.

I said that I would have to look in the book to see when they had been dropped off and to check whether someone else might have picked them up by mistake, but as I soon as I bent forward and started flipping through the pages, he produced a club from behind his back and swung it with all his might right down between the security bars and onto the top of my head.

I crumpled to the floor, only semi-conscious, and the next thing I knew, he had slid through the pass-through, ripped the phone off the wall, opened the cash register and took all the money—even the change. He then let himself out the back door.

All the while, I didn't move. I'm not even sure I was breathing, because I didn't want him to hit me again. When he was gone, I slowly got up, made sure the door was locked, and started crying again—and not just because my head was throbbing. Without a phone to call for help (cell phones were still decades away), I hastily made a sign to tape to the front door, locked up, and got in my car to drive home.

I knew only my brothers would be there, because my parents were on a twenty-fifth anniversary vacation trip to Nova Scotia. We quickly decided not to call them or even tell them what had happened until they got home, so I called the police, who asked me to meet them back at the store, and then I called my boss, whose first question was, "Well, who's running the store now?"

That was when I decided that I was quitting.

I gave as complete an account of the incident as I could to the officers. This time, I was able to tell them a little bit more about the thief's appearance than simply his race. When I gave them the name he had used to ask for the clothes—which I assumed had been a made-up name—they looked at each other as if it was familiar to them. One of them asked if I would be willing to come to the station downtown to look through mug shots, which was fine with me, and we made an appointment for Monday morning.

While the police began dusting for fingerprints and bagging up anything the thief might have touched (including the phone), an employee from one of the other stores showed up to take care of business for the rest of the day. I was eager to get out of there and go home again, so I asked one of the evidence technicians who was dusting by the front door if it was okay for me to leave. He said yes, he thought they had everything they needed from me. Then he looked across the street, and seeing the gas station that was located there, he asked, "Why didn't you just run across the street and call us when it happened?"

What I said was, "I didn't think about it; I just wanted to get out of here." But the true answer was, "I thought about it, but when I saw that all the people working there were black, I was afraid to go in."

Good Samaritan

* * *

At that point in my life, I felt a lot like the man who was making his way from Jerusalem to Jericho when he fell into the hands of robbers (Luke 10:25-37). They stripped him, beat him and left him half dead, after which a couple of holy people, a priest and a Levite, passed him by. We know they saw the man—Jesus specifically tells us that they did—but they did the conventional thing, the thing that most people probably would have done: they chose not to get involved with the victim and his wounds.

No one got involved with my wounds either, and I'm sure they must have been visible. Not physically—within a day or two after the robbery, I was fine physically—but spiritually. I was as wounded and broken as the man in Jesus' story, even though I tried to pretend that everything was fine. In my private thoughts, if I had built a brick wall of resentment and anger toward African-Americans before, now it was a reinforced concrete barrier topped with coils of razor wire. I wanted nothing to do with black people, period.

Come Monday, I found my assailant's picture in the book of mug shots, so I knew he already had a police record. He had, in fact, given me his actual name when he asked for the non-existent clothes, and his fingerprints were on everything. I was called to testify against him in court, and he was convicted, but because he was 17 at the time of the crime, and because I hadn't sought medical treatment for my injuries, the judge released him to the custody of his parents. Add another massive block to my wall of anger.

I can't help but wonder about how many people today are living with similar walls separating them from their neighbors. Granted, not everyone has had a violent or painful experience with someone from a different race or nationality, but even the smallest negative incidents add up over time, and contribute to the building of some pretty impressive walls. Every time we see news footage of a radical terrorist thrusting an AK-47 in the air, every time we hear about a tribal warlord refusing to give up power after a rigged election, every time a Central American refugee is described as an "illegal alien," bricks are being piled onto the walls that divide us from our neighbors.

If you are a member of a minority group in North America, you almost certainly have your own walls to deal with, built from negative images of white North Americans flaunting their wealth, living in palatial homes, and generally consuming far more than their fair share of the world's resources. The people you consider your real neighbors may be those who have to deal with discrimination, joblessness, or crushing poverty, and you wonder why lily-white America can't see the obvious need right at its doorstep.

The conventional response to this situation, on both sides of the wall, is to do nothing, because it doesn't feel to any of us as if we, personally, have done anything wrong. We weren't disobedient, someone else was, right? So it should be up to them to start making some changes. Maybe if they chose to be less sinful, some of those walls would come down, at least a little.

I can't begin to count how many otherwise kind and loving people I have known who have held something like this view, probably for most of their lives; for a long time, I was one of them. It wasn't my sin that got my money stolen when I was eleven. I didn't do anything to provoke the thief who clobbered me at the dry cleaners. So why should I be the one to do anything about tearing down the wall separating me from ethnically dissimilar Americans—or global citizens, for that matter?

Many churches are guilty of the same attitude. They say that they are totally open to minority visitors, and would even welcome new members from other ethnic groups, but in reality they aren't willing to confess their own sin so that they can begin the process of tearing down the walls that divide us from each other. They may not even be convinced that there is a wall—but if there is, it must be the responsibility of the people on the other side to do something about it.

As a result, I've met with a variety of church committees over the years that seemed a little stumped about why Hispanics or African-Americans—or more recently, LGBTQ persons—weren't joining their churches in droves. They weren't even visiting, even though they lived right in the church's neighborhood and the church had a large welcome sign out front.

When I've been invited into this kind of situation, the questions I always want to ask are, "Well, how often have you gone to visit a predominantly black church, or a Hispanic church? Have you gone to community meetings to understand the needs of your neighbors? Have you ever attended a PFLAG meeting?" In other words, what steps have you taken, in obedience, to love your neighbor as yourself? What have you done to show that you want to begin taking down the wall?

* * *

If we learn nothing else from the story of the Good Samaritan, we should at least be able to figure out that waiting for someone else to do something first is not an acceptable option. Jesus made it clear that it wasn't okay for the priest and the Levite to pass by the wounded man. They, of all people, should have done something. Yes, it might have made the priest late for mid-day services or for his turn at counting the temple tax, and the Levite might have become ritually unclean if the injured man inconveniently died while he was caring for him. But the need for mercy should have outweighed these concerns.

It was someone from the other side of an enormous wall who finally stopped to care for the man who had been robbed: a Samaritan. I'm not sure we fully grasp the meaning of Samaritan as a term of utter contempt when uttered by a Jew in the time of Jesus, but suffice it to say that no one in the crowd was saying, "Well, of course," when Jesus said that a Samaritan had stopped to give aid. They probably would have expected the Samaritan to check the man's pockets to see if the prior thieves had missed anything (give yourself two points if you just remembered that the original robbers had actually stolen the man's clothes).

The crowd would have been even less pleased when the Samaritan turned out to be the hero in the story. In caring for the wounded man, he acted almost as if there was no wall of division between Jews and the Samaritans! What was he thinking?

He was thinking that the half-dead person he found along the road needed someone to care for him. He was thinking that the differences between Jews and Samaritans weren't important in this situation. He was thinking that he was able to provide what the man needed.

Most importantly, he was thinking like someone on the road to Jericho—which is where the incident took place. Remember? Jesus said, *"A man was going down from Jerusalem to Jericho when he was attacked by robbers"* (Luke 10:30 NRSV). It almost seems like an unnecessary detail, but Jesus deliberately named the ancient city, and Luke recorded it. Could it be that Jesus was thinking back to the time of Joshua—both their names share the same Hebrew origin—when God had tried once before to teach his people about obedience and bringing down walls?

* * *

Five years after my second robbery experience, I was a freshly minted graduate of Hope College and on my way to Wayne State University School of Law in Detroit. When I had told my boss at the drycleaners that I wasn't going back to work at Franklin Street, he offered me a different job driving the pickup and delivery truck between stores. I didn't have to have any contact with the public, which meant that my interactions with African-Americans once again became virtually non-existent; and there weren't very many of them attending Hope College at that time either. My wariness, however, remained at just about the same level; that wall wasn't going anywhere.

You may find this hard to believe, but I had actually applied to the Wayne State Law School without having any idea where the campus was located, and I was accepted before I ever scheduled a visit. I knew that the mailing address was Detroit, but I assumed that the school would be in an appropriately leafy suburb somewhere.

Imagine my surprise, and not in a good way, when I found out that the Law School was between Midtown and New Center, adjacent to a part of the city that made the Franklin Street neighborhood in Grand Rapids look good. The university facilities were modern and well-maintained, and I had been assigned housing in a newer apartment building, but as I was hunting for a parking place during my first visit, I realized that this was not an area where I would want to wander very far from the security of the campus itself.

After I had settled into classes, I began looking for a part time job. Most positions on campus seemed to go to undergraduate students who needed to earn work/study money as part of their financial aid, so I began to apply at some of the shops and restaurants that were directly adjacent to the university. When I didn't hear back from any of those, I ventured out another block or two, until I finally turned in an application at TJ's, a restaurant with an unusual marketing strategy: Don't tell anyone where you are located. *Guy Fiery*

TJ's full name was (and still is) *Traffic Jam and Snug,* and the only reason I even knew it existed was because I was invited to go there with some other students. Other than a very small sign on the parking lot across the road, there was nothing on or near the exterior of the building to indicate that there was a restaurant inside. It was strictly a word-of-mouth place, and when people found it for the first time (especially if they were from the suburbs), they acted as if they were amongst the chosen few who had discovered its secret location. I never told them that the name came from the fact that the restaurant was so popular on Friday afternoons that it often caused a traffic jam at a nearby intersection.

It's hard to describe the décor at TJ's; the owners there were doing the exposed ductwork, industrial, antique, stained glass look long before any decorators discovered it and tried to replicate it in a thousand chain restaurants. The staff, on the other hand, I can describe in one word: Rainbow. I would be one of very few straight Americans of northern European descent working at TJ's.

I didn't know it when I started working there, but this was God's plan to help me take down the wall that had separated me from many of my neighbors for far too many years. I know it sounds like the script for an ABC After School Special, but as I got to know the African-American mother of two and the recently arrived young woman from Puerto Rico, the exuberantly gay server, and a variety of other people on the restaurant staff, I discovered—you already know what's coming, don't you?—that they were just people.

None of them tried to rob me, none of them seemed to be dangerous (although I wouldn't have wanted to be a guy who cheated on the girl from Puerto Rico), and the kinds of things we talked about when business was slow were as familiar and ordinary as could be. Again, forgive me for the cliché, but after a few months, I didn't think of any of the staff by their race, nationality, religion or gender orientation. I just thought of them by their names.

Since the restaurant was only a few blocks away from my apartment, and since finding free on-street parking was always a challenge near the university, I chose to walk to work, even on the nights when I would be coming home well past midnight. I definitely hurried the first few times, avoiding eye contact with anyone, but over time I began to become more comfortable with the area, and even began to think of it as *my* neighborhood. In this part of Detroit, I was the minority, and trying to maintain my wall of separation would have made me a very lonely person.

My new friends at TJ's were Good Samaritans to me, helping to heal my wounds from years before. Their patience with me, their exasperation at how narrow-minded I could be, their smiles when they told me, "You are so white!" all helped me to take down brick after brick. I often tell people that God sent me to Law School because I needed to learn how to study before I went to seminary, but I think the real reason he sent me to Detroit was to continue my training in obedience.

I don't think God could have come up with any better way to teach me to love my neighbor—all my neighbors—as myself.

* * *

As the early weeks of the Jericho series at Covenant Life got underway, I was still trying to figure out exactly what was going to happen on the final Sunday. I was confident that God would work it out, but I also wanted to be able to give people some idea of what to expect.

The Impact Team had done their job, beautifully. The six weeks of services on the different areas of obedience were all planned out, and I had finished the 43 daily readings and they were being printed and posted to the web week-by-week. For the final Sunday, I had told everyone that we would combine both morning services into one, we would gather in the ministry center, the trumpets would sound, we would walk around the church seven times while we prayed for walls to come down, and we would enter the worship center ... but then what?

I truly didn't know, but I wasn't too worried because of the way that God had worked out all of the other pieces of the series. For example, one of the things I had been thinking about since the very first time that God had put the idea for Jericho into my head was a fanfare and march for seven trumpets. I was hoping we could get someone to write a piece of music for us, but I had no idea how something like that got done.

What I did suspect was that it took time. Leigh and I used to sing in the Holland Chorale, and when the director handed out a piece that had been commissioned for the group, he often mentioned how far in advance some of the composers were working, which was more likely to be years than months. At Covenant Life, I knew that we didn't have years to wait for a trumpet piece.

Early in my tenure, I brought it up at a Wednesday worship design meeting, and discovered that one of the regular participants had a daughter who was a trumpet major in college, so that was a hopeful sign. But apparently playing the trumpet and writing for the trumpet are two different skills—who knew?—and as we were getting close to the beginning of the series, I still didn't have a trumpet piece.

About two months out from the Jericho start date, when it was impossibly late to think about commissioning an original composition, I started searching the web for an existing fanfare that might work. I found one—I can't remember the composer now—and played it for the worship team. It wasn't written for seven trumpets, and it didn't really have a marching section, but the team was okay with it, and we put it on the schedule for Jericho Sunday.

Very shortly thereafter, one of the elders mentioned to me that his son was working on recording a CD of worship music, and I half-jokingly asked if he thought his son would be interested in writing a trumpet piece. "I don't know," he said, "but it wouldn't hurt to ask him." I wrote down the son's e-mail address, sent him a note about what we needed, and pretty much expected to get back a note along the lines of "You want what? By when? Are you nuts?"

What I actually got, just a few days later, was a CD with a music file on it. All it said on it was "Trumpet Processional," and I didn't dare get my hopes up as I slid the disk into my computer. But as soon as I started listening I knew once again that it was God who was behind this entire Jericho idea.

It was perfect. It was as if the composer had read my mind. The piece started with a strong fanfare (in seven parts!) and then moved into a marching segment before returning to the opening theme. Although I was listening to a keyboard version of the piece, I could already hear the seven trumpets sounding as we set off on our march around the church.

Fortunately, the composer and the afore-mentioned trumpet major knew each other, so I asked them to get in touch with each other to make sure the piece would work (the trumpet major had to do a bit of revision—apparently it's easier to keep your finger on a keyboard key for a long time than it is to sustain a high note on a piccolo trumpet). Steve Caton knew a few trumpet players in the area and the college student knew a few more, so all of a sudden, we had an original trumpet processional and seven trumpeters to play it!

That kind of thing had been happening throughout preparation for the Jericho series, so I knew that God had something in mind for the final Sunday as well. But even so, I kept going through the steps in my mind: Gather, pray, sound the trumpets, march seven times around the church, enter the worship center.

But then what?

QUESTIONS FOR REFLECTION AND DISCUSSION

1. In the story of the robbery at the museum, a single act of disobedience created a huge wall of resentment. Was it really caused by just that one act? What else could have contributed to this wall?
2. Does the passing of time remove walls between neighbors? Will the bricks gradually come down of their own accord as time goes by? Why or why not?
3. What's the relationship between fear of the unknown and walls between the races? If we knew more about different cultures, would there be as many walls?
4. Many people assume that if there are walls between races, it must be the fault of the people on the other side, "because we aren't prejudiced." Are they ever right?
5. What first steps do we need to take to get to know our neighbors?
6. Has God ever placed you in a circumstance that forced you to deal with your prejudices? Can you give some examples?
7. With which person do you most readily identify in the story of the Good Samaritan—the victim, one of the passers-by, or the Samaritan?
8. What does "neighborhood" mean where you live? Is it an area marked by harmony and cooperation or by walls of separation?
9. Many churches send their members on cross-cultural mission trips. What effect do these experiences have on walls? Why?
10. The story of the Good Samaritan began when someone asked Jesus, "Who is my neighbor?" Who is your neighbor?

Guy Fieri

CHAPTER TEN: GENEROSITY

*Bringing Down Walls Be-
tween Coworkers*

W hat would you do if you were me in this situation? I show up a few minutes before 7:00 a.m. for my day shift at the hospital emergency room, and the third shift orderly is sound asleep on a gurney in a little-used treatment room. Should I immediately report him to my supervisor?

Before you answer, let me share some things that you might want to take into consideration. First, he might have had a really rough night in the ER. Second, the ER might be short-staffed on day shift, and if he's been asked to stay on to work a double, the night shift supervisor might have given him permission to take a nap. Third, maybe he has a wife and kids at home, and his wife got called away for some reason, and so this is the only rest he's going to get until she gets home later in the day. Fourth, maybe it was a really slow night in the ER, and he has restocked every treatment room, sterilized every gurney, dusted every light fixture, and organized every magazine in the waiting room. Maybe there was nothing left for him to do but go to sleep. There could be a lot of reasons why he's snoozing in treatment room nine at 7:00 o'clock in the morning.

So, do you immediately report him to the supervisor?

Neither did I. I just assumed that there must have been a good reason for his shuteye, gave him a cheery "Good morning," and sent him on his way.

Then it happened again, and another time shortly after that, and pretty soon it was a regular occurrence. Now what should I do? Not only was he sleeping on the job, but he never stocked the treatment rooms, never cleaned the gurneys, never dusted a light fixture, and if he ever touched a magazine, it was probably to read himself to sleep. The final insult was that he never even remade the gurney on which he was sleeping, so that I not only had to wake him up and send him home, but also had to put a fresh sheet, blanket and pillowcase on his grossly still-warm bed.

After a few months of this, I decided to report him, and instantly made an enemy. As long as I had kept my mouth shut, he considered us the best of opposite shift coworkers and maybe even friends, but when I had finally had enough of covering up for him, a huge wall went up between us.

From my perspective, his disobedience regarding the minimum requirements of our job had already contributed to a significant wall, but from his side, it suddenly looked like I was unfairly meddling in third shift business, and that I might even get his supervisor in trouble. He accused me of using my friendship with our ER director to my advantage, which was probably true since she knew that I was going to be attending seminary; I will readily admit that she often gave me preferential treatment. Further complicating matters was the fact that he did not, in fact, have a wife or kids at home, and that we had both been trying to date the same new day-shift nurse. As soon as I ratted him out for sleeping on the job, he told her how I was just trying to make him look bad, and maybe even get him fired.

Okay, yes, getting rid of him for good had crossed my mind; and within a month he was gone, so I won, right? I got rid of that annoying, lazy, and now literally shiftless co-worker, and I would never again have to deal with the wall that had grown up between us.

Ha! If only it had been that easy. On the one hand, I suppose I was right. Since I never saw him again, I never had to deal with that particular wall. But on the other hand, I hadn't taken into account how popular sleeping beauty was on his own shift; apparently, he was one of those people who made it fun to come to work. As soon as he was let go, many other walls quickly started to multiply between me and other ER staff, especially those on third shift who had been sympathetic to his point of view. Day shift staff tended to side with me, but even they seemed to be a little wary of my cozy relationship with the boss. For several weeks after my coworker's departure, break room discussions often focused on the uneasy relationship between third shift and first shift in general—with the unspoken accusation that I was the one who had started it.

Walls were popping up everywhere. Was there a different way—perhaps an unconventional, Jericho way—that I could have dealt with the original wall that had started this whole mess?

* * *

We don't have to think too hard to be convinced that there are walls of separation in nearly every workplace. We typically spend eight hours or more a day with people we didn't get to choose, and there's a pretty good chance that some of them are people with whom we would never willingly associate in any other setting. So it's not surprising that issues come up, some specifically related to the workplace, but also many others that have nothing to do with our jobs.

This was especially evident when some of my fellow college students and I got summer jobs at a bottling plant. It was a classic town-and-gown situation, and the town side wasn't particularly thrilled about welcoming the gown.

My work station was the Traymore machine that placed the cardboard tray under four six-packs of pop. The soda approached on the conveyor from the right, already harnessed into six packs by plastic rings; the machine automatically arranged these into groups of four which slid onto the flat cardboard tray directly in front of me. The arms of the machine then did a clever little mechanical dance by which they kicked up the four sides of the tray, spread glue on the tabs at each corner, held them in place for a brief moment while the adhesive set, and then sent the completed tray on its way down the line to be stacked onto a pallet for shipping.

All you really need to know about the Traymore is that when everything worked perfectly, there was nothing for the operator to do, other than feeding it a steady diet of cardboard. The secret to its smooth operation was making sure that the glue was up to temperature, that it didn't spill onto any other parts of the mechanism and that the trays were flat when you fed them into the machine (which required an occasional bit of back-bending the cardboard over your knee). If you remembered these few things, you spent hours and hours of time just watching cases of pop go flying past.

As you can imagine, training on the machine took about ten minutes, getting used to adjusting it took maybe an hour, the novelty wore off after two, and serious boredom set in before the day was half over. It got so bad that I actually looked forward to the times when something broke elsewhere on the line, shutting it down for repairs. This was when we were supposed to sort leakers.

Leakers was the in-house, catch-all term that included not only cases of pop that had been returned due to faulty lids (sometimes one bad lid on a can near the top of a stack would cause a whole sticky pallet to be returned), but also mislabeled bottles and bottles with foreign objects inside, usually bent straws (we were still washing and refilling glass bottles at that time).

Because it was so loud in the plant when both the bottle

and can lines were running—which meant that we all wore hearing protection—sorting leakers was one of the few times when we learned what the regular employees really thought of us college kids. First of all, even though everyone was supposed to be sorting, the regulars almost never did. Secondly, no matter what had caused the line to stop, you could be sure that it would be blamed on the college students who "sure didn't know much" considering that we were "paying so much to get educated." Third, we learned that there was nothing in the world more important than softball.

Wow, could these people talk about softball. If it wasn't last night's game, it was last week's or last month's or possibly that one game last year when that guy did that thing, and the regulars would all be laughing and bragging and having a wonderful time with each other as if the college workers didn't even exist.

In the three months that I worked at the plant, I can't think of a single instance in which a regular employee invited a college student to join in—or even just attend—a softball game. Neither can I remember any time when a college student invited a regular employee to do something outside of work. I can still picture the guy who trained me on the Traymore, but I can't come up with his name or whether he was married or if he had kids or any of those kinds of details. Neither of us ever tried to get past the wall that separated us; he knew that he was probably going to spend the rest of his life on the can line, or something like it, and I knew that those of us who were only there for the summer believed that we were going on to better things.

I confess that I was still guilty of this smugly superior attitude several years ago when my middle son got his own summer job at a factory. I didn't ask him about the people he worked with; I didn't tell him that he should try to show some interest in their lives. Instead, I said to him, "Now you know why you're going to college—because you don't want to be stuck doing this kind of work for the rest of your life."

I don't think I ever asked him a single question which would have indicated that I thought of his coworkers as actual human beings worthy of attention. I just helped him count the days until he could get back into the gown, leaving the town behind.

* * *

God's Word shows us a better way to deal with the walls that divide us at work. The first step is to simply be obedient to what our jobs require of us. If our idea of a good day at work is one in which we get to sleep on the job, or one when someone "accidentally" breaks a machine in order to stop the line for a while, we need to pay attention again to what Paul said in his letter to the Colossians. He was addressing slave workers, but the principle behind his teaching holds true for everyone who earns a paycheck: *"Slaves, obey your earthly masters in everything, not only while being watched and in order to please them, but wholeheartedly, fearing the Lord. Whatever your task, put yourselves into it, as done for the Lord and not for your masters, since you know that from the Lord you will receive the inheritance as your reward; you serve the Lord Christ"* (Colossians 3:22-24 NRSV).

What a novel idea: Do your job! Don't try to get away with doing as little as possible—which has become such a conventional attitude in the workplace today—but do the unexpected thing: work to the best of your ability. Do it not just because someone is watching you, or grudgingly, because you need the paycheck, but do it because being a faithful and honest worker brings honor to the name of Jesus. Imagine how many walls would come down in workplaces around the globe—or would never even be built in the first place—if everyone paid attention to this one small bit of wisdom.

Take, for example, the evening when Leigh and I were clothes shopping at a mall in New Jersey. This was during the late 1980s, a time when many retail stores out east were having trouble hiring enough people to simply work the cash registers. The only sales clerk we could find was talking on the phone, and it didn't seem as if she was going to hang up anytime soon. When she finally registered our existence by looking up and tilting the phone a couple of inches away from her ear, we asked if the store had a particular item in a different size. She never even looked at the dress Leigh was holding before she mumbled, "Nah, we haven't got that," and went back to her phone call. I spent the rest of the night spluttering about how I never could have gotten away with that kind of behavior when I was working the deli counter at Russo's. If I had ever treated a customer that way, I not only would have built a wall between me and the boss, I might have been thrown through one!

Unfortunately, Paul not only knew that there were plenty of slackers in the workplace, he also knew that their behavior was contagious. *"In the name of the Lord Jesus Christ, we command you, brothers and sisters, to keep away from every believer who is idle and disruptive and does not live according to the teaching you received from us"* (II Thessalonians 3:6-8 NRSV).

A few verses later, Paul concluded his thought by saying again, *"For we hear that some of you are living in idleness, mere busybodies, not doing any work. Now such persons we command and exhort in the Lord Jesus Christ to do their work quietly and to earn their own living"* (II Thessalonians 3:11-12 NRSV).

Those idle people often tempt us to ask ourselves why we are working so hard when they seem to be living nearly as comfortably as we are and yet are hardly doing anything. I think this question first comes up in about eighth grade when that kid gets assigned to your group project. You know the one I mean—it's not that he's incapable of doing good work, he's just lazy, and you know he's not going to get his part done on time. You're afraid that his last-minute work might affect your grade, but you're even more bugged that he'll probably get a better grade than he deserves because of your hard work. Even in eighth grade, you start to realize that you're going to have to deal with people like this for the rest of your life, and you wonder, "Why am I knocking myself out when I could just slack off like so many other people?"

Well, if you want to deal with wall after wall after wall, nearly all of which will be of your own making, fine, go ahead and be a slacker. But if you want to bring down workplace walls, Jericho-style, the first thing to do is your job; do it like you're doing it for Jesus himself. It's sad that what Paul said has become the *unconventional* approach to work, but there it is: "*Brothers and sisters, do not be weary in doing what is right*" (II Thessalonians 3:13 NRSV). Yes, it is tempting to go along with the world's practice of trying to get away with as little effort as possible, but the right thing to do is to be obedient to what our work requires of us.

* * *

A second lesson in God's Word about bringing down walls in the workplace has to do with the relationship between employers and their employees. Granted, not every boss is Christ-like (now there's an understatement), but the principle of working as if we are working for Jesus should make that irrelevant. Whether we love our boss and think that she is the greatest woman in the world, or despise our boss and want to see her career disappear faster than last year's fashions, our job is to be as obedient as Christianly possible to the person who has authority over us at work. As long as we aren't being told to embezzle or lie or shred the paperwork before the FBI shows up, we should make every effort to do what our boss tells us to do.

If it sometimes seems like we could get greater satisfaction out of making our boss look bad, well, we might, for a moment; we might even be able to use disobedience as a way to get rid of a bad boss. But in the long run, any walls we deliberately build between ourselves and our bosses will only come back to make our lives more miserable. It's far better to bring down those walls through obedience.

Toward the end of his earthly ministry, Jesus told several parables about doing the work we've been directed to do. In the first of the two that I want to consider (which actually comes after the other one in Matthew's gospel—I'm being unconventional), he was making a point regarding the Jews and Gentiles, about how the tax collectors and the prostitutes among the latter were actually being more obedient to what God wanted than were the Jews. But the lesson of the parable also applies to the choices we make about how we respond to those who have authority over us in the workplace.

"What do you think?" Jesus began. *"A man had two sons; he went to the first and said, 'Son, go and work in the vineyard today.' He answered, 'I will not'; but later he changed his mind and went. The father went to the second and said the same; and he answered, 'I go, sir'; but he did not go. Which of the two did the will of his father?" They said, "The first." Jesus said to them, "Truly I tell you, the tax collectors and the prostitutes are going into the kingdom of God ahead of you. For John came to you in the way of righteousness and you did not believe him, but the tax collectors and the prostitutes believed him; and even after you saw it, you did not change your minds and believe him"* (Matthew 21:28-32 NRSV).

To paraphrase Jesus just a bit, we might ask, "Which son built a wall between himself and his father?" to which the correct answer would be, "The one who never actually went to work in the vineyard." It's not enough to just say that we will be obedient; it's not enough to observe other people who are being obedient (as Jesus said was the case with the Jews and the Gentiles). It's not even enough to be the child of the person who is asking us to be obedient. Anything less than actual obedience builds walls of separation.

Note: Please bear in mind that I'm not making a point here about our eternal salvation, in which case I would say something quite different about being the child of the One who asks us to be obedient, and I would even add that his other Child, our brother Jesus, was perfectly obedient on our behalf. I'm only describing walls that exist in the workplace, where a t-shirt that says, "I'm a child of the King" probably won't get you very far with your earthly boss if you aren't actually doing your job.

* * *

While the parable of the father and his two sons is fairly obvious in what it teaches about obedience to those in authority over us (even the crowd gave Jesus the right answer), the other parable I want to consider, the earlier one in Matthew, may be one of the most difficult for us to accept. In it, Jesus shows us how conventional thinking can create huge walls between us and our bosses, and between us and our coworkers, too—maybe even between us and God, which was more or less Jesus' point in telling this story—even though no one has treated us unfairly. This is the story of the workers in the vineyard (Matthew 20:1-16).

If you've ever heard this parable, you probably haven't forgotten it, and like me, you may still be feeling a bit of sympathy for the characters who end up doing all the grumbling at the end. They're the ones who got hired first thing in the morning, agreed to work all day in a vineyard for a denarius (which was considered a fair wage), and who, at the end of the day, got paid precisely one denarius.

So why were they grumbling? Well, it seems that the boss went out and hired some additional workers about three hours after the first group was hired. He did the same thing around noon time and again in the middle of the afternoon. Finally, where there was just an hour of the workday left, he hired still more workers for his vineyard.

When it was time for the landowner to settle accounts, he told his foreman to start by paying the people who were hired last—and they were each paid a denarius. Imagine the joy at the back of the line when that news started to spread! If the landowner was paying a full day's wage to the men who had worked only an hour, the ones who had worked all day were sure to get more. But when they got to the head of the line, they got just the one denarius for which they had agreed to work. Cue the bitter grumbling.

This being a "the kingdom of heaven is like ..." parable, the most important lesson Jesus was teaching had to do with the same gift of salvation being offered to those who come to faith late as those who come to faith early (not that this should encourage us to gamble on a death bed confession; those workers who spent all day in the field shouldn't have discounted the value of knowing that they would be bringing home a paycheck at the end of the day). But along the way to this lesson about eternity, we also see a contemporary lesson about making unconventional choices for bringing down walls in the workplace.

When I first arrived at Covenant Life Church, I signed a contract that I thought was quite fair. I had given the leadership a copy of my most recent interim compensation package as a guideline, and one of the elders responded to me by looking at it and saying, "We can probably do a little better than that," which they did, and I appreciated it. I have often said that I've never known a church to go wrong by choosing to be generous.

About six months later, I was sitting with nearly the same group of people, discussing the proposed salary range which the Pastoral Search Team would be able to use as they were conveying information to candidates. To my surprise, the low end of the range under discussion was several thousand dollars *higher* than what I was receiving, and the high end figure was nearly thirty thousand dollars more!

I didn't say anything at the meeting, but went back to my study and played a few games of solitaire on my computer while I muttered about the injustice of it all. Why wasn't I worthy of that kind of salary? Wasn't I doing all the heavy lifting so that the new pastor could just slide in and reap the benefits of all my hard work? Shouldn't I have been offered even more than the pastor who would follow me?

* * *

Like the laborers in the parable, it's amazing how quickly we can go from thinking someone is being generous, or at least fair, to thinking that they are being stingy and unjust. This often happens when we compare ourselves to our coworkers, because clearly, they can't be worth more than we are, right? And they should always have to work just as hard or just as long as the rest of us before they get paid the same, too.

I can still recall my boss at the hospital telling me that she dreaded the time of the year when annual salary adjustments were decided. When I asked her why, she said that the employees always ended up finding out how much other people were earning, after which they immediately beat a path to her door to complain. (Isn't it amazing how much the workplace is like grade school? I remember when report cards came out and everyone wanted to know what grades the other kids got. Somehow, we always found out, didn't we?)

When I was a settled pastor, my salary and benefits were not only public knowledge if someone made a specific inquiry, they were often printed out with the church budget and left on a table at the back of the narthex for anyone who wanted to take home a copy. Mind you, I never knew what anyone else in the church was earning, but they knew—to the penny—how much I was being paid.

This hasn't typically been the case with interim assignments, for which I am grateful, because people treat you differently—and often build walls—if they know how much money you make; and therein lies a Jericho lesson about how to bring down the walls that are built when we compare ourselves to others. To put it simply: Stop comparing. No two people are exactly the same (not even identical twins have the same life experiences), so don't assume that everyone should be treated in exactly the same way.

Don't expect everyone to be able to work the way you do; don't presume that everyone will approach a situation in the same way that you would; and don't go out of your way to try and find out if other people are paid the same as you. Maybe you are an exceptionally good worker, and your boss would like to pay you more. Maybe you are lacking in some job skills, but you have other qualities that make you worth keeping around—but you're not going to earn top dollar. Maybe the boss knows something about your coworker's circumstances that you aren't privy to, and she wants to be generous.

This is what Jesus said at the end of the vineyard parable: *"Friend, I am doing you no wrong; did you not agree with me for the usual daily wage? Take what belongs to you and go; I choose to give to this last the same as I give to you. Am I not allowed to do what I choose with what belongs to me? Or are you envious because I am generous?"* (Matthew 20:13-15 NRSV).

If the laborers at the back of the line in Jesus' parable hadn't heard what the workers at the front of the line were being paid, they would have been perfectly content with their denarius—it was a fair wage. In the same way, if the employees in the hospital emergency room hadn't found out what their coworkers were making, they wouldn't have complained to our boss. If I hadn't sat in on the meeting where the future pastor's salary was discussed, I would have continued to think that I was being compensated generously.

This isn't to say that there aren't some real instances of injustice that need to be addressed. For example, I have always believed that nurse's aides are grossly underpaid. They perform a service that not many people would like to do, and they do it with humor and grace and even love, and yet their salary isn't much higher than minimum wage. As a group, they deserve more, and the same is true of people in many other professions (day care workers come to mind, as do military personnel, firefighters, safety officers, and anyone who has to work in an environment where easy-listening music is played all day long).

But getting back to what Jesus said at the end of his parable, the key word is *generous*. The landowner took pity on the workers who were hired last, and he generously chose to pay them a wage that would allow them to provide for their families just as well as those who were hired at the beginning of the day. The grumbling laborers had no such generosity of spirit, thinking only about how long they had worked instead of how much those other laborers must have been worrying as they waited all day for the chance to work. Would the ones who were hired first really have preferred to be in that uncertain situation for eleven hours—not knowing if they would bring home anything at all—instead of knowing all day that they would earn a full denarius?

Perhaps this whole chapter can be summed up with the word generous; nearly every wall in the workplace can be brought down if we choose to have a generous spirit.

* * *

Remember the sleepy-head I got fired by reporting him to my boss? What if I had chosen to have a generous attitude toward him instead? I could have actually gotten to know him a little better; I could have asked him what it was like to work third shift, and I could have tried to understand his situation. Over time, I may have decided that I was so glad not to be working third shift that it would be easy to overlook his napping on the job.

Alternately, if it turned out that he really was just a slacker who wasn't interested in developing any kind of relationship, I could have had a generous attitude toward his supervisor on third shift. I've worked with difficult employees before, and I fully understand that fine line between keeping someone or getting rid of him or her. I could have trusted that the third shift boss was dealing with the situation and had decided that on balance, it was better for now to keep his drowsy employee on the payroll.

Even if both of them had turned out to be first class goof-offs, I could have simply chosen to have a generous spirit toward my own situation. After all, it was my job to put sheets on gurneys and stock treatment rooms, and the minute or two it took to tidy up after third shift hardly affected my day. I had a job I loved and great people with whom to work, so why should I let the sour attitude of someone I hardly even saw (awake, that is), spoil my day? Far better to be generous of spirit, deciding that what happened on third shift was really no business of mine.

Paraphrasing Jesus, if the third shift supervisor or my own boss wanted to be generous, what benefit was there to me in being envious? All it would accomplish—all it *did* accomplish—was building walls, and that certainly didn't make my life any easier!

*　*　*

It was the generous attitude of my coworkers at Covenant Life that made the Jericho Series possible. At first, I think they had a hard time grasping the concept (notice that it's taking me a whole book to do now what I was trying to convey in a few Wednesday morning meetings at the time). As they started to grasp the idea and lived with it for a while, they began to make suggestions for how to improve on it, which then required a generous and trusting attitude on my part to allow them to make it better.

For example, one of the things that I had thought about from the very beginning of the series was the song, "Joshua Fit de Battle of Jericho." I had grown up with the Tennessee Ernie Ford version of this spiritual; it was on the 1960 album *Sing a Spiritual With Me*, which was one of three records that my brothers and I would regularly play on my father's stereo on Sunday mornings (the others were Tennessee Ernie Ford's *Sing a Hymn with Me*, and *The Lord's Prayer* by the Mormon Tabernacle Choir).

What I suggested to the worship design team was that we use some version of this song each week for all seven Sundays of the series—some vocal arrangements, some instrumental, some quiet, some rocking out (note: my daughter wouldn't be happy if she knew that I used the term "rocking out," so don't tell her I said that). When I made the suggestion, the members of the team just stared back at me, several of them with expressions on their faces that clearly conveyed what they were thinking: "Is he kidding?"

For several weeks in a row, I talked about the idea during our planning sessions and asked if anyone had tracked down different versions of the song for the different Sundays. Not surprisingly, no one had, and I started to get the sense that my enthusiasm for this idea wasn't catching. In fact, maybe they didn't like this idea at all.

It took me a while to grasp that it wasn't so much the song that the team didn't like, it was the gimmicky notion of using it every Sunday during the series. If there was one thing Covenant Life was not, it was gimmicky, and if I had been paying attention, I would have known this before I made the suggestion.

Nearly every element of worship at Covenant Life is carefully considered in order to make sure that it fits into the purpose of the weekly service. I can recall a popular praise song that was held back for over a year because of concern about how the phrase "He gives and takes away" would be received by several members of the congregation who were dealing with grief issues. It wasn't until we got to a Sunday in which dealing with loss would be part of the message that we finally sang the song.

I started to let go of the repetitive song idea, and at just about the same time, one of the worship leaders suggested that we might want to use a choir as part of the final Jericho Sunday (not a regular feature of the worship services). To my joy, she suggested that the choir could sing "Joshua Fit de Battle of Jericho."

That's what we ended up doing, and as was true of so many things at Covenant Life, if a thing was worth doing, it was worth doing well. Steve issued an open invitation for people to join a choir for Jericho Sunday, he set four different rehearsal times, he not only taught us the music, but taught us the background and meaning of the song as well, and he made it clear that everyone in the choir was a worship leader for that Sunday. They would be expected to take their commitment to the choir as seriously as all worship leaders were expected to take their roles for any given Sunday.

It would have been easy for the worship leaders to dismiss the idea of singing the spiritual altogether; it would have been easy for me to insist that we do it every week for seven Sundays in a row. Either of these choices would have built some serious walls of difficulty between us.

Instead, all of us chose to have a generous spirit toward the different possibilities, and even more importantly, toward the different people. If they didn't like the idea, I knew there had to be a good reason, and they trusted that I knew what I was saying when I said that some of the older members of the church would appreciate hearing a song they might remember from their youth.

We arrived at a good solution, and the choir became an important part of the final Jericho Sunday. In fact, I have to admit that it was much better than it would have been if we had already heard the song six times before.

You know that old saying, "If you want something done right, do it yourself?" It's not true. Sometimes the people we work with can make things much, much better than we ever could on our own.

QUESTIONS FOR REFLECTION AND DISCUSSION

1. Is it common for walls to build up between coworkers? Why? What kinds of disobedience contribute to these walls?
2. Do you enjoy going to work? What would it take to make your job more enjoyable? Does it have anything to with the people with whom you work?
3. How do walls multiply in the workplace? If I deal with one wall poorly, how can that create other walls of separation?
4. Do personal lives and work lives ever really stay separated? How do our personal lives sometimes contribute to walls in the workplace?
5. "What a novel idea: Do your job!" How would your workplace be different if everyone took this seriously? Would it remove any walls?
6. Is it generally true that people try to get away with doing as little as possible? If so, why? If not, why does this seem to be a common attitude toward our coworkers?
7. How would you work differently if Jesus was your boss? How would it affect your relationships with your coworkers?
8. In the parable of the workers in the vineyard, all of whom were paid a denarius even though some worked all day and others just an hour, with whom do you feel the most sympathy? Why? Did the boss treat anyone unfairly?
9. "I've never known a church to go wrong by being generous." Do you agree with this? If so, why are churches so often less than generous? How would an attitude of generosity make a difference in your workplace?
10. How does comparing ourselves to others build walls? What kind of obedience is necessary to bring these walls down?

CHAPTER ELEVEN: PRAYER

*Bringing Down Walls be-
tween Me and God*

I n nearly every congregation that I've served, there has
been at least one special member with a serious physical or mental disability. During my devotions, I pray for
everyone in the congregation by name—I try to do this at least
once a week—and when I get to that special needs person, especially if he or she lives independently, I almost always say,
"…and dear God, please keep so-and-so safe, healthy and free
from harm or injury."

Then I get a phone call saying that the person has been run
into by a car.

That was in Ohio. Other times, the people I've been praying
for have experienced seizures, or have been injured in falls. A
young woman who lived in a group home suffered a serious
emotional problem when a member of her family fell ill. An
elderly man wandered away from the home in which he was
living, only to be found later by the police (afterwards, he
loved to tell everyone that there were four officers and that
they all surrounded him with their guns drawn).

Part of me says, "Wow, God really isn't answering my

prayers when it comes to these special people. They are so vulnerable, and typically so trusting that you would think that God would have a special concern for them." That thought is quickly followed by the regular explanation (at least for me) which says that, a). we live in a sinful world; b). while we know that God will win the ultimate victory, we still have a few battles to endure along the way; and c). as is true in any earthly battle, innocent people are almost always the first victims. So, instead of blaming God for not answering my prayers, I try to work up some indignation toward the devil for making totally innocent people suffer.

A thought that has almost never come to mind, at least not until recently, is the one that says, "Hey, Mr. Piety, when you're done praying, why don't you go and see if there's something you can do for those vulnerable people. Has it occurred to you that maybe you're supposed to be the answer to your own prayer?" What? After I've entrusted them to God's care? Wouldn't that make it seem as if I don't have enough faith in God's providence for these blessed children?

Boy, I can sure sell it, can't I? Even to myself. Putting things into God's hands has been my *modus operandi* for most of my life. It has only rarely occurred to me—as a kind of nagging feeling in the middle of my prayer that I'm missing something obvious—that perhaps God has already equipped me with everything I need to answer some of my own prayers, and that only my obedience has been lacking.

Take the Ohio guy who was run into by the car, for example. He gets around in an electric wheelchair, and when I say "gets around," I mean that he seriously covers a lot of territory. Sometimes he's out well into the evening (his chair is equipped with lights), and he frequently has to cross busy roads. But that wheelchair just doesn't move all that quickly, which is why he got hit (the chair took the brunt of the collision; my friend got pitched out, but only suffered scrapes and bruises).

What if I had called him that week and had asked if there

was anywhere he needed to go, especially in the evenings? My guess is that he probably would have turned me down—he's pretty independent—but there's at least the chance that he might have said yes. What if I went to city hall on his behalf and lobbied for wheelchair warning signs to be put up near the area where he regularly crosses the road? What if I sent a letter to the editor of the local newspaper reminding people of the need to slow down in residential areas and to be aware of non-traditional vehicles?

There are a lot of things I could have done to make things safer for my friend. There's no guarantee that any of them would have worked—it *is* a sinful world and we *do* need to pray—but I could have been at least part of the answer to my own prayer.

A few thoughts here: First, I'm not trying to single-handedly increase the guilt factor of every person who hasn't done absolutely everything in his or her power to make the world a safer place for vulnerable people. I'm writing about making unconventional, obedient choices for the sake of our faith. But if we choose not to be obedient, that doesn't shorten God's arm in any way, to borrow a biblical image. God is still able to act even if we choose something other than perfect obedience.

Second, there are some people—like the young woman who had the seizures—for whom I'm not sure there is anything we can do, no matter how obedient we are trying to be. Sometimes, the best and most obedient thing we can do is to simply offer our presence and our prayers.

Third, and most importantly, prayer should never become a substitute for obedience. To cite just one example, we've all tried praying at the last minute rather than actually studying for a test, and we know how that worked out. We're doing essentially the same thing when we pray for the hungry to be fed, even though we haven't actually done anything to relieve hunger, or when we pray for traveling mercies, and yet choose to check text messages while we're driving.

People, God could use a little help here. He needs us to think "outside the prayer," so to speak. If the conventional thing to do when we pray is to just hand God a long list of what we want, then the unexpected thing, the Jericho thing, is to ask what obedience requires of us. It just might be that God can use our obedience to avoid some of those dreaded, hit-by-a-car phone calls in the middle of the night.

* * *

It seems contrary to logic that some prayers might actually build walls between us and God, at least from our perspective, but a quick look at the New Testament shows us that this is exactly the case. Disobedience always builds walls, even in prayer.

Consider, for example, the story Jesus told about the two men who went to the temple to pray. Luke gives us a pretty strong hint that someone's lack of obedience is going to build a wall when he introduces the story by saying, *"He also told this parable to some who trusted in themselves that they were righteous and regarded others with contempt"* (Luke 18:9 NRSV).

To his credit, the Pharisee, who was the first to offer a prayer, didn't hand God a long list of everything that he expected God to do. Rather, he stood up in the middle of the temple and gave a little presentation on how marvelously obedient he had been. *"God, I thank you that I am not like other people: thieves, rogues, adulterers, or even like this tax collector. I fast twice a week; I give a tenth of all my income"* (Luke 18:11-12 NRSV). In other words, he specifically obeyed commandments eight and seven, covered the rest of them by not being a "rogue," fasted when it was called for (and probably even when it wasn't), tithed everything (pre-tax, no doubt), and generally avoided being a reprobate like, ugh, this tax collector.

What's not to like about someone who can offer up a truthful prayer like this? In nearly every church I've ever served, this man would be considered not just a good member, but a "Pastor, we've got to keep him happy" good member (unfortunately, the tithing has a lot to do with that). If obedience is what brings down walls, how could all this impressive obedience actually result in a huge wall going up between the Pharisee and God?

At the same time, how could there not be a huge wall between God and the tax collector? He stood off at a distance, wouldn't look up, beat his breast, and all he could say was, *"God, be merciful to me, a sinner"* (Luke 18:13 NRSV). I'm thinking that he broke not only commandments eight and seven in the course of collecting taxes (if someone couldn't fork over the cash, I'm guessing some tax collectors would take what they could get, if you know what I mean), but pretty much every other commandment as well. It's probably safe to say that neither fasting nor tithing was high on his to do list.

Yet Jesus concluded the story by saying, *"I tell you, this man went down to his home justified rather than the other"* (Luke 18:14 NRSV). In this circumstance, the word "justified" can be interpreted as meaning "without walls." In spite of his admittedly sinful life, there were no barriers left separating the tax collector from God in heaven.

* * *

What we learn from this story is that what sounds like obedience, especially in the context of prayer, often isn't. In fact, some of our most eloquent prayers are often little more than the Pharisee's soliloquy in disguise.

One of my colleagues in New York delighted in pointing this out, especially if we were at a gathering of clergy. When our regional association of churches would hold one of its quarterly meetings, and we were supposed to be praying, my friend would often nudge my elbow and whisper under his breath, *"Listen! Pharisee's prayer."* Sure enough, the speaker was pointing out to God that we weren't like other people (since we had been so blessed to be called into the ministry, we lived in the greatest country on earth, and we enjoyed countless benefits from exercising our ministry); we certainly weren't like the godless heathen who needed to experience God's strong hand of justice (which usually applied to anyone who was currently putting our military in harm's way); and he closed by telling God how diligent we were in living out our faith daily, even by attending this very meeting to conduct the business of the church. In other words, it was a typical prayer, one that I myself have regularly offered in a variety of settings.

Therein lies the problem. We are becoming as casually disobedient in our prayers as we are in our TV habits, our speech, our driving, and just about everything else. Our conventional way of praying, which might sound good on the surface, will often mask an underlying lack of obedience. If anything, prayers of this kind leave us feeling as if God is more distant, rather than drawing us into a deeper and more joyful experience of God's presence.

If all we're doing when we pray is patting ourselves on the back for being included as one of God's children, well, that's not really much of an accomplishment. You may recall that God chose us first (Ephesians 1:4 and 2:4). If we go on to pray about people, places, things or events that we recognize as needing some godly attention, yet we aren't willing to participate in addressing the circumstances, whatever they may be, what do we expect our prayers to accomplish?

Consider what the Apostle James had to say about people who know all the right words, but fail to put any actions behind those words. "What good is it, my brothers and sisters, if you say you have faith but do not have works? Can faith save you? If a brother or sister is naked and lacks daily food, and one of you says to them, "Go in peace; keep warm and eat your fill," and yet you do not supply their bodily needs, what is the good of that?" (James 2:14-16 NRSV).

I have no doubt that James would apply the exact same principle to our prayers. If we have the ability to deal with the things about which we are praying, but all we do is talk about them to God, what good is our prayer? It's as if we're saying to

God that we can't be bothered, or that it's too costly, or that we're not sure if we're really the ones who are supposed to take care of this matter.

Hint: We are.

If we don't do it, who will? God? God alone? We don't really expect God to perform a supernatural miracle every time we pray about something, do we? I'm not saying that God can't act in that way, just that it isn't how God usually chooses to respond. So we know that when we pray, we're generally asking God to use one or more of his people to bring about the answer to our prayer. If we aren't willing to be those people, if we aren't willing to be obedient to whatever the Spirit is leading us to pray about, then who do we think will do it?

We should consider the very fact that we are praying about something as an action prompt from the Holy Spirit. Over the years, I've heard dozens, if not hundreds of people say, "God put this on my heart," and then they proceed to pray about whatever it is and leave it at that. Maybe we need to realize that God has also put it on our feet and in our hands. If the conventional approach to prayer is to just tell God what we think needs to be done, then the Jericho approach to prayer is to tell God what we think needs to be done, say Amen, and then go and do whatever we can to make sure that our prayer gets answered.

James himself gives us an example from the story of Jericho. After telling us about Abraham and how his faith was active along with his works, and that his faith was brought to completion by his works (James 2:22), James draws our attention to just one other person, someone who may have had a lot in common with the tax collector in Jesus' parable about prayer. *"Likewise, was not Rahab the prostitute also justified by works when she welcomed the messengers and sent them out by another road? For just as the body without the spirit is dead, so faith without works is also dead"* (James 2:25-26 NRSV).

That Rahab; she sure gets around (in the Bible). She didn't just say to the spies, "Someone ought to help you guys out," nor did she pray to the God of Israel saying, "Hey, a couple of your guys are here, and they could really use your help." What she said was, *"The Lord your God is indeed God in heaven above and on earth below,"* and *"Now then, since I have dealt kindly with you, swear to me by the Lord that you in turn will deal kindly with my family"* (Joshua 2:11-12). Maybe it wasn't exactly the format we use when we pray, but having acknowledged God's sovereignty and having made her request, she did what she could to make sure that it was fulfilled. She let the spies climb out her window, told them where to hide, and hung the scarlet cord from her window so that her home would be spared.

When it comes to obedience and doing the unconventional thing, I never thought that I would tell my congregation a story about a prostitute, and then say, "Go thou and do like-wise!"

But only when it comes to putting actions behind our words in prayer.

* * *

On the other side of the Jericho account, after Israel was defeated at Ai, we find Joshua in prayer, and this time it's defin-itely not a "go thou and do likewise" situation. I don't think Joshua necessarily realized that he was substituting prayer for obedience—in this case, the obedience of destroying all the devoted plunder from Jericho—but neither was he thinking about what he could possibly do to bring about an answer to his own prayer.

It almost seems as if he didn't stop to think about what really went wrong at Ai before he started praying. He knew what God had commanded back at Jericho, and he knew what the result would be if Israel was to disobey God's command re-garding the devoted goods; in fact, he passed on the order him-self: *"As for you, keep away from the things devoted to destruction, so as not to covet and take any of the devoted things and make the camp of Israel an object for destruction, bringing trouble upon it*" (Joshua 6:18 NRSV). Yet when Ai routed Israel, it seemed as if Joshua failed to connect the dots, and his prayer wasn't doing much to bring down the wall he perceived between himself and God.

We do the same thing. We know what God commands in his Word regarding all kinds of behaviors; yet when we fail to listen to what God says and life starts going off the rails, we quickly offer up prayer after prayer for God's intervention, but rarely stop and think about whether obedience could be the answer to our own prayers.

For example, I was guilty of acting like Joshua when the Lippizaner Stallions came to Grand Rapids. I was working for Manpower at the time (during a college break), and was assigned to go to the Civic Auditorium to help lay down a special floor for the high-stepping horses. It was a special material that cushioned the horses' hooves as well as protecting the auditorium floor, and each four by eight panel must have weighed at least fifty pounds. The trickiest part of the job was taping over the seams in the flooring without any wrinkles or raised adhesive edges that might catch on a hoof and injure one of the animals.

As it turned out, I was good at taping quickly and neatly, and when we had the floor completed by mid-afternoon, several of the roadies who traveled with the Lippizaners invited me to go to the bar with them, their treat.

I intended to just have a beer and then head back to the auditorium to wait for the show, but one became two and two became three and then I lost count. The roadies seemed to find this amusing, and when they got up to go back to the show, they told me I should just head on home (as if I could remember where that was). I managed to find my car, got in, and drove very slowly back to my parents' house.

Yes, I know that this was a phenomenally stupid thing to do, but I'm not going to lie to you and tell you that I took a bus. Alcohol impairs your judgment and I was behaving like an idiot.

When I got home, I mumbled to my parents that I didn't feel well, went straight to my room and fell on the rapidly spinning bed. I had one of the worst nights of my life and although I implored God to help me feel better, I got up the next day and thought I was going to die. In fact, it seemed possible that I had already died during the night, and that this was the beginning of my eternal torment.

Prayer was not what I needed just then (other than for forgiveness). What I had really needed was obedience when I was at the bar, or better yet, when I was still at the Civic Auditorium. I would need that same obedience in the future if I wanted to avoid a repeat of this utter misery. Prayer by itself wasn't going to keep me sober; I also needed to be obedient.

So did Joshua. After what must have been one of his worst days ever as the leader of Israel, God finally told him to get up and pay attention to what obedience required. *"Stand up! Why have you fallen upon your face? Israel has sinned; they have transgressed my covenant that I imposed on them. They have taken some of the devoted things; they have stolen, they have acted deceitfully, and they have put them among their own belongings"* (Joshua 7:10-11 NRSV).

God was gracious in reminding Joshua about the connection between disobedience and Israel's troubles; he showed Joshua what he needed to do to deal with the disobedience. That may be something that we want to consider in our own prayers: "God in heaven, if obedience is required of me in this situation, please show me what it is that I should do, and grant me the strength and determination to follow through on whatever obedience requires."

No one ever demonstrated this kind of prayer more clearly than Jesus.

* * *

"My Father, if it is possible, let this cup pass from me. Yet not what I want, but what you want" (Matthew 26:39 NRSV). Jesus

was in the Garden of Gethsemane, praying about a cup which he knew would include scourging, abandonment and his own death by crucifixion. It wasn't what he wanted to do, but it was what was necessary, and it was what obedience to his Father's will required.

Nearby, in a sad but perfect contrast to Jesus' obedience, Peter and the sons of Zebedee were sleeping. Jesus had asked them—maybe even commanded them—to keep watch with him. *"I am deeply grieved, even to death,"* he had said to them. *"Remain here and stay awake with me"* (Matthew 26:38 NRSV). But their eyes were heavy (v. 43), and although their spirits may have been willing, the flesh was weak (v. 41). So instead of watching and praying, they dozed off.

Sometimes we don't have to look very hard for the application, do we? Jesus was praying about an unimaginably difficult kind of obedience, one which would forever remove the wall of separation between God and humanity, while his three closest disciples couldn't muster up enough obedience to simply keep praying for an hour. Who do we most resemble?

I observed a discouraging reminder of the disciples' slumber exactly one week after the terrorist attacks of September 11, 2001. When the first plane hit the North Tower of the World Trade Center early that morning, I was outside, getting ready to paint our front porch. It was my day off, and I had just turned on my portable radio when I heard NPR's Bob Edwards saying something about a plane hitting a building in New York.

By the time I got the TV turned on and yelled down to the basement for Leigh to come join me, the South Tower had also been hit, and within minutes, there were reports of an attack on the Pentagon, and possibly another plane still in the air. We saw the towers fall, first one and then the other, and stayed glued to the TV for the rest of the day, unbelieving, feeling phenomenally helpless. What could we do? What did obedience require in an extraordinary circumstance like this?

A number of people from my congregation called during

the day and said that we should have a prayer service that evening. Fortunately, we always had a prayer meeting on Tuesday nights. Most weeks, six people came, but we always publicized it and encouraged others to join us.

That night, the sanctuary was full as we met for prayer. There weren't any rallying cries, no calls to arms, no brainstorming about other kinds of responses. All we knew to do was to pour ourselves out in prayer, and for more than an hour, we appealed to God for peace and mercy. It truly felt like the obedient thing to do—to watch and pray until a further course of action became clear.

Only we didn't keep watching and praying; we went back to sleep. Just a week later, we had our regular Tuesday prayer meeting again, and only a few more than the usual six showed up. It was as if the church had been roused from its slumber for a moment, but then, seeing that nothing new had happened for a whole week, our eyes grew heavy, and we went back to sleep.

I'm not accusing my congregation of being uniquely disobedient; every pastor I've ever spoken to about 9/11 has reported the same kind of one-time response. But it does serve as an excellent reminder of how like the disciples we are, how quickly we give in to our customary practices when it comes to obedience in prayer.

Would more time spent in prayer following 9/11 have accomplished anything? We'll never know, of course, but I think the Spirit might have used those opportunities for something good. Do you remember how, in the Garden of Gethsemane, Peter lashed out with his sword and cut the ear off one of the soldiers who had come to arrest Jesus? (Matthew 26:51). Maybe if he had been praying instead of sleeping, his actions wouldn't have been so rash; maybe the Spirit of God could have used his time in prayer to help him think more clearly about what obedience to Jesus required. *"Love your enemies,"* Jesus had said. *"Pray for those who persecute you"* (Matthew 5:44 NRSV).

Maybe the Spirit could have helped us to think about obedience to Jesus' commands in that way as well.

* * *

As I stood in the pulpit at Covenant Life on the first Sunday of the Jericho Week, I tried to think of ways to encourage the congregation to give radical obedience a try. I knew that prayer by itself wasn't likely to accomplish greater obedience in anyone's life. We also had to choose obedience.

Here's part of what I said to the congregation that morning:

The Jericho Week begins right now. Not later this afternoon, not tonight when you go to bed, not tomorrow morning. If you choose to participate, the Jericho Week begins now and lasts one full week until we get together again for worship at 10:00 next Sunday morning.

If there's one thing I've learned in my time here at Covenant Life, it is the concept of Covenant Life Time. In some cases, this just means that people show up late, but at least they show up, eventually. In other cases, though, I've learned that Covenant Life Time means "I intend to get around to it sometime," but there's no telling when that sometime might be.

So if I said to you, "Pick a time when you will start your Jericho Week," you might intend to start it today or tomorrow, but there's also the chance that you might never get around to it. So I decided that I would simply declare that the Jericho Week starts now, and if you had some particular disobedience planned for this afternoon or this evening, well, sorry about that.

If you are visiting with us today, you might be wondering, "What is a Jericho Week?" Even if you've been here for any of the last five weeks, and you've heard me talk about it, and you've heard me say again and again that it's a week of radical obedience, you still may be wondering what that really means. Let me first say what it *doesn't* mean:

It does not mean that we are going to spend this week strictly adhering to every rule and regulation that we find in the Bible, that way A.J. Jacobs did for his book, *The Year of Living Biblically*. For example, Leviticus 13 says that if you find mildew in any of your garments—any woolen or linen clothing, any woven or knitted material, or anything made of leather—if it is greenish or reddish and you suspect that it is mildew, you are supposed to show it to the priest. During this Jericho Week, I do not want to see your mildew.

In the same way, I don't care if you boil a baby goat in its mother's milk; I don't care if you trim the edges of your beard; I don't care if you eat pork or if you eat your steak rare, with the blood still in it; I don't care if you wear clothing woven of two different kinds of material—all of which are prohibited in the Old Testament. This week isn't about following a list of ancient rules, the meaning of which, in many cases, is obscure or even lost to us.

Another thing this week is not about is telling *other* people what they may or may not do. Parents, you'll have to make your own decisions about what you say to your children about this week, but between consenting adults, this is not a week to say to someone else, "You can't do that; this is the Jericho Week!" This is between you and God; you're not responsible for what someone else does or doesn't do this week, and they're not responsible for you.

Another thing this week is not is a week to beat up on yourself. What I'm suggesting that we do this week is not easy, and we are not going to be perfect. Go easy on yourself—I don't want your therapists to call me up and say "What are you doing to my client? You've undone two years of work on self-esteem!" I don't want to find out that half the congregation is calling the doctor for an anti-depressant. This is not a week to be discouraged or to beat up on ourselves for our lapses of obedience.

So what is it then? The Jericho Week is a week to choose to live differently. It is a week to choose to be mindful about obedience. It is a week to remember that Jesus said, "If you love me, you will obey my commandments." It is a week to remember that the greatest commandment says that we should love the Lord our God with all our heart, soul, mind and strength, and to acknowledge that we haven't been doing so well with that "all our strength" part. It is a week to say to God, "For this week, I'm going to try harder. For one week, I'm going to try to do things according to your Word, instead of just doing everything my way." It is a week to be aware, keenly aware, of obedience.

It is also a week to remember that disobedience builds walls, while obedience can bring them down. Every act of disobedience adds to the walls that divide us, some visible and very obvious, others less visible, maybe even invisible, but still very real. By choosing to live God's way this week, we are also choosing to be more aware of the walls that divide us, and we can be in prayer for those walls to come down. Every night this week, beginning tomorrow, we will meet in the Ministry Center at 7:00 for one hour to consider the different kinds of walls, and how our obedience can help bring those walls down.

If I was sitting where you are, right about now I would be very skeptical; I would need to be persuaded. It's kind of the way I felt when Leigh and I attended a Marriage Encounter weekend. I wasn't real "up" for that, to say the least. I was told later that I spent the first half of the weekend with my arms folded, hardly ever looking up. One of the leaders said that he was thinking about throwing his shoe at me just to get a reaction.

I don't like gimmicky things. Give me information; give me good *reasons* why I should do something; tell me what you anticipate the outcome will be; and then I'll tell you if I'm on board or not. Since those are the things I would need, let's consider them for a moment.

I've already given you some information; Jesus makes it clear that love and obedience are very closely connected. We see this in both the Garden of Eden and the Garden of Gethsemane. In Eden, God placed a tree, the Tree of the Knowledge of Good and Evil and he told Adam and Eve not to eat from that tree. It wasn't a cruel test; it was the gift of experiencing love. If there was no opportunity to be obedient, then there was no meaningful way to experience what it means to love someone.

Adam and Eve spurned love and chose disobedience in the garden, but in the other garden, in Gethsemane, Jesus chose obedience because of his love. "No greater love hath anyone than this, than that a man lay down his life for his friends." Jesus chose obedience for us; what will we choose for him?

I could spend all morning on information about love and obedience, but I'm going to hope I've said enough about that over the last few weeks. Turning to reasons then: Do you remember when we talked about Achan's disobedience?

Achan didn't think anyone was looking when he was disobedient, when he stole the devoted things from Jericho. He obviously didn't think that his disobedience would affect anyone else, but he couldn't have been more wrong. His disobedience affected all the people of Israel.

We are the people of God gathered in this place. What happens to any one of us affects all of us, in ways seen and unseen. My decisions to be obedient or disobedient affect you and your decisions affect me. Even when we think no one is looking, our actions have consequences.

If we choose to participate in the Jericho Week, probably more than 90% of the time, we'll be on our own as to whether or not we're being obedient. Nobody is going to check up on us; nobody's going to follow us around and watch us. This will test our character; it will be a measure of our integrity. When my family is around I can say "I'm not going to watch this or read that," but what about when no one is looking? If we remember Achan, we can never say that what we do in private has no consequences for anyone else.

One more reason to try the Jericho Week: Listen to these words from Luke: *"Whoever is faithful in a very little is faithful also in much; and whoever is dishonest in a very little is dishonest also in much. If then you have not been faithful with the dishonest wealth, who will entrust to you the true riches? And if you have not been faithful with what belongs to another, who will give you what is your own?* (Luke 16:10-12 NRSV).

If we want to make a difference in big ways, significant ways, we have to show that we can be trusted in small things first. When we prove ourselves trustworthy in the small things, especially when no one is looking, God may choose to trust us with bigger responsibilities.

As with giving you information, I could spend a lot more time giving you reasons why I believe this week is good idea. I will trust that you know, as I do, that obedience to God's way is never a bad idea. That doesn't mean it's easy, but if we are honest with ourselves, we already know that it is right.

That leaves the outcome. What do I expect that the outcome of this week will be? Let me answer that this way:

My personal devotions for the last few weeks have been in the Old Testament; I've been reading about all the kings of Israel and Judah. Every time a new king takes the throne, we read something like "So and so became king of Judah (or Israel); he reigned 25 years (or however long) over Judah or Israel." And then it says either, "He did what was right in the eyes of the Lord," or "He did not walk in the ways of the Lord." If the king chose to do what was right, the God blessed that king and the entire nation. If the king failed to do what was right, God withheld the blessings.

We are not living under the old covenant of the law, but under the new covenant of grace, and God makes it clear that blessings fall on both the just and the unjust. But I still think it is fair to say that if we choose disobedience, we shouldn't be surprised if we don't receive many blessings, while if we choose to obey God's way, we may also experience God's blessings.

I don't know what those blessings will be this week, or how this week of obedience may plant a seed that will bear fruit a long time from now. What I do know is that when Joshua and the people of Israel chose to obey God, the wall of Jericho fell down. It just fell down. God wanted to give his people the Promised Land, but he wanted them to do it in God's own way.

That's what this week is about. For one week, it's about trying it God's way, for a change.

QUESTIONS FOR REFLECTION AND DISCUSSION

1. Do all your prayers get answered? Do all your prayers get answered the way you would like them to be answered?

2. What does it mean to say that sometimes we are supposed to be the answer to our own prayers? Does this mean that we shouldn't pray about these situations?

3. Can prayer really build walls rather than bringing them down? How? Can you give an example?

4. "Prayer should never become a substitute for obedience." Do you think this a real problem?
Can you give examples of common prayers that illustrate this point?

5. In the parable of the Pharisee and the tax collector praying in the temple, what did the Pharisee do wrong? How did his disobedience in prayer build walls, and who was affected by these walls?

6. What is the relationship between the word "justified" and the phrase, "without walls?" When the tax collector went home justified, were there any walls left in his life?

7. Do you agree that we are casually disobedient in our prayers? What effect has this had on our desire to spend time in prayer? Why?

8. Do you expect a miracle every time you pray? Why or why not? Short of a miracle, how do we expect God to answer our prayers?

9. Do we stop and consider all the possible answers to our prayers before we pray? If not, how could this lead to disappointment with God? How can greater obedience before we pray help us experience God's grace more clearly?

10. Jesus asked his disciples to watch and pray with him in the Garden of Gethsemane. How can watching and praying in advance of something prepare us for the obedience which may be necessary to prevent or remove walls?

CHAPTER TWELVE: HONESTY

*Bringing Down Walls Between
Me and My Secret Self*

So this is what it feels like to be a leader.

There are nearly 500 people stretched out behind me, which means that there are almost a thousand eyeballs staring at my back—and I can feel every one of them. These people have got to be thinking that this is the most ridiculous thing they have ever done. The shofar just sounded again, which means that we're starting our second lap around the outside of Covenant Life Church—five to go—and then we head back into the worship center, where we will ... what? Today is Jericho Sunday, and I still don't know what's going to happen when we finish this march.

Is this what Joshua was thinking as he led his army around Jericho?

* * *

As much as the gentle rain had turned out to be a blessing on the day of our prayer walk, I was praying for fair weather on Jericho Sunday. God was gracious (not that I think God takes a vote on the weather, but rather works all things together for good), and the day was perfect. For a Sunday in July, the sky was cloudless, the temperature was right around 70, the humidity was low, and there was a light breeze blowing. It could not have been a more beautiful morning.

We were just having the one combined service at 10:00 o'clock, so I didn't need to get to the church as early as I usually did, but Leigh and I left home at around 7:00 anyway. I don't remember talking much in the car on the half hour drive from Holland to Grand Haven. I was nervous and was probably running through the sequence of the day's events in my mind to make sure that I didn't forget anything. I didn't actually have a lot to do; other people had stepped up to take charge of nearly everything that was going to take place. There wasn't even the usual half hour sermon for me to practice; just a few comments before the march began and an abbreviated message about Jericho and walls near the end of the scripted part of the service.

This was it; this was the culmination of the whole Jericho series. I was fighting that anti-climactic feeling that sometimes precedes a long-planned event. After such a huge buildup—nearly a year of talking about it, three months of planning, six Sundays exploring every possible angle of the Jericho story, 43 daily readings, a week of intentional obedience, six nightly meetings with a single walk around the church each night—I was afraid that people would think, "Is this it? This is all you've got?" I knew, intellectually, that the day didn't belong to me and that whatever happened wasn't up to me, but it still felt to me, emotionally, as if I was personally responsible for everyone's Jericho experience. It was kind of like the way you feel when you've been to a restaurant you really enjoyed and so you invite some friends to come with you and you are willing them to have as good an experience as you had. I was willing the whole church to have a great Sunday.

I'm embarrassed to admit that I was so wrapped up in my own worries that I can't even remember what Leigh did when we got to the church. I'm sure she was praying (probably for the return of my sanity), and that's how I began the morning, too. Just sitting in my study, trying to breathe normally, trying not to be anxious, trusting God. That always sounds so good when I say it, but then I still find myself peering over God's shoulder, ready to give advice about how I think things ought to be done.

One of my biggest worries was about who would show up. I knew my core volunteers and worship leaders would be there, but the only thing we had ever done that was remotely like this was the prayer walk, and we had suffered some fairly significant attrition on that Sunday. Not to put too fine a point on it, this was a lot stranger.

Attendance at the previous six evenings of the Jericho Week hadn't been as consistent as I had hoped. We had started with a good crowd on Monday, talking about our need for knowledge of God's Word in order to be obedient, but by Saturday, when the subject was obedience in private, there had only been about 35 people in attendance. I had expected a slight decline each night, especially since I hadn't put a lot of emphasis on attending every meeting, but not as much as we had experienced. I was pretty sure that those few who had stuck it out for the entire week would show up, but how many others would join them?

God forgive me, but I can be as sinfully fixated on numbers as any other pastor.

After finishing my prayer time and reviewing my notes for the morning, I wandered out into Main Street—the gathering space between the north and south entrances, with the worship center to the east and the ministry center and coffee shop to the west—and saw that the music team was already in the worship center, rehearsing. A couple of the trumpeters had also arrived and were warming up on the platform in the ministry center. That got my heart beating a little faster; I was eager to hear the new Fanfare and March live—and actually played on trumpets—for the first time.

Steve Caton's schedule for the morning had the band rehearsing from 8:30 to 9:10; the seven trumpeters were supposed to join them for the last ten minutes to go over the two hymns we were using, both of which called for brass accompaniment. The trumpeters would then rehearse the Fanfare and March from 9:10 to 9:30, accompanied by our liturgical dancers. The choir took over the worship center from 9:30 to 9:55, and worship was supposed to start at 10:00 sharp, in the ministry center.

It was just a little before 9:00 as I walked through Main Street, and I noticed that some of our Frontline Team members were already hanging their name tags around their necks and heading toward their places near the north and south doors, at the information center and in the coffee shop. One of them said to me that she wanted to make sure she spotted every single visitor, since the unusual nature of the service would certainly take some explaining! I was grateful that she said it with a big smile.

As carefully as Steve and I had scheduled the pre-service activities, I couldn't possibly have planned what happened over the course of the next hour—except that I sort of did, accidentally. I had decided early on, for no particular reason other than logistics, that we would begin Jericho Sunday in the ministry center, rather than in the usual worship center. I was thinking that this way, people would only have to go through one set of doors to get outside for the march, rather than first exiting the worship center and then heading through the exterior doors—in other words, one bottleneck instead of two. Although the ministry center is a fairly large space which opens into both the coffee shop and Main Street, I hadn't really thought about how crowded it would become if people from both services were present. I had only ever seen it filled with about half the members of the congregation.

Clearly, some of the regular early service people didn't know what to do with their extra hour on this particular morning; either that, or they forgot that we were starting at

10:00. Many of them arrived early, and finding the worship center doors closed, they started to congregate in the coffee shop and ministry center. With more than half an hour to go before the service, it already felt like we had a pretty large crowd, and the feeling of being packed in shoulder-to-shoulder seemed to increase everyone's sense of anticipation.

As 10:00 drew closer, the second service people started streaming in, and they were greeted by an already sizable crowd. It seemed to energize everyone; I think they had all come to find out the answer to the same question I had been asking: Who would show up?

Answer: nearly everyone. I allowed myself the same kind of fleeting moment of hope that I had experienced when I was first being considered as the interim pastor for Covenant Life. Maybe something good was going to happen at this service.

* * *

At exactly ten o'clock, the seven trumpeters took their place on the ministry center platform and called us to worship with the Fanfare and March. I don't exactly know how to describe it; to say that it sent tingles up and down my spine doesn't really cover it—it was a much, much deeper feeling than that. To borrow a biblical image, it was as if the sound was a wordless call from God, penetrating us to the "joints and marrow" (Hebrews 4:12). I think we had a small hint of why God says that it will be a trumpet call that announces the return of Christ.

When the Fanfare ended, I welcomed the people who were gathered, greeted anyone who was visiting, and told them that they had chosen an interesting Sunday to be with us. I said a few words about how obedience to God's way often requires us to do things in an unconventional manner, and briefly described the unconventional service we had prepared. After the musicians led us in several songs, I shared this introduction to the march:

At this time, we invite those who are able to join us in a walk of prayer and obedience. Joshua and the people of Israel walked around Jericho once a day for six days; in the same way, all this week, those of us who have been meeting each evening have also been walking around the building once every night. We've been praying about each of the areas of obedience that we've covered for six weeks, praying specifically that God would bring down the walls that have been built by our disobedience.

On the seventh day, Joshua and the people walked around Jericho seven times—not speaking, not shouting, led only by the sound of the shofar, the ram's horn, and by the Ark of the Covenant, the symbol of God's presence. As a symbol of our desire to be obedient to God's way, we're going to walk, too, seven times around the church. It will take about half an hour if we keep up a fairly steady walking pace.

If that's more than you are able to walk, we invite you to walk as much of it as you can; or if you aren't able to walk, we invite you to remain here in the ministry center —or perhaps you would like to wait outside on the patio and watch us as we go by.

While we are walking in silence, or waiting here or on the patio, I invite us to pray. Specifically, I invite us to pray that God would bring down walls. Not these literal walls, of course, but walls created by sin and disobedience. We've talked at length about six areas of obedience: Obedience to the Word of God, obedience with our families, obedience with our neighbors, obedience in the workplace, obedience in prayer, and obedience when no one is looking. Think about each of these areas, and ask God to show you the walls that are there—walls between you and your spouse, or you and your children or parents; walls between you and your fellow church members or between you and your neighbors; walls between you and the people you work with; walls between you and God; walls that you've created in yourself as you've tried to keep a secret part of your life separate from the public part of your life.

Ask God to help you be aware of these walls as you walk and pray, and ask him to bring those walls down. Like Joshua and the people of Israel, we will walk in silence, and when we have finished walking, I would like us to continue to be silent, to refrain from speaking to each other until we are instructed to do otherwise.

At that point I offered a brief prayer, Steve gave three blasts on the shofar, I hoisted the Bible high above my head, and led the way to the north door.

* * *

Another blast on the shofar, and the artist on the patio is finishing a colorful three on the easel; we're starting lap four. So far, all I've thought and prayed about is ... pretty much nothing. I've just been thinking about how thankful I am that it's a nice morning and that we aren't going to lose anyone to heat stroke. I guess I've also been thankful that our maintenance man, Joe, did such a nice job of clearing out the weeds here along the back side of the building. It looks so nice you would almost think that we walked here every week.

Okay, Case, time's running out; concentrate. Start praying about something. Think about some walls that need to come down. Are there any church people you've offended? Any neighbors that have issues with you? Is there something you need to talk about with Leigh or the kids? How about your prayer life or your scripture reading? Anything there?

Why am I not thinking of anything? I know I'm not perfect, and I'm sure there must be some walls that have to come down.

Maybe it's the walls-in-private thing that I'm supposed to

work on. Do I have anything there? Is there a secret part of my life that I'm not willing to face?

Yes.

Wow. I didn't see that coming. I thought that was completely done and over with. Now what do I do?

I guess have to be honest with myself and admit that I knew there was still an internal wall there; but I also know that it would take a miracle for that wall to disappear. I wonder if God will work a miracle for me.

He did once before.

* * *

It was a long time ago, when Leigh and I were still in New Jersey. It was a day a lot like this one, only it was in October. Friday the 13th of October, to be exact. That's a date I'll never forget.

Leigh was at work. I was outside in the back yard with our kids, who were about two, three and five at the time. I was watching them and reading, and they were playing peacefully with each other. After we had been outside for maybe half an hour, Abby called over to me and asked me to go get their ball. It had gotten away from them and rolled off the lawn and across the church parking lot, ending up on the other side of the busy street that passed in front of the church.

At almost exactly the same moment that Abby was asking me to get the ball, the neighbor's seven-year-old daughter must have come out the back door of her house. I couldn't see her because of some pine trees that cut off my view of her door and driveway. I was just getting up from my chair and was turning to go down to the road when I saw that she was standing by the entrance to the parking lot, right at the curve in the road, clearly intending to go across and retrieve the ball. In the space of about a second, I saw her look left, look right, wait for a car that was just passing from the right—I was just about to yell—and she stepped out into the road. She never saw the car coming around the curve from the left.

I've never been so angry with God. I tried to hide it, and tried to say all the right things, but it was eating me up inside. I didn't want to steal from our neighbors' grief; they were the ones who had lost a daughter while I still had all three of my children. I don't know how Leigh and I got through the first week, or the second, but we did. After a month or two, life started to seem sort of normal again, but I wasn't myself. Not even close.

I thought I was going to carry my anger toward God forever. I wasn't thinking in terms of walls in those days, but it was a huge wall that I thought would always be there, at least until the end of my life or Christ's return, whichever came first. Everyone has their own first question that they want to ask God when they get to heaven; mine was going to be, "What were you thinking when you took a seven-year-old from her family?"

Several months after the accident, I was having another sleepless night. As soon as I closed my eyes, I would see the car coming again. My feet were in molasses, my voice was frozen in my throat. I could never get down to the road in time, and I always woke up agitated and angry all over again.

It was about 4:00 in the morning when I tried to lay down again, and I fell asleep. This time, I didn't see the car. I saw an angel.

As I said at the beginning of this book, I'm not the mystical type, and I wouldn't normally claim to have supernatural experiences, but as soon as this dream began I knew it was different. For one thing, it was more vivid than any dream I'd ever had before, almost like the difference between night and day; it was that much brighter. Also, in the dream, I knew that I was asleep as I was seeing the angel, but I was also as alert and wide awake as I have ever been. I knew even as I was experiencing the dream that I would have no trouble remembering it when I woke up.

At first, my eyes were fixed on the angel's face. It was

a woman's face with an understanding smile that conveyed deep joy and peace. Then I noticed her wings. They seemed to be made of paper and they were decorated in vivid crayon colors; they were beautiful. I stared at them for what seemed like several minutes. Then the angel spoke:

"When children die, they go to heaven and color the angels' wings."

That was all she said. I slept peacefully for the rest of the night and when I woke up, my anger was gone.

* * *

One final blast on the shofar; a number seven on the easel. Time to go back through the doors and into the worship center.

Everyone has been amazingly disciplined during this entire walk; I haven't heard anyone say a single word to anyone else. Actually, I may have been the only one to break the silence, because at about lap four, I was surprised to see that my brother, Ty, and his wife Deb had suddenly joined the march. He seemed amused to walk in on the middle of something so unusual. I hadn't told anyone in my family what we were up to, so I quickly whispered that we were marching in silence and that I would explain it to him later.

As we went into the worship center, people actually found seats more quickly than I thought they would. No one tried to stop at the coffee shop first (I had told the servers to put away all the pots from when the march began until after the worship service was over), and both early and late service people seemed to make room for each other without any difficulty.

When everyone was assembled—in perfect silence—I got up and said, "When Joshua finished leading the people of Israel around the city of Jericho seven times, he told the people to shout. Stand up, and let me hear you say 'Hallelujah!'"

"Hallelujah!"

"Let me hear you *shout* 'Hallelujah!'"

"HALLELUJAH!"

"Let me hear you shout 'Our God reigns!'"

"OUR GOD REIGNS!"

"Let me hear you shout, 'Blessed be the name of the Lord!'"

"BLESSED BE THE NAME OF THE LORD!"

We repeated that last shout three times, and when we were done, there was spontaneous applause, something else I hadn't seen coming. As soon as the people were seated, the seven trumpeters, gathered on the left side of the platform, played the Fanfare and March again, this time accompanied by the liturgical dancers. If we hadn't already gotten the point that this was a day about walls coming down, the dancers made it clear for us.

As soon as the trumpeters and dancers were finished, the lights came up on the opposite side of the platform where the choir members had been instructed to sit when the march was over. They sang a lively version of "Joshua Fit de Battle of Jericho," after which I returned to the center of the platform, and invited the congregation for one last time to turn to Joshua 6:1-21, the heart of the Jericho account. After reading the passage, I continued with these words:

> When God wanted to give the people of Israel the Promised Land, he truly wanted to give it to them as a gift. For 400 years, they had been living in Egypt, becoming a captive nation, slaves who hardly even remembered that their ancestors had once settled in the land of Canaan. God raised up Moses and Aaron to lead the people into the wilderness, and there God had to teach them about how to be the people of God. God provided for them with water and manna and quail; God led them by a pillar of smoke and a pillar of fire; most importantly, God taught them about obedience through the Law.
>
> But the generation that departed from Egypt was rebellious; they didn't want to obey, so the people wandered. God continued to provide and protected them for

forty years, until it was finally time for Joshua to lead the people into the Promised Land.

The first major challenge they encountered was Jericho, a fortified city with enormous walls. Forty years earlier, when spies had been sent into the Promised Land, it was cities like Jericho that made ten of the twelve spies say that they would never be able to conquer the land. Only Joshua and Caleb had believed that it could be done. Now, forty years later, it was time to see if they had been right.

As Joshua approached Jericho, a messenger from God appeared, the commander of Lord's army. He wouldn't say if he was on Joshua's side or on the side of the enemy; it was as if that was to be decided based on what happened next. The commander had a message for Joshua: God wanted him to march around the city once a day for six days, and on the seventh day to march around it seven times. When he had done that, the commander said, the wall would collapse.

God truly wanted to give the people of Israel the Promised Land as a gift. If they chose to believe God and were willing to approach the city in obedience, trusting God's way, the wall would just fall down.

Like the people of Israel, we also are on our way to a Promised Land, and again, God wants to simply give it to us as a free gift. He sent his Son, Jesus, to take care of all the obstacles in our way, and all we have to do is accept what God is offering.

Let me make this as clear as I can: Our salvation does not depend on our obedience, but only on the obedience of Jesus on our behalf. Salvation is God's gift to us. It has already been accomplished, and we live in the freedom and the joy of knowing that we are forgiven people. "Nothing can separate us from the love of God in Christ Jesus our Lord."

But even though we know that God has given us the gift

of faith, and even though we know that we have been forgiven through Christ, we continue to build walls though our disobedience and our sin. God wants us to already begin experiencing the joy of eternity right now, but we build walls that separate us from that joy; and sometimes those walls can leave us questioning whether we believe God's promise, that forgiveness is already ours.

The way we bring those walls down is the same way Joshua and the people of Israel brought down the walls of Jericho—through obedience, by listening to God, by doing things God's way. Many of us have made a particular effort to do this all this past week. We've been listening and praying and walking, and now we've come to the end of the week, which is when, according to the story, the walls are supposed to come down.

I want to give us an opportunity to allow that to happen. As Joshua and Israel devoted the city and everything in it to God, I want to devote these next few moments, and everything that happens in them, to God.

This is what I would like us to do: First, I would like us to stack up all the chairs and place them around the perimeter of the worship center. Then I want us all to move to the edges of the room, and as we do that, I would like husbands and wives and older children to go to opposite sides (by all means, please keep your younger children with one of you). When we've got the chairs all stacked up and we've made a circle around the perimeter of the room, I'll have just a few more words to say.

I was amazed at how quickly the chairs disappeared, and that instruction about husbands and wives, parents and children moving to different sides of the room? I had thought of that (been told to do that?) just a couple of days earlier. The lights had been slightly dimmed as we were moving the chairs and I could see that people were trying to spot their family members across the open space (it's a large room). When everyone had found a place in the circle, I continued:

Thank you for doing that so quickly.

This is a time to let God answer our prayers. This is a time to let walls fall down. As you stand around the edges of this holy place, where we learn so much about God and where we sing God's praises, where we laugh and pray and sometimes cry, look across to the people you know and love—your husband or wife, your child or parent, your neighbor, your coworker, your friend.

God doesn't want us to be divided by walls, and yet we know that sometimes we are. We say something a little more harshly than we intended, we forget to say "I'm sorry," we put ourselves first and forget to pay attention to someone else's need. In a hundred ways, in a thousand ways, bit by bit, we build walls.

If you are willing and if you feel prompted by the Holy Spirit, this is a chance to at least begin letting those walls fall down. We've removed all the visible barriers that we can in this space; the ones that we can't see are up to you.

Let me just quickly say what this time is *not*. When we cross this space to be reconciled with each other, it's not a time to build new walls. For example, this is not a time to go up to someone and say, "You know what, you don't know this but you really offended me once and I'm here to give you a chance to say that you're sorry!" That's not going to bring down any walls; that's going to build a really big new wall. You might want to find a way to connect with that person sometime soon in another setting to talk about that wall, just not now.

This also is not the time to make a first-time confession about something like unfaithfulness to your spouse or embezzling from your boss, or something else that you have been keeping hidden; that also would create an instant wall. Again, you may decide today that you are going to deal with that wall, but that isn't what this time is for.

This is a time to be reconciled with the people you know and love, to deal with the situations where both of you know that something has come between you and you want to give God the chance to bring down that wall. You may need to set a time to get together to really talk; maybe this time will be nothing more than that, saying, "Can we get together?"

I said to our worship leaders that this is a pretty savvy congregation. "I think they'll know what this time is for. It's a time to bring down walls, not build them; it's a time to be reconciled, not create new problems; it's time to give God the chance to answer our prayers."

For those of you who either don't have any walls to deal with here, or who know that this isn't the time or place to deal with them, I invite you to pray where you are for the people who are being reconciled with each other. Pray with all your might that walls will come down.

Before I invite you to move, let me say that we're going to worship just a little more when this time is done; I'll gather us back together. Now, let me read these words from II Corinthians 5: *"From now on, we regard no one from a worldly point of view. Though we once regarded Christ in this way, we do so no longer. Therefore, if anyone is in Christ, the new creation has come: the old has gone, the new is here! All this is from God, who reconciled us to himself through Christ and gave us the ministry of reconciliation: that God was reconciling the world to himself in Christ, not counting people's sin against them. And he has committed to us the message of reconciliation."*

In this Spirit, let the walls fall down!

* * *

From this point on, I didn't know what would happen. As I said before, Covenant Life Church does not appreciate gimmicky things, and here we had just managed to get nearly 500 people to march around a building seven times and now we had them lined up around the walls of the worship center. If they didn't judge that what was happening was real, I was convinced that not a single person would move. It would just be the most awkward, uncomfortable church moment ever.

I shouldn't have worried; it was real. People started moving almost instantly. Husbands and wives crossed to meet each other in the middle of the floor, parents and children were bowing their heads in front of each other; entire families were embracing in hugs and tears.

I could see that people were coming together for a few moments, and then were leaving to go and work on walls that they might have with other people. Leigh and I did the same; there were some walls between us, and with a few words, we let them start to tumble down. I then went to find my brother; I don't hug him very often (I can count those occasions on one finger), but I embraced him this day (I still didn't tell him about the *Rolling Stones* record, though; one step at a time).

Several members of the congregation caught my eye as they were moving about, and the way they smiled at me with streaks of tears running down their cheeks told me everything I needed to know about how the Spirit was moving to bring down walls in Covenant Life.

I had arranged with the worship leaders to have the band begin playing quietly on my signal. After about ten or fifteen minutes, when it became evident that people weren't moving about quite as much, the band started to do a quiet instrumental version of *Did You Feel the Mountains Tremble*. After a few times through, the lights came up and the leader asked the people to come forward and join in. I don't know that I ever heard Covenant Life sing with more enthusiasm.

A verse near the end of the songs says:

Did you feel the darkness tremble?
When all the saints join in one song

And all the streams flow as one river
To wash away our brokenness.

As I sang along, I realized that the inner wall I had prayed about on the march around the building was also falling down. I don't know if I would call it a miracle, and it wasn't completely gone, but I had peace that in time, it would be.

* * *

Miracles did happen at Covenant Life on Jericho Sunday. For example, I heard afterwards from a person who had never been to Covenant Life before. She told me that she had no idea why she had chosen that particular morning to visit, until she was standing in the circle and saw one of her neighbors on the other side of the room. "When I saw her standing there, I knew, instantly, why God had me come to Covenant Life."

I heard dozens of brief comments from many different husbands and wives during the fellowship time after the service, and the stories of walls coming down between couples and families continued for several weeks after the march. One woman told me about the struggle she was having with her own private wall during the walk itself, moving from "This is ridiculous," to "Maybe there's something to this," to "This is the greatest spiritual experience I've ever had," all within seven laps of the church.

For the next few weeks, I preached on themes of how to continue living in obedience after something like the Jericho experience. I went back and personally read the whole story of Jericho again, too, even though I had read it so many times during the preceding months. But this time I started with chapter one of Joshua, instead of starting at chapter two, where the spies meet Rahab.

In the first chapter, I saw these words that God had spoken to Joshua upon the death of Moses: *"Be strong and courageous; for you shall put this people in possession of the land that I swore to their ancestors to give them. Only be strong and very courageous, being careful to act in accordance with all the law that my servant Moses commanded you; do not turn from it to the right hand or to the left, so that you may be successful wherever you go. This book of the law shall not depart out of your mouth; you shall meditate on it day and night, so that you may be careful to act in accordance with all that is written in it. For then you shall make your way prosperous, and then you shall be successful. I hereby command you: Be strong and courageous; do not be frightened or dismayed, for the Lord your God is with you wherever you go"* (Joshua 1:6-9 NRSV).

When I read these words, I thought again about Joshua standing on the road to Jericho, confronted by the commander of the Lord's army. "Are you for us or for our enemies?" Joshua had asked.

"Neither," he replied, "but as commander of the army of the Lord, I have now come." The question wasn't whose side the commander was on, but whose side Joshua was going to be on. Would he walk in obedience, or would he choose to go his own way?

Through the whole Jericho experience, I've become more convinced than ever that God's peculiar way of doing things is always the best. Period. I don't care how out of step it is with the conventional way of doing things, God's way is better.

Only God's way brings down walls.

QUESTIONS FOR REFLECTION AND DISCUSSION

1. Does being a leader mean that you have all the answers? What does it mean? Does it require a different kind of personal integrity?

2. How do our private lives affect our public lives? Is it possible to truly keep the two separate?

3. If your pastor said that you were going to do something like the Jericho march, would you participate? Why or why not? What other opportunities do you have to address your personal walls?

4. Many people expressed gratitude for the half hour that it took to walk around the church seven times; several said that it gave them time to think. Do we set aside enough time for personal reflection?

5. "God forgive me, but I can be as sinfully fixated on numbers as any other pastor." Are numbers the best measure of a successful program? What are some other ways that we can measure success or effectiveness?

6. A lot of effort went into the worship for Jericho Sunday, even to the point of commissioning an original piece of music. Should this be the exception or the rule for worship? Why is it so often the exception?

7. Several people reported that it took several laps to begin focusing on the purpose of the walk. Is the same true of all our prayers? Can we get to the heart of prayer in the space of just a few minutes?

8. How do tragic events build internal walls of division? Who is divided? Who can bring these walls down?

9. If you had been in the large circle on Jericho Sunday, who would you hope to see standing on the other side of the circle? Given a chance to participate in a time of reconciliation, what would you do when the pastor said, "Let the walls fall down!"

10. Is it possible to experience the Jericho effect in any way other than obedience?

PART THREE: DAILY READINGS

The Jericho Effect

Daily Readings

There are 43 daily readings in the collection which follows, one each day for six weeks, plus a final Jericho Sunday. Individuals may choose to use them as part of a personal Jericho experience, or a group may wish to use the readings together as part of a Bible study or congregational Jericho series.

Both individuals and groups are encouraged to try a week of radical obedience during the sixth week of readings (as described in the text of the book). This is the week which also covers our behavior in private—obedience when no one is looking.

A few questions follow each reading; some are obviously personal, while others would be appropriate for group discussion. Group leaders who are using this material will want to be sensitive to the difference when selecting questions for group use.

Individuals and groups may also wish to think about participating in some kind of symbolic march during the final week of readings, as well as a seven-times-around march for the final Sunday. It is a wonderful opportunity for prayer, and a sign to God of our desire to be as obedient as Joshua in choosing to do things God's way.

Daily Reading for Week One, Day One

Week One: Obedience to the Word of God

READ: Romans 3:21-26

My children make fun of me when I start reminiscing about the dark ages—you know, the days before cell phones, microwave ovens, DVD players, and perhaps most unimaginable to them, computers. We've had a computer in our home since the summer of 1984 (taking out a hefty loan to pay for that first one), and since our oldest was born at about the same time, none of my children have ever known what it was like to type on—gasp!—a typewriter.

In other words, they don't share my memories of jammed keys, inky fingers, smudged pages or fiddling with correction tape. Their very first grade school "documents" looked more professional than the philosophy thesis I turned in as a college senior. If they do happen to catch a typo, it doesn't mean the agony of retyping a whole page. They just pull up the saved document, make the correction, and print out a fresh sheet.

If only correcting all our mistakes was that easy! Unfortunately, our daily lives have a lot more in common with the typewriter than they do the computer.

The first thing we have to acknowledge is that everyone sins. Everyone. No one's life is letter perfect. The second thing we have to acknowledge is that while we all sin, we don't have to sin as often as we do. We can do better. We should do better.

So why don't we? Is it possible that our assurance of salvation in Jesus is making us lazy in our obedience? I know that I have become a sloppier typist because corrections are so quick and easy on my computer; I can probably hit backspace and retype a word faster than you can notice that I made a mistake. Could it be that I am suffering something of that same attitude when it comes to my daily obedience? Since I know that "Jesus Paid it All" (as the hymn says), could it be that I am becoming complacent in my efforts at obedience?

Whatever the reason, for the next six weeks, we are going to be thinking about how we can be more deliberate in our obedience, even though it is true that Jesus paid it all. That fact alone should make us desire obedience more than we ever have before!

To think about:

1. If you're near your computer, open your word processor and quickly type, "The quick brown fox jumped over the lazy dog." How did you do? Any mistakes? What would you have to do differently to get it right every time?

2. You turned in a sloppy paper—lots and lots of typos—and your teacher said she'll fix them for you. What do you make of that?

3. What motivates you to do better? At home? At work? In sports? For God?

Daily Reading for Week One, Day Two

Week One: Obedience to the Word of God

READ: Psalm 119:1-8

My middle brother got married on a beautiful Saturday in June, back in the late 1970s. I was his best man. This was the era when the style mavens had decreed that colored tuxedos were the latest thing, so there I was with the rest of the groomsmen, all of us in yellow tuxes with black trim. Yes, we looked like a bunch of bananas.

Since this was only the second wedding I had ever attended, I wanted to make sure that I did all my best man duties "by the book." I actually went and found a bridal magazine at the library which spelled out all the things the best man was supposed to do, the most important of which was to get the groom to the wedding on time. I was surprised, however, by how many other things I was expected to take care of, everything from picking up and returning the groom's tux to verifying the reservations for the honeymoon (I let my brother take care of that one himself).

On the day before the wedding, we had a rehearsal. The minister walked us through the entire ceremony, twice. It seemed like overkill, but his point was very clear: Let's make sure we get this right. The only way for us to do that was to know in advance what we were expected to do.

This is the reason I chose the reading from Psalm 119 for this first weekday of the Jericho series. These six weeks are going to be all about obedience, and the only way for us to be obedient is to know in advance what God expects of us in as many situations as possible. The Psalmist reminds us, in every single one of this psalm's 176 verses, that God has provided us with a Holy Word. God has given us a book that teaches us how to do things God's way.

I think it's also worth noting that when everyone in a wedding party knows what they are supposed to do—and does it—it is a tremendous blessing to the bride and groom. Jesus tells us that in the kingdom of God, he is the Groom and the Church is his bride. In other words, our obedience is a blessing to both our Savior and to his Church.

That's a pretty good incentive for studying in advance how God wants us to obey his Word. The more times we rehearse it, the more automatic it becomes.

To think about:

1. Look at all the different words the psalmist uses to describe God's instructions for us (laws, statutes, commands, precepts, etc.) Are some more positive than others? Do any of them strike you negatively? Why? Can you think of other words that the psalmist doesn't use?

2. How would a wedding be different if there was no preparation in advance? What would the ceremony be like if no one knew what they were supposed to do?

3. What makes a person wear a yellow tuxedo? What makes a person want to please God?

Daily Reading for Week One, Day Three

Week one: Obedience to the Word of God

READ: Luke 8:19-21

It was my first day on the job in the emergency room at St. Mary's Hospital. I had been hired as a Cast Tech, someone who worked in what was then called the plaster room, where the orthopedic doctors took care of broken bones. My job was to assist the docs when they were wrapping plaster, as well as making sure that the room was clean, organized, well-supplied and always ready for the next patient.

My on-the-job trainer was going to be Tony, a gray-haired LPN who had been a fixture in the ER for many years. It was obvious that he had trained many techs before me, because when we walked into the plaster room for the first time, he handed me a spiral notepad and a pen, and said, for the first of many times, "Write this down ..." By the end of the day, I had filled dozens of pages with notes about how many rolls of plaster were needed for a below-the-knee cast, how to scrub and glove for a sterile procedure, how to roll stockinette over a broken arm, how to wrap up a tray of used instruments to send to central processing, and countless other instructions.

Taking notes as I was being trained was the easy part. The hard part was putting the notes into practice. Nearly every time I encountered a new situation, I recalled that Tony had taught me something about it, and when I dug through my notes, I almost always found what I was looking for. For the two years that I worked in the ER, I was never without my notepad.

God's Word is also meant to be put into practice. The Bible is more than a book of theories or suggestions; it is a practical book of instructions for dealing with nearly every situation we will ever encounter. Obviously, the instructions do us no good if we ignore them and do whatever we please.

Imagine how quickly I would have been booted out of the ER if, every time a doctor was ready to apply a cast I had to ask, "Um, what am I supposed to do again?" I might not have gotten fired the first time, but I certainly wouldn't have been of much use. Putting the Word into practice is what makes us useful to God.

To think about:

1. Have you ever had a job where you had to follow detailed instructions? What would have happened if you ignored them and did things however you thought was best?

2. The Bible addresses some situations directly while in other cases it teaches principles to help us make our own decisions. Why do you think this is? Which is more helpful?

3. If you were a patient in the ER, would you want to be attended to by someone who put their training into practice, or someone who just did it their own way?

Daily Reading for Week One, Day Four

Week one: Obedience to the Word of God

READ: Numbers 15:32-36

I debated whether I should include this passage as part of our series on obedience. It portrays God in a way that we don't think about very often today—a God who intends that the law be taken seriously! If it also seems to us that this story shows us a God who doesn't care about mercy, then it may be that we need to give this a little more thought.

The story itself couldn't be any simpler: While the Israelites were still in the wilderness, a man was found gathering wood on the Sabbath. While gathering wood was not expressly forbidden, God's law did say that no work was to be done on the sabbath. It also clearly stated, "You shall kindle no fire in all your dwellings on the sabbath day" (Ex. 35:3 NRSV). Apparently, the tribal leaders couldn't decide if gathering wood in anticipation of a fire violated either the prohibition against work or against making a fire, so they brought the man to Moses. Moses brought the issue to the Lord, who said that the whole assembly was to stone the man to death outside the camp.

For Israel, the lesson was clear: God was trying to fashion twelve tribes into a single nation, and was also trying to protect this nation as they made their way through a hostile land. If God had been lenient toward the man who was gathering wood, the next person would have gathered wood and stacked it in the fire pit near his dwelling. The next one would have gathered it, stacked it, and set fire to it. The one after that would have gathered it, stacked it, ignited it and carried part of it into his dwelling. You can hear the rationalization, can't you? "Hey, the law says 'Do not light a fire *in* your dwelling,' right? Well, I lit it outside."

If God had ignored what seemed like a minor infraction of a sabbath law, a law which was supposed to teach the people to trust that God would provide for them, even if they ceased to work for an entire day, how long would it have taken before all of God's laws were ignored? In a very short time, it would have been chaos, with every man and woman doing as they thought best. Only in the New Testament, after Jesus' death and resurrection, do we come to understand the full story of God's mercy.

But God's commandments are still for our good. Although we can expertly rationalize our casual attitude toward nearly every one of them, a more thoughtful examination of the law will reveal that it is still intended for our individual good and for our good as the people of God together. Obedience will teach us trust, and trust will reveal God's mercy.

To think about:

1. An elderly parishioner once told me, "Maybe we were too strict in sabbath observance years ago, but at least we believed something." How would you respond to that?

2. How would your life be different if the people closest to you didn't think it was necessary to obey any of the Ten Commandments? Is our society moving in that direction?

Daily Reading for Week One Day Five

Week one: Obedience to the Word of God

READ: Luke 24:13-27

Okay, true confessions time: I'm not a big fan of small group Bible studies. When I was in college and law school, I usually only agreed to attend if I knew that there were single girls involved, an unfortunate attitude which God still managed to use for my good. It was through one of these female-led Bible study groups that God steered me back toward the church, and eventually into seminary, where I met my wife, Leigh!

My oft-repeated complaint about these groups is that no one brings any particular knowledge to the table, so we end up with a nice social interaction—which has some value, I admit—but I don't really learn anything. Of course, it probably doesn't help that I don't usually look at my Bible study material until just a few minutes before the study is supposed to begin.

You too, right?

Imagine how much more profitable our study time would be if we were determined to take it seriously. We could finally move beyond the milky platitudes ("God wants us to pray more"; "God wants us to love each other") and sink our teeth into some meat ("God has an answer for my perpetual struggle with coveting"). Instead of mindless fill-in-the-blank questions, we might actually begin to fill in some gaps in our knowledge.

The key—and this may sound as simplistic as some of the pious phrases above—is to walk with Jesus when we study. On the road to Emmaus, Jesus led his companions in a thorough study of the law and the prophets, explaining everything that was said in the Scriptures concerning himself. Wow, would I have loved to have been in that study group!

I still can be, and so can you, if we pause to invite Jesus to be our guide when we study the scriptures—and then study them *seriously*. You know, we all moved beyond the "Dick and Jane" readers a long time ago. Isn't it time for us to go deeper into God's Word, too?

To think about:

1. Why do we so often ignore the instruction manuals that come with electronic gadgets? When do we usually start reading them?

2. Which book of the Bible do you think is the hardest to understand? What steps would you have to take in order to not only understand it, but to be able to explain it to someone else?

3. A lot of people complain that the Bible is a really big, difficult book. Have you ever seen a law library? A medical library? The United States Tax Code? Shouldn't we be asking, "How can the Bible be so short?"

Daily Reading for Week One, Day Six

Week one: Obedience to the Word of God

READ: Matthew 5:17-20

Quick: What are jots and tittles? If you guessed that they are a new kind of candy, you guessed wrong. No points if you thought they were brands of clothing or shoes either (although I seem to recall the names "Dots" and "Jellies" when my daughter was younger).

No, jots and tittles are parts of Biblical Hebrew, the very smallest marks that give the words their meaning. If you read today's Bible passage in an older translation, you would have found these words in verse 18, where Jesus says, "Till heaven and earth pass, one jot or one tittle shall in no wise pass from the law, till all be fulfilled." In other words, every part of God's Law will continue to be important as we await the final return of Christ.

We've been thinking about obedience to the Word of God for several days now, and it's time to address the question that's probably on all our minds: We're really not supposed to be serious about this obedience business, are we? It's one thing to sort of take it seriously—to mind our language, most of the time; to be pretty good to our parents; to make Sunday a slightly different day; to mostly tell the truth —but are we supposed to make more of an effort than that?

Yes, we are. Seriously.

And let me be very clear about this: It's not so that we can say we are perfect, because we never will be. It's not so that we can feel superior to our feckless neighbor, because we're nothing to boast about. Above all, it's not so that we can curry favor with God and win a spot in heaven. He's already offered that as a totally free gift through his Son, Jesus Christ.

So why should we be serious about our obedience? Out of love. For the sake of honor. To show respect. For the simple joy of knowing that it pleases God when we are willingly obedient. Theologically, our obedience gives visible evidence of our faith in God; it is an outward sign of the spiritual gift that God has granted us. Practically, however, our decision to be serious about obedience is a gift we return to God out of gratitude.

It could also be that our feckless neighbors will notice that there is something different about us. Willing obedience is so rare, it might encourage them to think about faith in God.

To think about:

1. When you were a child, how did your parents react when you did something you were supposed to do without being asked?

2. Which statement is more true? "Obedience is hard" or "I am lazy."

3. Is there one area of obedience which is particularly hard for you? Pray about that today.

Daily Reading for Week One, Day Seven

Week one: Obedience to the Word of God

READ: Deuteronomy 21:10-14

Okay, men, so it's not all that likely that you will soon be going into a battle in which you will see a beautiful woman amongst the captives whom you desire to take as your wife (although that may not be a bad description of the modern dating scene); and women, there's not much chance that you will soon be captured by a dashing warrior who oddly insists that you shave your head. In the same way, there are only about two or three percent of the people reading this who are likely to spend any time on a tractor, so why should the rest of us worry about the Bible's command to not harvest our fields all the way to the corners? And I've never seen my neighbor's donkey wandering around free, so why should I care what the Bible says about wayward beasts?

There are a lot of instructions like these in the Old Testament, and no, we're not expected to take them literally today. Even within the time period of the Bible itself, the application of God's laws changed drastically—from many wives to one wife; from eunuchs forbidden to enter God's house to eunuchs being baptized; from death for adulterers to forgiveness for the woman caught in adultery. Since Jesus began many of his teachings by saying, "You have heard it said ...," and then continued, "But I say to you ...," the temptation is to think that these ancient laws have nothing to teach us.

You already know that that's a mistake. Of course, these laws are valuable; it just takes a little more effort to discern the meaning of the "beautiful captive" law than it does a commandment like "Thou shalt not steal." In fact, the case law of the Old Testament—the many passages that give examples of the Ten Commandments being applied —may be even more helpful to us than some of the commandments themselves, because the specific cases illustrate the principles behind the laws: mercy, grace, respect for life, kindness, generosity, etc. Those principles have never changed—not within the Biblical time, not today.

In the particular example of today's passage, God was requiring greater mercy of the Israelites than any other nation at that time would have practiced. To take a captive, treat her as a wife, and if she proved displeasing, to just let her go free? Unheard of! Modern readers may shudder at the entire notion, but at the time, God was moving Israel toward greater and greater mercy, a principle which is still valuable today—even if we never go into battle.

To think about:

1. Why do you think God cared about the way captives were treated? Why should we care?

2. Some of the Old Testament case law seems harsh: Death for a rebellious son. Death for adultery. Death for sabbath-breaking. What was different at that time? Why were these laws necessary?

3. If you could declare one new law for God's people, what would it be? How would it honor God?

Daily Reading for Week Two, Day One

Week two: Obedience with my family

READ: Genesis 3:1-7

As our attention this week turns to obedience with our families, we begin with the very first wife and husband, Eve and Adam. In particular, we begin with perhaps the clearest example in all of Scripture about why it is so important that we be obedient in our family relationships.

There's one phrase I especially want us to notice: "She also gave some to her husband." Eve had chosen to eat the forbidden fruit, and having completed her act of disobedience, she passed it along to her spouse. If misery loves company (a phrase that hadn't yet been invented, since up until this time there was no such thing as misery), Eve's actions toward Adam made sure that she would never be alone in her sinfulness.

By the way, we should probably note than Adam didn't have to say "Yes."

In spite of our ability to choose otherwise, we often continue Eve's disobedience today. It could be that my spouse begins to mirror my less-than-honorable values. My children may pick up on my choice of language, and they undoubtedly will notice what I watch on TV. My siblings may choose to compete with me in terms of material success or serial marriage relationships.

I recall a news story from Jamestown, New York, that was widely reported several years ago. A twelve-year-old girl was selling drugs from her mother's home while her mother was at work. That girl didn't decide on her own to become a drug dealer; she was filling orders for her mother. In the same way, our children might become dealers in prejudice, materialism, unfaithfulness or dishonesty.

The good news is that we can spread obedience through our immediate and extended families just as surely as disobedience. Yes, our children notice what we watch on TV, but they also notice what we choose not to watch, and they will listen as we explain the reasons why we choose not to watch it. Just as they hear and copy our sinful words and opinions, they will also copy our obedient choices. Our spouses will also be more likely to choose obedience if we choose it first for ourselves.

In other words, we can choose to break the Eve and Adam cycle. Just because she also gave some to her husband doesn't mean that we have to do the same.

To think about:

1. What values did you receive from your family? Do you wish that any had been different?

2. Do the people closest to you make you more or less likely to be obedient? Why?

3. If you knew for certain that your family would become like you, what would you change?

Daily Reading for Week Two, Day Two

Week two: Obedience with my family

READ: Genesis 27:1-13

If you're not familiar with the story of Jacob and Esau, you might want to complete the rest of chapter 27 before you continue with this daily reading. In a peculiar way, I find it comforting that Jacob could so easily lie, cheat and steal, and still be used by God to become the father of a great nation (not that I'm recommending any of these actions as a way to get ahead).

What I am recommending is that we take a close look at Isaac and Rebekah's roles in their children's life stories. It is pretty clear that their opinion toward their boys had not changed much since they came of age. At that time, the author of Genesis tells us that "Isaac loved Esau, because he was fond of game, but Rebekah loved Jacob" (Gen. 25:28 NRSV). When Isaac was near death, and ready to give his blessing to his eldest child, Rebekah saw to it that the blessing went to Jacob instead. Needless to say, having grown up in this poisonous environment of parental favoritism, things weren't exactly rosy between the brothers.

The favoritism that I have witnessed in families today is rarely as blatant as what we see with Jacob and Esau, but it is just as real—and destructive. In one family, an athletically gifted child was praised to the heavens while the quieter, bookish son was occasionally treated as an afterthought. In another family, an overweight child was severely disciplined—and sometimes even mocked—while the rest of the family enjoyed their fill of potato chips and ice cream.

Obedience toward our family doesn't mean that we treat every family member the same. Rather, it requires us to respond to each person's gifts and needs in as loving a way as possible. Everyone's gifts are different, but equally worthy of praise. Everyone's needs are different, but everyone is worthy of our attention.

If favoritism has become a pattern in your home, it can be hard to break. It can also be hard sometimes to tell the difference between favoritism and simply responding to the needs of a more demanding child. In either case, the future well-being of our children—and their relationships with each other—is being shaped by how we treat them today.

To think about:

1. Was favoritism evident in your family as you were coming of age? Would your siblings agree with you? Why or why not?

2. In your present family (even if everyone is grown), is there anyone whose gifts or abilities are being overlooked? Is it possible to make up for previous neglect?

3. Was Jacob responsible for his actions in the story of the blessing? How would you respond to him if he said that it was all his mother's fault?

Daily Reading for Week Two, Day Three

Week two: Obedience with my family

READ: II Timothy 1:1-7

Let's imagine that we're getting a sneak preview of Judgment Day, and we're found standing in front of the Divine Bench. We hear our name read aloud, and then the Prosecutor says, "You are charged with being insincere in your faith. How do you plead?"

I don't know about you, but I'm going to have to go with "Guilty" on that one (confident that through Jesus, the verdict will ultimately be "Forgiven!"). There have been many times when my faith has been more motion than meaning, more behavior than belief. I've often given a good imitation of faith, while inside I was mostly trusting in myself.

If no one else ever knew that I was faking it, I might be able to say that I was still being obedient—but in front of my family, I'm not that good an actor. I think my wife and children know me well enough to tell when I'm going through a dry spell, faith-wise, even though I try to keep up the motions of faith.

I wish that I could be more like Timothy. I wish that people could always say about me, "I am reminded of your sincere faith." Like Timothy, my mother and both grandmothers (father and grandfathers, too) were faithful people, but for some reason, it doesn't always "take" with me. I go through seasons in my faith—some rich and verdant, others dry and dreary.

My greatest fear in the dry spells is the effect it may have on my children. If they sense that their father is having doubts, it may fuel their own uncertainties. As I said, I can try and fake it, putting on my spiritual smiley face and acting as if all is well, but I don't think they'll be fooled for a moment.

No, I think what sincerity and obedience require of me is honesty. I think I will serve my family far better by showing them that I am trusting God to carry me through a difficult time, rather than pretending that all is well. "Thank God!" and "Praise Jesus!" may not be on my lips, but I can at least be patient, trusting that the Holy Spirit hasn't left my heart, and that God's presence will soon make itself known again.

Come to think of it, maybe that's what it really means to have a sincere faith.

To think about:

1. Have you ever felt as if you were just going through the motions of faith?

2. What good can God accomplish through our dry spells? What good can come of it for our families?

3. How can we remain obedient when our faith is weak? Can we do it on our own?

Daily Reading for Week Two, Day Four

Week two: Obedience with my family

READ: Acts 16:25-34

There have been many times in the last 35 years when I have encountered Christian families in which the children have not been required to go to church or to take part in any kind of faith instruction. When I've queried the parents as to this choice, they've invariably responded with some version of, "We want to let our children make up their own minds about faith when they grow older."

The traditional clergy response to this is, "If they were sick, you wouldn't let them decide whether or not to take medicine, would you?" I suppose I could come up with a theological argument describing these churchless children as sin-sick and in need of a cure, but I'm guessing that their parents don't see them that way. Remember, these are the folks who are already so convinced of their children's basic goodness that they think the little darlings are going to joyfully choose faith when they hit their teenage years.

Rather than wait for time to possibly prove them wrong, I think we need to come up with a new argument based on the joy of sharing something exciting that we've experienced ourselves. Why would we want to keep that from our children?

The Philippian jailer had experienced a miracle of grace. An earthquake shook his prison, the chains were released, the doors opened —but none of the prisoners escaped. In obedience to the authorities, Paul and Silas chose to stay put, which gave them the opportunity to witness to the jailer—and his whole family! (maybe there should be a sequel to this book called The Philippian Effect). The jailer didn't keep his joy to himself; he took it home with him.

Maybe this is a more persuasive argument than the one about "sick-and-in-need-of-medicine." If we believe that Jesus is the Savior of the world, and if we have experienced the joy of faith in our own lives, why wouldn't we share that good news with our children? If we place a high value our own faith (and I suppose that's the key question in all of this: do we?) our children will come to share that same value.

The old word for this faith sharing, often negatively perceived, is "indoctrination." I say, if I go to the doctrine of faith and discover joy, why wouldn't I take my children to the doctrine?

To think about:

1. Who first took you to church, or from whom did you first learn about faith? Have you ever wished that they had left you alone to make up your own mind when you were older?

2. What words would you use to describe teaching your family about faith? Is it a duty? A chore? A privilege? A joy?

Daily Reading for Week Two, Day Five

Week two: Obedience with my family

READ: I Timothy 5:1-4

One of the hardest jobs I ever held did me in within a week. I've unloaded semis by hand, I've worked on a factory production line, I've done landscaping, I've worked in a hospital emergency room, I've waited tables, I've worked a deli counter—but by far the hardest job ever was working for a week as a nurse's aide in a nursing home.

It wasn't the physical labor that got to me as much as the emotional. Within the course of a single shift, I got to know "my" people as real people, not just empty human shells waiting to die. Within a few days, I learned which of them got regular visits from family, friends or church members, and which ones never received a caller. One woman's family had placed her in the nursing home's care in Michigan, and promptly moved to California. I'm sure there was a lot more to the story than I learned in my week of care-giving, but all Mom knew was that she hadn't seen her family in three years (and it wasn't a case of faulty memory—I've known residents like that, too, who say "No one ever comes" even though their families are there every day!)

It's easy to overlook the obedience that we owe to our parents and grandparents. Especially today, when seniors are living healthier and longer lives, it's easy to think that we have no responsibility toward them. In fact, we might think that they should be helping us out a little more, maybe financially, or with child care. But when their situation changes, or their health suddenly takes a turn for the worse, we have no procedure in place, no regular habit of honoring and respecting them to fall back on. It's hard to suddenly go from zero to a hundred in caring if we haven't been cruising along at somewhere near fifty all along.

It may be that obedience toward our parents or grandparents will require nothing more of us than listening to the same story for the tenth—or hundredth—time. But it could also be, at the other end of the care spectrum, that we will be asked to take them into our homes and provide for them just as they once did for us. Every situation is different, and God doesn't ask for exactly the same kind of obedience in each circumstance.

What is important is that we begin to develop an attitude and practice of obedience today, before the demands on us seem instantly over-whelming. If that seems hard, pause for a moment and remember the word Paul used to describe what we are doing: repaying. What would it take to truly repay your parents and grandparents for all they've done for you?

To think about:

1. If they're still living, what is one thing that your parents or grand-parents would love to have you do for them? What, if anything, is preventing you from doing it?

2. Make a list of the blessings we receive through obedience toward our parents. Any surprises?

Daily Reading for Week Two, Day Six

Week two: Obedience with my family

READ: II Samuel 18:24-33

My wife, Leigh, and I have been blessed with three children who have all chosen as adults to be involved in the church. It wasn't always this way, as it wasn't for me, either; but it gives us joy to know that they are sharing their gifts today in the company of God's people.

On the rare occasion (lately) when all of us have been worshiping in the same place, Leigh and I have sometimes been asked, "What's your secret? How did you raise three children who all want to be in church?" Leigh and I both wish that we had a definitive answer to that question that we could share with others. We did try to be obedient toward our children, raising them with respect, encouragement, discipline, expectations and joy. But perhaps the most honest response is the simple fact that God didn't give us rebellious children.

David's son, Absalom, is an extreme example of a rebellious child. David clearly loved his son (see verse 33), but love alone wasn't enough to prevent Absalom from pursuing his own interests, even when those interests meant removing his father from power, and possibly even killing him! It was a complicated relationship, difficult to understand in an era when fathers had multiple wives and oddly blended families. But even considering all those elements, David and Absalom showed that love alone wasn't a guarantee that a child would remain faithful.

Parent/child relationships continue to be complicated today. I've known parents who have tried to be obedient toward their children, but whose children still chose to wander far from their parents' values. Other parents never taught their children anything spiritual, and yet these children have chosen to be fully involved in the church as adults.

When it comes to a sure-fire plan, complete with a faith commitment guarantee, there really isn't any such thing. But this doesn't mean that we should neglect what God has equipped us to do: loving our children and caring for them to the best of our abilities, praying for them and teaching them as much as we are able. Will it guarantee their success? Not necessarily, but we will know that we did our best in obedience—and that can only be a blessing to our children.

To think about:

1. Why do you think some children grow up to be rebellious? What are some factors that we can see in Absalom's life?

2. At what age should children be allowed to make their own decisions about spiritual matters?

3. How does obedience get handed on from parent to child? In what ways do you recall your parents' obedience?

Daily Reading for Week Two, Day Seven

Week two: Obedience with my family

READ: Genesis 4:1-9

"Am I my brother's keeper?" God had asked Cain if he knew the whereabouts of his brother Abel, and Cain had foolishly lied to God, saying that he didn't know. He did; Abel was lying dead in the field. Cain then asked this famous question, one that brothers—and sisters, too—have been trying to answer ever since.

For example, when I was a college student and knew that my roommate was out drinking, if his mother called, asking if I knew where he was, how was I supposed to answer? A few years later, when my hospital supervisor asked if I knew where the third shift orderly was (he was sleeping in a treatment room), what was I supposed to say? These weren't literally my brothers, but the question still ran through my mind.

The questions have only gotten harder as I've grown older. "Pastor, could you loan me just $50? I promise I'll pay you back next week." "Rev. Van Kempen, why weren't you here when my wife passed away?" "Pastor, I'm pretty sure that Mary is seeing someone other than her husband; shouldn't you go talk to her?"

In every situation, I want to do the right "brother's keeper" thing—but half the time (or more) I'm not even sure what the right thing is. In the examples above, is it okay to just say that my roommate is "out," even though I know what he is doing? Can I tell my supervisor to just check treatment room 9, and let her find the other orderly?

Do I have to loan money to my brother whenever he asks? Could I say to the bereaved husband that no one ever contacted me to tell me his wife was ill? Is it really my job to determine if Mary is being faithful to her husband?

"Am I my brother's keeper?" It's not an easy question, but obedience requires us to think about it and do our best to answer it in a way that is honest and which also blesses our brothers and sisters. If those two things are in conflict (and they often seem to be), it might help us to imagine that God has come to us as he did to Cain, asking us about our brother or sister. Thinking about the answer we would want to give God may help us decide what we should do.

To think about:

1. What are some of the ways that we clearly should consider ourselves to be our brother or sister's keeper? How have you been called on to serve others in that way?

2. What are some examples of times when we are not responsible for our brothers/sisters? Is there anything we can still do for them in those circumstances?

3. Why do you think God included this question near the very beginning of the Bible?

Daily Reading for Week Three, Day One

Week three: Obedience toward my neighbor

READ: Luke 10:25-37

If you could look back in time a few decades, you would find me near the backyard of the house six doors down from where I grew up. If you watched closely, you would catch me jumping the fence and snitching grapes off the neighbor's vines. I can still remember the feel of the thick skins and the tart taste of those sun-warmed concord grapes—yum!—but I still feel the shame, too.

This week's readings are all about obedience toward our neighbors, and we might experience a bit of shame as we consider what God is teaching us. As we start out, we have to (painfully, perhaps) acknowledge that Jesus wasn't exactly filled with praise for how religious people fill the role of neighbor. Being a good neighbor means more than just keeping my hands off of my neighbor's grapes, or staying on my own side of the fence. If all Jesus meant was something like, "don't steal" or "respect your neighbor's property line," the majority of us would be experts when it came to neighbor obedience. But passive, non-interfering obedience wasn't what Jesus had in mind.

As the story of the Good Samaritan unfolds, we see that the Biblical mandate to love our neighbor may require us to take some direct, cross-cultural, messy, and even costly action. My neighbor isn't just the person next door, or across the street. He or she is the person whose need becomes apparent to me, the person I can't pretend not to have seen.

I'm sure a post-parable interview with the priest or the Levite in the story would have revealed familiar excuses: I was too busy; running late; can't stand the sight of blood; didn't want to get involved; already doing too much. Our own neighbor neglect stories are probably filled with similar reasons for our non-involvement.

We can do better. Like the religious expert who encountered Jesus, we too can ask, "Who is my neighbor?" and keep our eyes open as God shows us the answer.

(Oh, and keep your hands off your neighbor's grapes, too!)

To think about:

1. A note in my church bulletin said that someone needed a ride for medical treatment. I was free that day but chose not to respond. Was I disobedient? What else would you need to know?

2. No one individual can help every person in need, so how do we decide which of them are our neighbors? Does the Holy Spirit play a part in this?

3. The commandment says "Love your neighbor as yourself." Is that an impossible standard? Could it be that we are "loving" ourselves at the expense of our neighbors?

Daily Reading for Week Three, Day Two

Week three: Obedience toward my neighbor

READ: Leviticus 19:9-18

Let me see if I can illustrate what we're up against today when it comes to being obedient toward our neighbors.

Several years ago, I heard that a popular comedian had been invited to speak at the annual White House Correspondents' Dinner, an event which is regularly attended by the President and the First Lady. I had also heard that his routine had not gone over well—dead silence in the room. I knew that I could probably find the video of the event online, which I did, and when I watched it, I knew why the comedian bombed: he wasn't funny, he was mean. His jokes weren't gentle jabs at the White House or the press, they were vicious, personal attacks on the President. You could tell that the people in the room were embarrassed by what they were hearing.

When I finished watching the video, I noticed an ad on the side of my computer screen. It said something like, "How low can humor go?" and gave the web address for a site that apparently made fun of people with disabilities.

This is what both entertainment and public discourse have become today. We have developed into a society that attacks anybody and everybody with sarcasm, cynicism, and often, outright cruelty. It isn't just the late-night comics or the tabloids or social media trolls. It is in the prime time shows, must-read websites, popular books, and even our daily conversations.

Look at that list of commandments in Leviticus again. I know it's a lot of "Do nots," but think about what God is saying in comparison to the way we treat people today—especially verse 17, "Do not hate your brother in your heart." If we're going to take obedience toward our neighbor seriously, we're going to have to be seriously out of step with what's happening all around us.

I'll be the first to admit that it's hard to be deliberately out of step, to be kind and generous when everyone else is being oh-so-cleverly sarcastic. But it's a step we have to take if we want to be obedient to what God teaches us about loving our neighbor.

To think about:

1. Do you agree that our society is becoming increasingly sarcastic and cynical? If so, why do you think that is?

2. Why is it hard to be different?

3. One of the judges on a popular reality show used to tear into the contestants, often mockingly, and would then say, "I'm just being honest." Is honesty a legitimate excuse for being unkind to our neighbor?

Daily Reading for Week Three, Day Three

Week three: Obedience toward my neighbor

READ: Proverbs 27:10

Leigh and I used to live in a historic, downtown city neighborhood where the houses were built very close to each other. I couldn't quite reach out my kitchen window and shake hands with my neighbor, but I could certainly see him in his kitchen (and I had to remember that he could see me in mine!)

This isn't the way most new neighborhoods are being built. People today prefer what the real estate agents call "woods and water" developments, country homes that are often isolated from the next house down the gently curving road. There aren't any sidewalks, no shared driveways (does anyone still have one of those?), and no one walks by the front porch to stop for a chat.

I've lived in dairy farming country (upstate New York), so I know that it is possible to have good relationships with neighbors who aren't just a few feet away. In fact, it may be easier if you aren't awakened each morning by the neighbor whose car desperately needs a new muffler. But I also know that the new suburban neighborhoods can be isolating, with every home an island.

That was my family's experience when we lived in New Jersey. In five years, I never met our nearest neighbor. I know that he (she?) threw a huge Kentucky Derby party once a year, but other than that, I didn't know anything about the people in that house.

Not surprisingly, the book of Proverbs has a lot to say about neighbors, and one of the things it tells us is, "Better is a neighbor who is nearby than kindred who are far away." The author, King Solomon, was thinking about times of need. Of course, we can call on our distant family members for help, and they almost have to offer it, don't they? After all, they're family. But how much better would it be to know that in a crisis, we can call on the neighbor who is close by?

Are we that kind of neighbor to the people who live near us? Are you obedient toward them in that way? Do your neighbors know, without a doubt, that they can call on you in a time of need?

To think about:

1. Is it possible to live next door to someone and not be a neighbor?

2. If your neighbor threw lots of parties (for the Kentucky Derby, for example) and never once invited you, how would you feel? Do you invite your neighbors to events at your home?

3. Why do you think people moved away from densely populated cities toward more sprawling suburbs? As the trend begins to reverse, with many people moving back into city centers, do you think they will be better neighbors to those who live near them?

Daily Reading for Week Three, Day Four

Week three: Obedience toward my neighbor

READ: Luke 14:7-14

Many years ago, a group of my fellow seminarians and I were Sunday dinner guests in the home of one of our friends. His mother had spread a great table. There was a lot to choose from—meats, vegetables, breads, fruits. As we all sat down at our places gazing over the feast, the mom politely asked, "Can I get anyone anything?" I hardly even noticed the question; it's one of those things that you hear people say, but unless there's been an obvious omission—like when they forget to give you silverware in a restaurant—you politely say "No," and maybe make some pleasant comment about the abundance of food that's been prepared.

This time, though, someone spoke up. "Do you have any cheese?"

I had just been getting ready to bow my head for prayer when I heard this request coming from across the table. One of my friends—always a bit of an awkward presence—had apparently noticed that there wasn't any cheese on the table, and since the hostess had asked if she could get anyone *anything*, he asked. She looked a bit flustered, but went into the kitchen and returned a few moments later and set some nicely cubed cheddar in front of my friend.

It's tempting to exclude uncomfortable people from our guest lists, or even from our circle of friends and acquaintances. They can embarrass us with their lack of manners, they can cause other guests to squirm, they can even penetrate our pretense of sophistication. But being obedient to our neighbors requires us to include everyone in our circle, no matter how awkward they might be.

Based on several scripture passages, including today's reading, I'm pretty sure that Jesus was an awkward guest. He not only commented on where people chose to sit at the table, he suggested a completely different guest list to his host!

We, too, are challenged to include our all neighbors, especially those who may never get a nice invitation: the poor, the lame, the blind. It might seem awkward at first, but we had better get used to it—because we'll be sharing the Lord's Table with those same people in eternity.

To think about:

1. Who do you already know who you suspect might be an awkward presence in your home? Have you ever thought about inviting that person to something?

2. If you found out that someone was excluding you from their circle because they didn't think you would fit in, how would that make you feel?

3. Have you ever seriously considered who will be in heaven? Shouldn't our churches—and our homes—already reflect that glorious mix of neighbors from every avenue of life?

Daily Reading for Week Three, Day Five

Week three: Obedience toward my neighbor

READ: Leviticus 18:20

You know, this is the daily devotion that I wish I didn't have to write, but after more than three decades in the ministry, I know that it's necessary. We can't talk about obedience toward our neighbor for a whole week and not mention our neighbor's wife (or husband).

I guess I was pretty young and naïve when I first started in ministry. I would occasionally hear that there was trouble in a marriage, but I generously assumed that it was about money or time, or communication. It rarely occurred to me that one of the partners might be having an inappropriate relationship with the spouse of a neighbor.

I was probably in my third year when a young husband and father from a different church came to my parsonage door and asked if he could speak to me for a while. He told me an amazing tale about bowling, drinking, and flirting with the barmaid—which had quickly become quite a bit more than flirting. His wife suspected, he told me, and he knew that what he was doing was wrong, but up until the previous day, he hadn't been willing to stop seeing the young woman.

"So what happened yesterday?" I asked. He told me that he had gone to the bowling alley after work, had drunk quite a bit, had been, shall we say, overly friendly with the barmaid, and then had to pick up his young son on his way home. Between that stop and getting to his house, he had driven off the road, totaled his truck, and very nearly caused the death of his son.

"It was as if I woke up," he said. "I suddenly realized what I was doing to my wife and family; that if my son had been killed, I never would have forgiven myself; and if I had been killed, my wife never would have known for sure if I loved her." We talked for quite a bit longer, but in that moment of confession, I knew that this young man had experienced a conversion.

I don't know if anyone reading this is involved with a neighbor in this way, and I know that I don't even have to say that it is wrong; we all know that already. What I do need to say is that it is possible to stop, to return to the spouse whom God has given you as your life partner.

It may not be easy. There could be painful consequences. But it is the way of obedience.

To think about:

1. Is there such a thing as harmless flirting?

2. What about the Internet? Is it obedient to view adult material on-line? Are online relationships safe?

3. What do you think about the man's comment, "It was as if I woke up"? What kind of a wakeup call do you need from God?

Daily Reading for Week Three, Day Six

Week three: Obedience toward my neighbor

READ: Deuteronomy 19:14, 27:17

First, for the technologically challenged, a definition of GPS: GPS is the acronym for Global Positioning System, a navigation tool using earth-based receivers that acquire precise timing signals from dozens of orbiting satellites, allowing the user to know precisely where he or she is on the face of the earth. Regular GPS is accurate to within two meters; more sophisticated versions (not the kind we regularly use) can be accurate to within a centimeter.

Most of us have GPS on our phones or in our cars. Before that, I used GPS when sailing, having once emerged from a sudden Lake Michigan fog bank to a GPS-determined spot directly between the pier heads in the harbor channel. I also use it when running, keeping track of the distance covered no matter what kind of a convoluted course I travel. GPS is used by the military, farmers, surveyors, the airlines, and increasingly, by golfers ("you've got 129.23 yards to the front edge of the green").

If we could rewind the calendar about 3,500 years, we would see that the GPS system at that time was: Big rocks. Really big rocks. If you wanted to mark a precise location—say, for example, the boundary line between your property and your neighbor's—you would identify it with a boundary stone.

Now imagine if your neighbor wanted to gain a little more grazing ground for his livestock. All he would have to do is move that boundary stone a few feet—or perhaps a few hundred feet. It would be hard to prove without going through a very arduous measuring process.

Those boundary stones signified much more than just a property line. They were a symbol of trust and honor in the community, a standing agreement between people who might not agree on much else. You might have different opinions on everything from the king's politics to what the priest said in the tabernacle last sabbath, but you agreed on that boundary stone.

Just because we can easily verify boundary lines with GPS today does not mean that we are excused from the obedience which requires us to share honor and trust with our neighbors. We may not agree on many day-to-day issues, but we can and must respect each other's rights: the right to own property, the right to security, the right to earn a living, and perhaps most important, the right to worship in our own way.

To think about:

1. Which of your own rights do you judge is most important? Is it important to your neighbor?

2. What are some ways that people disrespect their neighbor's rights?

3. What do you and all your neighbors all agree on, absolutely? Why these things?

Daily Reading for Week Three, Day Seven

Week three: Obedience toward my neighbor

READ: Romans 7:7-12

I should probably begin by noting that this reading is only a few verses out of a long theological point that Paul is making with the Romans. The reason I had us read just this small selection is because of the particular sin that had Paul tied up in knots. Remember, this is the man who had stood quietly by as Stephen, one of the first deacons, was stoned to death. Since then, Paul had been visited by Jesus himself (on the way to Damascus), he had been beaten, imprisoned, ship-wrecked, run out of town, and vilified, sometimes even by other believers.

So what was it that Paul struggled with? Was it a murderous heart? Did he deny God because of all his troubles? Had he lied his way out of a jam? Had he stolen things in order to survive?

No. Paul's struggle was coveting. I'm guessing that this isn't a sin that makes it into our confessions very often, but it's the one that had Paul saying, "Wretched man that I am!" (Romans 7:24 NRSV).

Dictionary.com defines coveting this way: "to feel blameworthy desire for that which is another's." Experiencing simple desire is just normal human behavior. For example, when I see a Ferrari drive by, it's very easy for me to imagine myself behind the wheel. But when that desire rises to the level of "blameworthy," in other words, when I allow myself to consider a sinful course of action to fulfill my desire —whether I actually follow that course or not—I've crossed the line into coveting.

Coveting's effect on our relationship with our neighbor can be devastating. The simple fact that my neighbor owns something, enjoys something, or is in a circumstance different than mine can cause me to think all kinds of wicked thoughts: "She doesn't deserve it." "What makes him better than me?" "Who does she think she is?" And finally, "He's nothing but a big jerk!" Be honest now—haven't you sometimes thought those things about people you didn't even know?

If coveting was easy to remedy, the Apostle Paul probably wouldn't have struggled with it as much as he did. He does, however, tell us where the cure begins: with Jesus. Our Savior, who owned nothing but his robe, can help us to think far more charitably about our neighbor.

To think about:

1. What do you covet most? What effect does this have on your relationship with your neighbor?

2. What do you have that other people might covet? How does this affect your relationship with them?

3. Why do you think coveting is so destructive? And why is contentment such a blessing?

Daily Reading for Week Four, Day One

Week four: Obedience in the workplace

READ: Matthew 21:28-32

Am I crazy, or did I used to work with one of the two sons in this parable (the second one)? If it wasn't him, it was certainly one of his close relatives—all, "Yes, sir! Right away, sir!" But he never actually got anything done.

This week's readings are going to be all about the workplace, and how important it is for us to demonstrate obedience at work (even if we're self-employed). We spend a lot of our lives doing something to provide for our families and ourselves—and the church—and the way we perform that work says a great deal about our relationship with God.

Work, of course, is about more than just making money (although I won't deny that that is important). It is about being engaged in some productive activity, living our faith day-by-day in the company of others who may or may not be followers of Jesus. The manner in which we do our work probably says more about our obedience to God than we could ever say in words.

Consider the parable again: Jesus was speaking to religious leaders in the temple about how quick they were to say "yes" to God with their mouths, but then never followed through with actual commitment to God's kingdom—they were more interested in satisfying themselves. By contrast, the tax collectors and other "sinners" didn't say yes to God as quickly, but when they did, they followed through on what God was asking of them in obedience.

In our places of work, we have the opportunity each day to show God and others that we are not only saying yes to being faithful servants in terms of our attitudes and behaviors, but also are willing to do yes as a sign of our faith in God. In other words, we want to demonstrate the best of both sons in the parable: we say yes to God, and we follow through with our commitment.

You know that guy that I mentioned at the beginning of this reading, the one who never followed through at work? We actually started to refer to him as "that guy," as in "Boy, I don't want to be like that guy." When it comes to the workplace, we want to be the person who can be trusted to do what we say we will do. By doing so, we honor both God and our fellow workers.

To think about:

1. How are work and witness related?

2. If your co-worker always talked about her church, but was an un-trustworthy worker, would it affect your opinion of her church? Her faith?

3. If everyone was exactly as committed to their work as you are to yours, would that be a good thing or a bad thing? Why?

Daily Reading for Week Four, Day Two

Week four: Obedience in the workplace

READ: Genesis 2:8-15

Every now and then, someone will tell me that they think heaven sounds kind of dull. "All that sitting around on clouds, singing and playing harps; I think I'll get tired of that." I would, too; fortunately, that isn't the biblical image of paradise.

The heaven I find described in the Bible is a lot like the world we live in now, only without sin or any of the consequences of sin. The Garden of Eden prior to the Fall, and the closing chapters of Revelation each describe a very recognizable world—with hardly a cloud or harp in sight. They also describe a world in which we have work to do.

That's right. We will have jobs in paradise, even as Adam did in Eden. God put Adam in the Garden not just to sit around and enjoy it, but also to "till it and keep it" (Genesis 2:15 NRSV). As hard as it may be for us to believe sometimes, work is good for us. We were made to work.

So why doesn't it feel that way? Why do we so often find ourselves reluctant to go to work? In a word—sin. Just as sin has corrupted every other part of God's creation, it has also corrupted the work we do and our attitude toward it. Instead of accepting a job that perfectly matches our gifts, we might greedily take a job that pays more—and suffer because of it. Or else our pride might cause us to accept a job that requires more of us than we are able to give, and we fear that our inadequacy will be discovered.

Sin also causes bosses to demand more of us than is reasonable, or tempts them to pay us less than we are worth. Sin makes some jobs more dangerous than they need to be, and others more pointless than they should be. In countless ways, sin has taken the joy out of work—and joy is what God intended for work in the Garden.

Obedience in the workplace may not completely restore that joy, but it can certainly move us in that direction. Anything that we can do to lessen the impact of sin will be a step toward God's original intent for work.

Work, just like everything else, will never be perfect in this life. But it can certainly be better than it is now if we are willing to be obedient to God's plan: to believe that work is good for us, and meant to be a source of joy.

To think about:

1. Do you like your work? Why or why not? What would have to change for you to enjoy it?

2. If money was no object, what job would you choose to do?

3. If you aren't in the right job now, what steps would you have to take to get the right job?

Daily Reading for Week Four, Day Three

Week four: Obedience in the workplace

READ: Matthew 4:18-22

Quick, other than the fishermen—Peter, Andrew, James and John—what kind of work did the rest of the twelve apostles do before they were called by Jesus?

You came up with Matthew, the tax collector, right? And maybe Paul, the tent maker? (sorry, no points; he wasn't one of the original twelve). How about Luke, the physician? (nope, not one of the twelve either). If you're scratching your head, wondering why you can't recall any of the other seven, it's because the gospels never tell us. On the one hand, this means that Jesus probably called people from ordinary walks of life to be his disciples. On the other, it suggests that we should take special note of the fact that we do know that four of them were fishermen.

Let's look at both hands: First of all, it is pretty clear that the kind of work we do has no bearing on whether or not we can be effective disciples of Jesus. Over the course of my ministry, I've occasionally had people decline church positions because they weren't college-educated, or didn't hold what they perceived to be jobs that were important enough. They thought that only the business types, executives and professional people should hold church offices.

True statement: I've had lots of professional people serve on church boards. I've also had farm hands, factory workers, HVAC installers and at least one reformed car thief. I can't honestly say that one group was better than the other, although the latter might have been more teachable.

The point, of course, is that if you are obedient in what you do, God can use you, no matter what your occupation might be.

Now for the other hand: If we pay attention, our occupation might equip us for gospel work. When Jesus first called Peter and Andrew, he said, "Follow me, and I will make you fish for people" (Matthew 4:19 NRSV), a challenge that made sense to them due to their familiarity with nets, boats, the Sea of Galilee and the fickle nature of fish.

How about your job? What can it teach you, and how has it prepared you for the work of the gospel? It's pretty clear that the Kingdom of God will include people from every occupation, a reality that should already be reflected in the church. So it doesn't matter what you do —if you are obedient and faithful in your occupation, the church can use your service.

To think about:

1. Jesus called the first four disciples to "fish for people." What might he say about you? Are you challenged to be a "Carpenter of the church?" "Accountant of the spirit?" "Salesperson of the truth?"

2. Should someone who is known to be disobedient in his or her daily occupation be asked to serve in a church capacity? Why or why not? What about Matthew?

Daily Reading for Week Four, Day Four

Week four: Obedience in the workplace

READ: Acts 18:1-4

I wonder, whatever happened to Maggie? She was the girl I worked with at Pizza Hut who ended up pregnant when she was 18 and single. And what about Carl, one of the other cooks? He had a dream that he would become a teacher, but did he ever finish his college degree? Did Tina, the nurse I worked with at the hospital, ever leave her abusive husband? Did Max, manager at the restaurant in Detroit, ever hit it big when he was playing the ponies at Hazel Downs? Did Marlene, the waitress, ever find the man of her dreams?

These are all real people (although I've changed their names). I got to know them just through work. We weren't in class together, we didn't spend time at each other's homes, and we rarely even talked to each other on the phone, unless it was to trade a shift.

We also didn't stay in touch when we went our separate ways; I was usually the one leaving to go to the next thing. Even though we had talked daily, and had gotten to know quite a few things about each other, when the work was done, so was our relationship.

I still think about these people, and regret that I didn't make the effort to keep up some kind of correspondence with them; today, Facebook would have made that a lot easier. I think several of them would have liked to stay in touch, but I never took the time to write or call them.

As I look back, it now seems that at least some of these encounters were God-given opportunities. I had the chance to be a long-term friend to a number of people for whom faith was not currently an important issue. Over time, as my own faith developed and grew, I may have been able to share some of my experiences with them. We may have been able to encourage one another; I may have even had the chance to lead someone to Jesus.

Paul, the apostle and tent-maker, did a much better job of remembering his co-workers. In the book of Acts, we find him side-by-side with fellow tent-makers Aquila and Prisca, Jews who had been driven out of Rome. At the end of the book of Romans, after they had been allowed to return home, we find Paul saying, "Greet Prisca and Aquila who work with me in Christ Jesus" (Romans 16:3 NRSV). Clearly, he had not allowed an opportunity to pass him by.

How about you? Could it be that someone with whom you work represents an opportunity for a growing, long term friendship, and possibly a chance to influence another person for Christ?

To think about:

1. When is it appropriate to share our faith in the workplace? If a co-worker asked you about something that makes a difference in your life, would you mention your faith?

2. What would be an acceptable way to let co-workers know that your faith is important?

Daily Reading for Week Four, Day Five

Week four: Obedience in the workplace

READ: I Timothy 6:3-10

It had been at least half an hour since the custodian had come into my study, complaining about things that were, essentially, part of his job —setting up rooms, making equipment available, cleaning up after events, and other routine activities. I wasn't sure why I had to hear all these things until he mentioned money. "Bingo," I thought, sighing to myself. "Here we go again."

If you have ever had a co-worker who is obsessed with money, you know how phenomenally annoying that person can be. If that person happens to be you, consider this your official notice: Your co-workers don't want to hear you, a). complain about how little you make, b). boast about how much you make, c). ask how much they make, or d). tell them how they can make more. What they really want is to see if you are able to think about anything besides money, because well-adjusted people, particularly people of faith, know that there is more to life than money.

Paul told Timothy that "there is great gain in godliness combined with contentment" (I Timothy 6:6 NRSV). As long as our basic needs are met (vs. 8), we don't really have a right to complain. Notice that it's not the rich who "fall into temptation and are trapped by many senseless and harmful desires" (vs. 9). No, it is those who *want to* get rich. Money itself isn't the problem; it is the love of money, being eager for money that leads to trouble (vs. 10).

Since the workplace is where nearly all of us get our paycheck, it is also the place where we need to be most on our guard when it comes to our attitude about money. Of course, we should be paid a fair wage for our labor (employers, take note of I Timothy 5:18: "The laborer deserves to be paid." Read Deuteronomy 24:14-15, too). We should also make sure that we give our employer a day's work for a day's pay. Once we have agreed to do a job for a certain rate of pay, if our employer honors that agreement, we shouldn't be constantly pestering our co-workers about how little money we earn. At the risk of sounding like you mother: Remember, there are plenty of people in the world who would trade places with you in a heartbeat.

Obedience in the workplace in this case means obedience in our attitude toward money. There are very few things that can erase any outward evidence of faith in God quicker than an obsession with money. It is an obsession that can only lead to grief—for you and those who have to work with you!

To think about:

1. Has God been faithful to you in the area of money? What evidence supports your answer?

2. Do you give your employer a day's work for a day's pay? If not, why not?

3. Who benefits most from your pay? You? Your family? The Church? Is there any imbalance in how your pay is divided? Is there evidence of obedience?

Daily Reading for Week Four, Day Six

Week four: Obedience in the workplace

READ: Luke 5:1-11

When the FedEx envelope was delivered on a Monday afternoon, I didn't think much of it. The church I was then serving was soliciting pastoral profiles, and it wasn't the first one to arrive via overnight delivery. I threw it on a stack of mail to be dealt with later in the week.

A few days later, my wife, Leigh, noticed the envelope still sitting on my desk. "Aren't you going to open that?" she asked. Mostly to satisfy her curiosity, I pulled on the opening strip, and removed a letter which said that I had won a contest sponsored by the Visa company.

In fact, it said that I was the Grand Prize winner.

Thinking that it had to be a hoax, I reread the letter and had Leigh read it a few times, too. There was a number to call, and when I spoke to the person at the other end, I was finally convinced that it was for real. I had won back everything I had spent on my Visa card the previous year (note: Leigh and I use our Visa for nearly everything—and pay it off monthly). It was an amazing gift, a powerful reminder that God can provide for us in completely unexpected ways.

I imagine that my feeling that evening was a lot like Peter's on the morning that Jesus got into his boat. After a long night of fishing —with nothing to show for it—Jesus told Peter to let the nets down once more; and the boat was filled to overflowing. Peter was so overwhelmed by his awareness of God's power that he asked Jesus to go away, saying, "I am a sinful man."

Jesus could do the same for each of us, if that was his will, but it doesn't seem to be. Some people work hard every day and are frustrated, judging that they have little to show for their efforts. Others receive an astonishing windfall after doing almost nothing at all. It's in God's hands, and as today's passage makes clear, God could make any of us instantly wealthy, if that was what was best for us, according to God's will.

What God desires is our obedience and trust. We shouldn't automatically assume that wealth is a sign of God's blessing; Peter walked away from his windfall to follow Jesus. In the same way, if our resources are meager, we shouldn't assume that God is displeased with us. The widow of Zarephath was richly blessed with only a little flour and oil (I Kings 17).

It's really up to God. God will provide as God chooses. All we can do is obey and trust.

To think about:

1. Have you ever thought that God was being unfair, giving someone less deserving greater blessings than you? What does the Bible say, repeatedly, about wealth?

2. Should harder work always be rewarded with more money? Why or why not? Who would be the wealthiest if that was how God chose to provide for everyone?

Daily Reading for Week Four, Day Seven

Week four: Obedience in the workplace

READ: Mark 6:30-31

We were sitting in Chicago on a Friday morning, waiting for our agent at Apartment Finders to return, when I noticed that the agency had a public computer terminal. This was in the pre-smartphone era, and getting up from my seat, I said to Leigh, "I'm just going to check my e-mail a minute." She mumbled something, and when I started to turn back, she repeated herself.

"You're addicted, you know." She was smiling as she said it, so I knew it was okay to go and respond to my messages, even though it was my day off.

Our last Scripture passage for this week about obedience in the workplace is actually about *not* working. Sometimes obedience requires us to put down our tools (hammer? phone?) and take a break. Just because everyone else seems to be in constant work mode doesn't mean that we have to do likewise.

It's almost as if we are unwilling to admit that the human body needs rest. People boast about how little they sleep, how many days they are on the road, how many hours they put in every day. At the same time, people who take regular time off for themselves or their families are perceived as not ambitious enough, not on the fast track, not eager enough to get ahead.

The truth is that we require down time. We're made in God's image, and even God rested after a week of hard work. Jesus rested (remember him sleeping in the boat?) and he recognized when his disciples needed rest. They had been working so hard that they didn't even have time to eat, so Jesus said to them, "Come away to a deserted place all by yourselves and rest a while" (Mark 6:31 NRSV).

That's good enough for me. I know that I am a much better worker when I have had a full night's sleep. I think more clearly, I am nicer to other people, I'm even more patient with other drivers during my commute.

I also know that I periodically need longer breaks from my work. Sometimes I take a study leave as a change of routine; other times it's a family trip. More recently, it has become Leigh and me in Chicago for a couple of nights.

It's okay to rest. It's even obedient to rest. "Six days shalt thou labor ..." As I said, that's good enough for me.

To think about:

1. Do you work too much? If so, why? Could different choices allow you to work less?

2. Many other nations work fewer hours and take longer vacations than we do. Why do you think that is? Are they on to something?

Daily Reading for Week Five, Day One

Week five: Obedience in Prayer

READ: Deuteronomy 4:1-8

Moses may not have been entering the Promised Land with the people of Israel, but he knew what was waiting for them across the Jordan. They would be surrounded by other nations, people who worshipped different gods and followed different laws. He knew that the fickle Israelites would be tempted to follow the ways of their neighbors, instead of remaining true to the way of their one true God.

"What other great nation has a god so near to it as the Lord our God is whenever we call to him?" (Deuteronomy 4:7 NRSV).

Moses' question is an excellent reminder to us as we begin a week in which we will be thinking about obedience in prayer. As he knew from his intimate relationship with the Almighty, there is no other god like the one true God; there is no other global deity who proves to be near to his or her people when they pray. Human-conceived gods of wood and stone might have had a safe, controllable feel about them, but they weren't able to answer, or even listen to prayer.

Nothing about the uniqueness of praying to God has changed since Moses' time. Try directing a prayer to Wall Street, and see if you get a response (I know people who believe the stock market controls their destiny). Try directing a prayer at your TV set and see how well it provides for you (I know people for whom TV is their first love). Close your eyes and invoke the name of your favorite athlete; did you get an answer? (I know people who make athletes their model for living).

Only God hears prayer; only God *desires* prayer. Ever since the Garden of Eden, when God walked and talked with Adam and Eve, God has wanted to be in close contact with humanity. God loves us and longs for us to respond in kind.

Brief aside: You know all those prayer studies they've been doing lately? The ones where they take a group of sick people and have people pray for half of them and not the other half? I wouldn't spend too much time thinking about those results. All they prove is that scientists don't understand the purpose or meaning of prayer.

Prayer isn't a spiritual ATM, where we shove in our prayer card and withdraw an automatic blessing. It is more like a conversation between parent and child; and there's nothing our heavenly Parent loves more than to hear from the kids.

To think about:

1. Why do you pray? Why do you think God wants us to pray? Are your reasons the same?

2. Many people try to worship a false god alongside the one true God. Who or what are some of these false deities? What do they offer to their adherents?

Daily Reading for Week Five, Day Two

Week five: Obedience in Prayer

READ: Luke 18:9-14

At the fall Classis meeting, the pastors and elders of my denomination's churches in southwestern New York were gathered for worship. Not having any responsibilities in the service, I got to sit next to my favorite curmudgeon, the pastor of our congregation's sister church in my town. As soon as one of the prayers ended, I heard my friend mutter something about "Pharisees." I leaned over and quietly asked, "What did you say?"

He hoarsely whispered back, "He just offered his own version of the Pharisee's prayer. Ministers do it all the time, and it drives me nuts!"

After the service, we talked about the prayer some more, and I've never listened to public prayers in the same way since. My friend was exactly right; it is amazing how often the clergy—and many others—sound just like the Pharisee in the temple.

For starters, even though Jesus told us not to be hypocrites in prayer (Matthew 6:5), we are often like those whom Jesus described by saying that "they trusted in themselves that they were righteous and regarded others with contempt" (Luke 18:9 NRSV). We would never admit that we look down on others, but we pray for the hungry to be fed and the naked to be clothed, and then go off to indulge in classy gourmet dinners while wearing our designer fashions. If we're not going to make a significant and self-sacrificing difference in helping the needy, we probably shouldn't ask God to take care of them, either.

We then proceed to thank God that we're not like these unfortunate others, only not in so many words, of course. We do this by praying for a carefully edited list of sins, being cautious not to include our own (pornography: bad; smutty TV: okay; drug dealing: bad; six pack of Bud: okay), and close by listing the many ways we perceive that we have been blessed, thanking God for the opportunity to worship, pray, gather with other believers and offer our tithes, all the while implying that others would do well to be a little more like us.

It's sweet-sounding, all this careful self-exaltation and humble bragging, but it doesn't make much of a difference. How much better, and how much more obedient, to pray like the tax collector. In humility, he couldn't even raise his head. "God, have mercy on me, a sinner."

I think that's how an obedient prayer is supposed to begin.

To think about:

1. Have you ever prayed the Pharisee's prayer? Do you ever pray for things you've done nothing to change?

2. Why was Jesus pleased with the tax collector's prayer? What did he really ask for? If you were the tax collector, what would be the second line of your prayer?

Daily Reading for Week Five, Day Three

Week five: Obedience in Prayer

READ: Matthew 26:36-46

My first church was in dairy farming country, and several of my parishioners came to church directly from the barn (well, they stopped in the house for a quick shower and change of clothes first, but you know what I mean). On any other day, they would be riding a tractor or baling hay or tending to the heifers. But on Sunday, they came into a warm, quiet sanctuary, sang a few hymns, sat down, got ready to hear the sermon or the pastoral prayer ...

... and went to sleep.

I didn't mind. I knew they worked hard and most of the time they managed to stay awake, but on those few occasions when they just couldn't keep their eyes open, I figured that at least they dozed off hearing about God.

I'm guessing that many of us fall asleep while praying, right? I can't be the only one! Is it disobedient? If I compare it to falling asleep while I'm calling on someone for a pastoral visit, it might be. I only did that once; it was in the nursing home, it was warm, and the resident had kind of a quiet, droning voice ... Zzzzzzzzzzzzzzzz. But if I compare it to snuggling up in a big armchair with my young grandchildren, reading to them and talking, and having them fall asleep on me, no, then I think it is just fine. As long as we don't do it every time, I don't think God minds if we fall asleep while we're being held in prayer.

Obedience, however, demands something different from us if we are supposed to be in prayer for someone else, especially in the middle of a crisis. We often say, "I'll pray for you," or "you'll be in my prayers." In those circumstances, we should make a concerted effort to keep our word and pray. In the same way, if we have met together to pray for a particular cause—remember the night of 9/11?—we should make every effort to stay alert as we pray.

In Gethsemane, Jesus encouraged the disciples to "stay awake and pray" so that they would not fall into temptation, the temptation to be concerned only with themselves and their own physical needs. He longed for their spiritual support, as do many of the people who count on us for prayer, but they let him down.

In summary: If God is holding us in prayer, it might be okay to fall asleep in God's arms, but if we are holding someone else in prayer, sleep should wait until after the "Amen."

To think about:

1. If you were invited to meet your favorite celebrity or athlete, do you think would you fall asleep? How is that like meeting God in prayer? How is it different?

2. Why is it important to follow through when we say "I'll pray for you?" Who would know?

Daily Reading for Week Five, Day Four

Week five: Obedience in Prayer

READ: Romans 8:22-27

At age 14, I learned a lesson in prayer that I didn't really understand until I was 16. The lesson is "Thy will be done," and I remember it almost every time I think that God isn't answering my prayers according to my wishes.

As a tweener—no longer a child, but no adult privileges, either— nothing in the world seemed more important to me than buying a minibike, one of those short, lawnmower-powered precursors to today's deluxe scooters. I knew that I would need my parents' permission to raid my savings account, so I approached them at the breakfast table with my petition: "Mom and Dad, I don't want you to answer right away, but I want you to think about this and give me an answer tomorrow. I'd like to use some of my savings to buy a minibike ..." I told them how much it cost and how I would use it, certain that they would be impressed with the maturity of my approach and the careful consideration I had given to the subject.

Following dinner the next night, I asked them if they were ready to answer me. They were, and the answer was "No." I was disappointed, and maybe even a little angry—it was my own money, after all! But two years later, when I bought my first car with money from that same savings account, I was grateful for the "No" I had received.

The Apostle Paul reminds us that we sometimes don't know what we are asking for in our prayers. In our human weakness, we may pray for the wrong things, and then wonder why God hasn't gone along with our plans. Even though we are told that the Spirit intercedes for us "according to the will of God," we still wonder why things don't go our way more often.

This is when I remember the minibike. My parents could see my situation more clearly than I could, and their will was wiser than mine. In a similar, but infinitely greater way, God's Spirit intercedes for us with a will that is never wrong. The Spirit cleanses, refines, purifies, edits and even completely rewrites our prayers until they are in line with what our Father knows is best.

"Thy will be done" is always an obedient prayer, even if it takes us some time to understand the answer.

To think about:

1. Did you ever ask your parents for something to which they responded, "No?" What do you think about their answer now?

2. If the Holy Spirit is going to intercede for us anyway, why should we put any effort into getting our prayers right? What difference does it make?

3. If we could see our lives as God sees us, how would it change our prayers?

Daily Reading for Week Five, Day Five

Week five: Obedience in Prayer

READ: Jonah 2:1-10

Talk about hitting bottom. Jonah was being as deliberately disobedient as anyone can be, choosing to do exactly the opposite of what God wanted him to do. Instead of marching east to preach in Nineveh, he was sailing west to hide from God in Tarshish. When the boat encountered a freakish storm, the sailors determined that Jonah was the cause of it, and they reluctantly pitched him overboard.

Which is when he got swallowed by the big fish.

There's not a whole lot a person can do while waiting to be digested; one's options are limited, which is often true when we finally sink as low as we can go. The one possibility that is always available to us, no matter how deep our disobedience, is prayer. No matter what we have done, for the sake of Jesus, God will always listen to prayers of the disobedient.

I encourage you to stop and think about that for a moment. "No matter what we have done ..." Eve ate the apple, Moses struck the rock, Sarah laughed, David had Bathsheba's husband killed, Peter said, "Nope, don't know the guy," Paul stood around while Stephen was killed, Jonah tried to run—and God was willing to listen to all of them.

Jonah's prayer—presumably written down some time after he was no longer fish food—is filled with an awareness of God's mercy. The prophet knew that he deserved his punishment: "I am driven away from your sight" (vs. 4), and today, too, our disobedience may carry severe and painful consequences. But as Jonah said in verse 7, "As my life was ebbing away, I remembered the Lord, and my prayer came to you, into your holy temple" (Jonah 2:7 NRSV).

In other words, disobedience never has to have the last word. There is no bottom so deep that we lose the opportunity for one last act of obedience—prayer. We can always turn to God in prayer, and know that God will listen.

You're not sure you agree with me? Try asking the thief on the cross when you meet him in Paradise.

To think about:

1. Why do you think God always leaves open the option of prayer?

2. Think of a few kinds of disobedience with which you struggle. What would be the likely course of events if you became increasingly disobedient in these areas? Do we always have to hit bottom before we turn to God in prayer?

3. If Jesus took the punishment for our sins, why do we still get eaten by big fish?

Daily Reading for Week Five, Day Six

Week five: Obedience in Prayer

READ: Psalm 51

I credit my, um, "unique" friend and one-time mentor, Rev. Cal Steck, with helping me to become serious about obedience in prayer. Before you read any farther, I should warn you that I'm going to quote him directly (if you knew him, you would know why that requires a warning!)

I was still in my first parish when I met Cal at a weekly minister's breakfast. He was everything I wanted to become in ministry: smart, funny, well-read, widely-respected and, beneath his wise-cracking exterior, sincere. A few months after meeting him, when I seemed to be growing more fatigued in my work by the day, I called on Cal to see if he could give me some advice.

After we talked about ministry in general for a while, he asked me some questions about my daily devotional routine, as well as the prayers that I used when leading the congregation in worship. He challenged me to start a prayer journal, and when he reviewed it the following week, he pointed at one entry and said, "What is this?" I had quoted a line from the old Ogdon/Gabriel hymn, "Brighten the Corner Where you Are," identifying that as one of my goals for my ministry.

"Well, that's just crap," he replied, not without a hint of a smile. "I want you to spend some time praying other people's prayers." He suggested that I start with the Psalms, especially Psalm 51 and others like it, and also recommended some anthologies of prayers. In addition, he thought I would benefit from a reading of the ministry classic, *Diary of a Country Priest* by Georges Bernanos.

A few weeks passed, and I realized that my spirits were much improved. When I returned to Cal to tell him about my experience, he didn't look too surprised, but rather seemed a bit smug and satisfied as if, perhaps, someone had led him through a similar exercise early in his own ministry. He then handed me a book, his personal copy of *A Minister's Prayer Book*, by John Doberstein. "There's only one catch," he said. "If you ever stop using it, I want it back."

35 years later, I still have it.

To think about:

1. Whose prayers do you wish you could read? How can reading someone else's prayers improve our own obedience in prayer?

2. Have you ever tried writing out a prayer to God? If not, how do you think it would be different than a spoken or silent prayer?

3. Psalm 51 was written for a very specific reason (David's sin with Bathsheba). How does knowing that change your reading of the prayer?

Daily Reading for Week Five, Day Seven

Week five: Obedience in Prayer

READ: Matthew 6:5-15

I stood before a congregation of kind, gentle, loving, but largely uninvolved worshipers. A few were paying attention to what I was saying, but most of them seemed to have their thoughts elsewhere. Several were asleep. One kept plucking at imaginary insects on her leg.

You've probably already guessed that I was at the nursing home. As I made my way through the overly complicated message I had prepared, I looked forward to the one part of the service that I knew would involve most of the participants: The Lord's Prayer. Sure enough, when I started to speak the familiar words, first a few voices, then nearly everyone joined in. That pathway had been well-preserved in these fading memories.

No week on obedience in prayer would be complete without a consideration of the Lord's Prayer. Actually, let me rephrase that: No week on obedience in prayer would be complete without *praying* the Lord's Prayer.

It's easy to read or recite the Lord's Prayer; we do it all the time. Even largely non-religious people have learned it along the way. For example, when I incorporate it into a wedding or funeral service, nearly all of the people in attendance are able to join in.

We also spend time, either in church or on our own, studying the prayer or reading about it. A quick glance at Amazon.com reveals that there are currently over 10,000 titles related the Lord's Prayer. It's a popular subject.

But how often do we really pray it, in obedience to our Lord's direction? How often do we think about what we are saying when we ask for God's will, or our daily bread, or to be forgiven as we have forgiven others? This requires more than just a recitation of the words; we have to slow down and think about what we are saying.

I think it's safe to say that this is what Jesus meant when he said, "Pray then in this way." He didn't mean for us to simply race through the words again and again, but to thoughtfully consider each petition, to offer each one to God in sincerity and conviction, and to do so for the rest of our lives, even when everything else has grown dim.

To think about:

1. Which petition of the Lord's Prayer seems most significant to you at this time in your life? Has that always been true? Have other petitions been more important at other times?

2. When did you learn the prayer? When were (or, are) you able to recite it from memory?

3. Take time to slowly offer the Lord's Prayer to God, if not right now, sometime today.

Daily Reading for Week Six, Day One

Week six: Obedience in Private

READ: Luke 12:1-3

Here's the premise for this entire week; you might want to take a moment to memorize it:

There are no secret sins.

That's it. Just five words. Everything we read this week will point us back to these words—every scripture passage, every story, every illustration, every question we consider. Everything having to do with the theme of obedience in private begins with this premise. There are no secret sins.

We know, of course, that we can't hide anything from God; we can barely hide anything from each other, and we're not nearly as all-seeing and all-knowing as God (except, possibly, our mothers). That dime I snuck out of my savings bank to buy candy as a child? That was discovered when my bank had less money in it than my brothers'. That time I was speeding on my way home from work? That was found out when the officer pulled me over in front of my own house. That magazine that I found in the woods and hid in my brother's closet? Well, actually, I don't know what became of that. All I know is that one day it wasn't there anymore; someone found it. The point is that the vast majority of our sins don't remain secret; they have a way of revealing themselves.

Even if we do manage to keep a sin concealed from the people around us, we're still not fooling God. Jesus told the disciples that, "Nothing is covered up that will not be uncovered, and nothing secret that will not become known" (Luke 12:2 NRSV).

He was talking about the hypocrisy of the Pharisees, but he might just as well have been talking about us—the way we act when others are looking versus the things we do in private. None of it will be concealed forever.

I don't say this in order to frighten us or shame us or to cause us to worry about our relationship with God. For the sake of Jesus, all our sins are forgiven, including the ones we commit in secret. In gratitude for this forgiveness, though, if our desire is to offer God the gift of our obedience, it also has to include obedience in private. Otherwise, all our obedience is just hypocrisy. If we're only obedient when others are around, well, I don't think God is too impressed by that.

Meaningful obedience begins in the same place where sin begins: in the human heart. To choose to love and honor God when no one is looking is the beginning of real obedience.

To think about:

1. Were you ever caught in a secret sin that became known? Did you really believe you could keep it secret?

2. What's your opinion of people who act one way in public, but another in private? Can they be trusted? If you knew they would listen to you, what would you say to them?

Daily Reading for Week Six, Day Two

Week six: Obedience in Private

READ: Acts 5:1-11

I played golf with several of my friends on the day I graduated from seminary. I even posted a pretty good score, because I chipped in from about 50 yards on one particularly difficult hole. My three friends all witnessed the shot, and before I ran up to the green, I made one of them go up to the cup to make sure my ball was really in there. If I was going to brag about this shot—and I intended to!—I wanted witnesses.

As we walked up to the next tee, it occurred to me that it would be very easy to agree with one or two people to lie about something like a hole-in-one, or a low score for 18 holes. You would really need only one person to share your secret sin, after which you could reap the benefits for as long as you liked.

Something like this must have been on the minds of Ananias and Sapphira as they agreed to defraud the church with a shared secret sin. They sold a piece of land, and wanted to give their fellow believers the impression that they were sharing all the proceeds with the faith community, when in fact, they were keeping some of it for themselves. Their sin wasn't in choosing to keep part of the money—Peter made it clear that it was theirs to do with as they chose—but in lying to the church, and to the Spirit of God.

In addition to golf, it's easy to think of other contemporary examples of this kind of sin: A husband and wife decide together to cheat on their taxes. A couple of friends shoplift and lie together to cover it up. Two people connect on the Internet and agree to meet, without telling their spouses. A couple of students share answers on a test. In each case, the deceit is supposed to stay between just the two—but how often does it, really?

Not every shared secret sin will result in the same consequence suffered by Ananias and Sapphira (who both fell down dead), but something does die when we agree with one or two people to conceal a deliberate sin. Truth dies; trust dies; relationships die; community dies; even faith itself can begin to die when we choose to deliberately deceive not just people, but the Spirit of God.

As great as it would be to tell you that I once scored a hole-in-one, it's even more satisfying to say that a pretty good chip shot was as good as my game ever got; because that's the truth.

To think about:

1. Did you ever share a secret sin with one or two people? How did it turn out? Did it stay secret? What effect did it have on your relationship with those people?

2. Did God kill Ananias and Sapphira? Does God hand out punishments to people who try to cover up their sins today? Who is responsible for the consequences of our secret sins?

Daily Reading for Week Six, Day Three

Week six: Obedience in Private

READ: Psalm 139 (read the devotion first today)

If you're like me, there are probably one or two secret sins in your life that you can't manage to shake. You may have first come under their influence as a young adult, or possibly even earlier, and now they just seem to hang around, coming back into your life again and again, even if you have done everything in your power to deal with them, seek forgiveness, and move on. They never seem to go away completely.

By now in this series, you know that I've been pretty willing to share many of my own stories, but not this time. Today, I'd rather you thought about the sin that gives *you* the most trouble. I'm sure you've prayed about it; I'm sure you would prefer that it wasn't such a strong influence or temptation, but there it is. It may be that you've begun to wonder if you will ever learn how to be obedient in the face of it.

Psalm 139 can help. I don't want to hold out false or oversimplified hope in the battle against a persistent sin, but this Psalm is our reminder that we are never alone in our battle against temptation and shame. Nothing is hidden from God, and God can help us conquer even the most tenacious enemy.

In a moment, when you read the Psalm, notice how in the first part David recognizes that God is always with us, always aware of what's going on in our lives. It's not a condemning or judging presence, but a guiding hand (vs. 10), a source of security. In the second part, the flawed king reminds us that in spite of our sinful flaws, we are still of tremendous worth to God. We were "fearfully and wonderfully made," and God had a plan for every day of our lives even before we were formed. It's never too late for us to choose trust in God's plan.

In the last part of the Psalm, David asks God to slay our enemies—for him, probably literal enemies like the Philistines; for us, enemies like envy, coveting, deceit, anger, abuse, or lust. For God, enemies who occupy our hearts and minds are no harder to vanquish than the flesh and blood enemies who surrounded King David in the hills of Judah.

David closes the Psalm with an earnest prayer, one that we can make our own if it is truly our desire to be free of our secret sin. As you

Case Van Kempen

turn to the Psalm now, keep your hidden sin in mind as you read it, and when you get to verses 23 and 24, I invite you to offer them to God as your sincere prayer, a sign of your willingness to turn every part of your life, including the secret parts, over to God.

To think about, after reading the Psalm:

1. Do you believe that God can conquer your secret sins?

2. How can you cooperate with God to avoid this sin in the future?

Daily Reading for Week Six, Day Four

Week six: Obedience in Private

READ: Matthew 5:27-30

I think very few people would disagree with me if I said that many of our secret sins are sexual in nature. It's not that we're necessarily more casual about revealing non-sexual sins, but rather that sexual sins have a particular stigma attached to them. Example: I can think of a half dozen or more ministers who have been dismissed from their churches because of sexual sin; I can't name a single one who has been dismissed for theft.

One of the things that makes obedience difficult in this area is the fact that we live in a culture which constantly confronts us with sexual images and sexual situations. I know that I am dating myself by saying this, but when I was coming of age, the raciest thing on television was Goldie Hawn dancing in her bikini on "Laugh In." In college, it was the ubiquitous Farrah Fawcett bathing suit poster. Even that fully-covered image was scandalous to my parents' generation, whose movies and TV shows made sure that any hint of sexual activity took place off screen.

Sending a letter by typewriter and snail mail didn't offer the instant gratification—and effortless sexual opportunity—which the Internet affords today. There was no such thing as Facebook, Snapchat or any kind of text messaging, all of which make secret sexual sin as easy as checking the weather forecast.

I am not so naïve as to think that our culture is going to quickly reverse course on public sexuality (although there are some positive signs as a result of the "Me, too" movement), which leaves me wondering how we can obey Jesus' teaching about adultery and lusting without locking ourselves in our closets. I think I know the answer, and it isn't easy, but neither is it impossible. It requires us to make many deliberate decisions for obedience.

Consider these common situations: The TV show becomes inappropriate. Decision? Turn it off. The magazine cover boasts inappropriate contents. Decision? Don't pick it up. The appearance of a particular person at the gym is becoming a temptation. Decision? Go at a different time. The Internet relationship is becoming too personal. Decision? Stop! In nearly every situation, there is a choice we can make for obedience.

Are these easy choices? No, they aren't; but they are much easier than dealing with the consequences of a secret sin—and remember, as we said at the beginning of the week: There are no secret sins.

To think about:

1. Is it realistic to think that we can choose obedience in every sexually charged situation?

2. How do we prepare the next generation for the world they are going to inherit? What difference can our obedience make?

Daily Reading for Week Six, Day Five

Week six: Obedience in Private

READ: Psalm 90

Before you read any farther, did you happen to notice who wrote the Psalm for today? That's right—it was Moses, the same Moses who led the Israelites as they escaped from captivity in Egypt. We don't know exactly when he wrote it, but it's not hard to imagine that he had been out in the wilderness for a while, dealing with the grumbling and complaining of the recently freed slaves, some of whom wished they had never left Egypt (see Numbers 11, for example).

Moses was keenly aware of the many open and obvious sins of the Israelites—after all, he appeared to be the "go to" guy for just about any complaint—but he also knew that the people were guilty of secret sins (vs. 8). None of them were hidden from God, and Moses pictured a heavenly scene in which all the secretly written sins of God's people were laid bare, painfully exposed by the light of God's own presence.

God had a right to be angry. That much was clear to Moses, and he knew that God would be perfectly justified in simply obliterating the rebellious ingrates. But Moses also remembered God's "steadfast love" (vs. 14), the love that had provided for the people at the Red Sea, at Mt. Sinai, in the gift of manna and quail, in the pillars of cloud and fire, and in countless other ways.

It is that same steadfast love that sent Jesus to free us from our captivity, our enslavement to sin which so often seems to have a tight grip on us, and which makes it possible for us to reveal our secret sins before God. We no longer have to be overwhelmed by God's wrath or fear being consumed by God's anger. God's love doesn't excuse the seriousness of our sins, but it allows us to approach God with the assurance that God wants to help us, not sweep us away.

The other thing I like about this Psalm is its reminder that this life is but a blink of an eye compared to the eternity which awaits those who trust in God. Our years are "soon gone," which means we don't have a lot of time to waste trying to hide our sins from God and each other. The sooner we trust God's love, and the sooner we confess our sins, the sooner we will already begin to experience the blessings of eternity in this life.

To think about:

1. What are some of the ways that you have experienced God's favor in your life? Were these favors deserved?

2. What does it mean to "count our days that we may gain a wise heart" (vs. 12)? Can we have a heart of wisdom and also harbor secret sins?

3. How long have you been dealing with your most tenacious secret sin? How has it prevented you from experiencing God's kingdom in this world?

Daily Reading for Week Six, Day Six

Week six: Obedience in Private

READ: Judges 16:4-21

So what exactly did Samson do wrong in this story? I know that in the Biblical account of his life, he comes across as arrogant, immoral, rude to his parents, and occasionally, frighteningly violent. But in the specific instance of his relationship with Delilah, what did he do wrong? Shouldn't people in love be able to share their innermost secrets?

We've been thinking about secret sins this week, and a closer look at Samson's life reveals that he is practically the poster child for the consequences of harboring secret sins. The fact that he was felled for sharing a non-sinful secret proves to be bitter irony, considering how a pattern of secrecy set him on the path which led to his ultimate betrayal by Delilah.

His first secret act (Judges 14:5-6), not necessarily a sin, was to kill a young lion with his bare hands. The secret which followed, definitely sinful, was when he went back to the same lion's carcass and found bees and honey. As a Nazirite, Samson was not supposed to come near any dead thing, but he ignored his vow, ate the honey, and turned the whole episode into a riddle with which to take advantage of the Philistines. His young, unnamed Philistine wife pried the secret out of him, and in fierce anger, Samson killed thirty men to pay off the wager on his riddle.

This episode led to still greater violence with the Philistines, and eventually to his downfall through Delilah. As happened earlier with his wife, Delilah also managed to pry his secret out of him—this time a non-sinful secret—but the sharing of it proved to be Samson's ruin.

It was no doubt easy for Samson to believe that harboring secret sins didn't matter. Every time he was in a bind (literally; see Judges 15:13-14), his strength allowed him to escape the situation. In the same way today, we often manage to use our unique talents or abilities to escape the consequences of a secret sin. It may be a cleverly constructed cover story, a timely quip, an assertion of integrity, or simply an emphatic denial. Whatever means we use, if it works once, we are likely to believe we can get away with it again. And again. And again.

But as Samson's life reveals, our secret sins will eventually prove to be our undoing. It's remarkable to note that God can use even our disobedience to accomplish a godly purpose, as was the case with Samson and the Philistines, but this is not an excuse to continue in our sin. Real strength comes from living a life based on truth.

To think about:

1. What unique ability do you have that allows you to get away with hiding secret sins? Do you think you will always be able to count on it?

2. Think of some examples of secret sins that can have consequences many years down the road. What prevents us from dealing with them and putting them behind us for good?

Daily Reading for Week Six, Day Seven

Week six: Obedience in Private

READ: Luke 22:1-6

All this week, we've been thinking about our obedience when no one is looking. I wanted to end the week by considering the story of Judas, because his example illustrates, in so many ways, the dangers of thinking that we can control the consequences of our secret sins.

One of the first things we notice about Judas is that he planned his sin. He left the other disciples to make a secret deal with the chief priests and the officers of the temple guard. It wasn't that he stumbled into his secret sin accidentally, or spontaneously. It was premeditated.

A second thing we notice is that the people with whom he was planning his sin were delighted, and even agreed to give Judas money. The same is often true today—there is almost always someone who is delighted when we choose to harbor a secret sin, and we may even experience something like a payoff. We shouldn't be surprised if our sin feels good in the short term, but like the 30 pieces of silver Judas received, the payoff for sin doesn't last; the feeling is fleeting.

A third, and perhaps obvious element of Judas' decision to sin is that someone was going to be harmed. We're often aware of this, too, when we sin, but we may think that the harm is minimal, or that we'll be able to deal with it if necessary. What is less obvious in the verses we read is that it isn't clear if Judas realized that Jesus would be killed (see Matt. 27:3-4). Our secret sins often have unintended consequences.

Finally, we have to note the fact that Satan entered Judas. Putting ourselves in a frame of mind which is open to sin gives Satan opportunity. Many people, as they are recounting an episode of sin, will say that it was almost as if they were being led along. Exactly.

The bottom line is that every sin is a betrayal. Whether our sin is discovered sooner or later, (and remember, it is always known to God), we betray the people we love, we betray the people who should be able to count on us, we betray our fellow believers, and above all, we betray our Savior. If we say that we are Jesus' followers, but we live with a secret sin, well, how is that different than what Judas did?

Although our sin may be like that of Judas, the consequences don't have to be. Jesus already paid for our sins, and he lives to set us free— free from the weight of our sin for all eternity.

To think about:

1. What's the payoff for our sins? How does it compare to the possible harm if our secret sins were to be discovered?

2. How can a decision to be obedient when no one is looking help us to keep Satan at a distance? What else can we do to resist his deception?

Final Daily Reading

READ: Joshua 6:1-21

Today is the last day of devotional readings for *The Jericho Effect.* For six weeks, we've been thinking about various aspects of obedience, and how doing things God's way can demonstrate our gratitude and bring down walls. As the series draws to a close, maybe it's time we looked at the story of Jericho itself!

Joshua and the people of Israel were finally approaching the Promised Land. The forty years of wandering in the wilderness were coming to an end, and it was God's desire to give the region of Canaan to the descendants of Abraham, Isaac and Jacob. (Note: It can be tempting to feel sympathy for the citizens of Jericho and the other residents of Canaan, but consider Genesis 18:16-33, in which Abraham pleads for the city of Sodom. There weren't even ten righteous people in the entire city.)

A traditional attack on Jericho would have been nearly futile; its walls were enormous, and the Israelite blood almost certainly would have flowed freely. God, however, had another plan, an approach which required radical obedience on the part of Joshua and his army. God instructed them to march around the city with trumpets and the Ark of the Covenant for six days, and on the seventh day, to march around it seven times. Only then were they to shout, at which time the walls would come tumbling down.

Obedience, doing it God's way, was the key to victory, which has been the theme of these past six weeks. Our sins create walls between us—walls between husbands and wives, walls between parents and children, walls between neighbors, walls between races, walls between co-workers—the list goes on and on. In every case, the way to bring down these walls is to do things God's way, to commit ourselves to the way of obedience.

Our willingness to obey isn't a means to prove that we deserve salvation. It doesn't purchase God's love and it isn't a sign that we are better than anyone else. It is simply a demonstration of our desire to respond to God's grace and mercy in the best way we can—by doing things God's way.

And the result? God willing, we will see a change. God's way is always the best way for us to proceed, and if we faithfully seek to do things

God's way, we will see walls coming down—or at least beginning to crumble.

Like Jericho, these six weeks have only been a beginning; the real test of our desire to do things God's way starts right now. Are you willing to keep on doing things God's way, for a change?

To think about:

1. What will you choose to do differently after thinking about obedience for six weeks?

2. Prayerfully consider: What walls does God want to tear down in your life?

ABOUT THE AUTHOR

When someone asks Case Van Kempen if he was born in a barn, he always answers yes, and then says, "Only it was spelled differently." Case was born in the town of Baarn, in the province of Utrecht, the Netherlands, emigrating to the United States as an infant with his family in 1956. Case attended Seymour Christian School and Ottawa Hills High School in Grand Rapids, Michigan, then attended Hope College in Holland, graduating with a degree in philosophy in 1977. From there he went on to Wayne State University Law School. It was while there that he heard the call to ministry, and enrolled in Western Theological Seminary. Since Case had never intended to be a seminarian, he needed to take a crash course in Biblical Greek, which is where he met his wife, Leigh (Boelkins). She was also a student in the summer Greek course, and after a brief courtship, they were married in 1981. After graduating, Case and Leigh moved to the Clymer Hill Reformed Church in Clymer, New York, then to Union Reformed Church in Franklin Lakes, New Jersey, and from there back to Holland, to serve the Maplewood Reformed Church. While in New Jersey, Leigh was ordained to chaplaincy, serving as the multi-faith chaplain for Northwest Bergen Hospice. After ten years at Maplewood, Case took the training for interim ministry, and has served churches across the upper midwest. He has also written several books and Bible study guides, all for Faith Alive Christian Publishing: Hard Questions People Ask About the Christian Faith, Daniel: Daring faith for Dangerous Times, and 1, 2, 3 John: Living in the Light of Love. Case and Leigh have three adult children.

Made in the USA
Middletown, DE
15 February 2020